Library of
Davidson College

THINKING
DIRECTED, UNDIRECTED AND CREATIVE

THINKING
DIRECTED, UNDIRECTED AND CREATIVE

K. J. GILHOOLY

Department of Psychology
University of Aberdeen
Scotland

1982

ACADEMIC PRESS
A Subsidiary of Harcourt Brace Jovanovich, Publishers.
LONDON   NEW YORK
PARIS   SAN DIEGO   SAN FRANCISCO   SÃO PAULO
SYDNEY   TOKYO   TORONTO

ACADEMIC PRESS INC. (LONDON) LTD.
24/28 Oval Road
London NW1

United States Edition published by
ACADEMIC PRESS INC.
111 Fifth Avenue
New York, New York 10003

Copyright © 1982 by
ACADEMIC PRESS INC. (LONDON) LTD.
Second printing 1983

All Rights Reserved

No part of this book may be reproduced in any form by photostat, microfilm, or any other means, without written permission from the publishers

British Library Cataloguing in Publication Data

Gilhooly, K. J.
Thinking.
I. Cognition
153.4   BF311

ISBN: *(cased)* 0-12-283480-1
ISBN: *(paperback)* 0-12-283482-8

Photoset by Dobbie Typesetting Service, Plymouth, Devon.
Printed in Great Britain by St Edmundsbury Press, Bury St Edmunds, Suffolk.

To my parents

Preface

This book is intended as an introduction to recent research and theory concerning thought processes in normal human adults. Inevitably, only a very selective account can be given in any one book on this now very large area of research. The major topics dealt with are (i) thinking directed at solving well defined problems, (ii) less directed forms of thinking such as are found in daydreaming and (iii) creative thinking. While these topics are largely considered from the perspective of the information processing approach, which is currently dominant in cognitive psychology, some historical background is also provided (particularly in the first chapter). In the final chapter, an attempt is made to assess the progress achieved within the information processing approach to thinking and to indicate promising directions for future research. To help the interested reader go more deeply and widely into the various topics raised in the book, I have made suggestions for further readings at the end of each chapter.

The level of treatment is pitched at students who already have some background in psychology. As well as students and teachers concerned with courses on the psychology of thinking, I hope that the book will also be of interest to researchers, teachers and practitioners in other areas of psychology and in related disciplines, such as education and artificial intelligence.

A book such as this, is the end product of many influences on the author's cognitive system. Clearly, I am indebted to the "founding fathers" of the information processing approach. I also owe more immediate debts of gratitude to my teachers at Edinburgh and Stirling Universities and to my colleagues and students at Aberdeen University, who have influenced me by word or deed. Production of this book was greatly facilitated by the good working environment provided by my Head of Department, Professor Salzen. I should also like to thank very much our Departmental typists Alison Grant and Sheena Clark who worked cheerfully and quickly on the manuscript, despite excess of work and shortage of staff. Finally, completion of this project was due, in large part, to the encouragement provided by my wife Mary, who deserves my special thanks.

August, 1982.   *K. J. Gilhooly*

Contents

Preface	v
1. INTRODUCTION	1
I. Preliminaries	1
II. Approaches to thinking	4
III. Summary and concluding comments	14
IV. Further reading	15
2. SOLVING NON-ADVERSARY PROBLEMS	16
I. State-action representations	17
II. Problem reduction approach	22
III. Experimental studies	24
IV. Summary and concluding comments	46
V. Further reading	47
3. SOLVING ADVERSARY PROBLEMS	48
I. Game trees and the minimax principle	48
II. Artificial intelligence and chess	49
III. Experimental studies of human adversary problem solving	51
IV. Summary and concluding comments	64
V. Further reading	66
4. DEDUCTIVE REASONING	67
I. Syllogistic reasoning	67
II. Summary and concluding comments	83
III. Further reading	85
5. INDUCTIVE REASONING	86
I. The four card selection problem	86
II. Generating and testing hypotheses	95
III. Summary and concluding comments	100
IV. Further reading	103

6. DAYDREAMING	104
I. Psychometric approaches	105
II. Experimental approaches to daydreaming	108
III. A conceptual model of daydreaming	120
IV. Summary and concluding comments	121
V. Further reading	122
7. CREATIVE PROCESSES	123
I. Studies of creative individuals	125
II. Stage analyses	129
III. Increasing idea-production	134
IV. Theoretical approaches	141
V. Summary and concluding comments	147
VI. Further reading	163
8. THINKING: THEORETICAL OVERVIEW, PROGRESS AND PROSPECTS	150
I. Modal model assumptions	151
II. Theoretical progress?	160
III. Research trends	161
IV. Concluding comments	163
V. Further reading	163
REFERENCES	164
Index	176

1
Introduction

Thinking is an activity that has long intrigued and puzzled psychologists and philosophers — and continues to do so. Since all valuable innovations in the arts and sciences originate from fruitful thinking, it is a process of evident importance. At a more prosaic level, thought is frequently required to deal effectively with the various frustrations that arise in everyday activities. Even when not dealing with any pressing problems, thinking is always occurring, during periods of wakefulness, albeit often in a free-floating day-dreaming fashion. It is desirable to obtain a good theoretical understanding of thinking, not only for the sake of pure knowledge, but also with a view to helping people think more effectively. This book aims to review recent attempts, involving new approaches, techniques and experiments, to increase our understanding of thinking. The focus will be on thinking in normal adult humans, particularly problem-directed thinking, undirected daydreaming and creative thinking.

I. PRELIMINARIES

A. Characterizing thinking

The term "thinking" will be taken as referring to a set of processes whereby people assemble, use and revise internal symbolic models. These models may be intended to represent reality (as in science) or conceivable reality (as in fiction) or even be quite abstract with no particular interpretation intended (as in music or pure mathematics). This text will be mainly concerned with the first case, which is typical in problem-solving. Thinking directed toward problem-solving may be regarded as exploring a symbolic model of the task to determine a course of action that should be the best (or at least be satisfactory). A symbolic model often enables the thinker to go far beyond the perceptually available information (Bruner, 1957), and to anticipate the outcomes of alternative actions without costly overt trial and error. The first psychologist to explicitly describe thinking in terms of running symbolic models, appears to have been Kenneth Craik (1943; *see also* Zangwill, 1980). To illustrate his analysis, Craik used the example of a bridge builder determining a viable design by exploring symbolic models of possible bridges, rather than by overt and costly trial and error with real bridges.

The general view of thinking adopted here, is "reflexive" in that it encompasses the activity of psychologists as well as the activities of psychologists' subjects. Psychologists seek to assemble symbolic models of how humans (including themselves) assemble and utilize symbolic models. As Wetherick (1979) has put it, cognitive psychology seeks to model man's model-making capacities. To aid in the development of models of thinking, psychologists present experimental tasks to their subjects and record the resulting behaviour in varying degrees of detail. The psychologist's interpretation of the behavioural data should, on the approach presented here, take account of the way in which the subjects model (or interpret) the experimental task. As will emerge in later Chapters, it is frequently the case that behaviour which seems unintelligible or irrational becomes clear and sensible when an understanding is achieved of how the task has been interpreted by the subjects.

As well as varying in degree of directedness (problem solving *v.* daydreaming), thought is also often considered to vary in modality. Subjectively, thinking often seems to involve inner speech or visual, auditory or other forms of imagery. For example, reporting the 6th letter in the alphabet after "E" would generally involve the experience of inner speech. On the other hand, deciding whether one irregular shape was the same as another irregular shape at a different orientation (Shephard and Metzler, 1971) would generally involve an experience of visual imagery. Subjective experience, then, suggests the existence of different internal "languages", or distinct sets of symbols (verbal, visual, etc.), with their own rules of combination. Some translation rules must also exist to enable one to go from a word to an image and vice versa. Although the *experience* of imagery is not denied by current theorists, the *functional role* of imagery has been questioned. Imagery might be merely epiphenomenal, i.e. like factory noise, a non-functional by-product of the important processes. For instance it has been strongly argued (Pylyshyn, 1973) that the *meaning* of both verbal and non-verbal representations is conveyed by an underlying abstract, conceptual code. On this view, a visual image is generated on the basis of a symbolic description of the object being imaged, but it is the symbolic or propositional description that is important, rather than the image itself. To use one of Pylyshyn's examples, two images of a chessboard might be *pictorially* identical, but one image might be based on an abstract encoding that includes the relationship "black queen attacks white bishop", while the other image might not. On Pylyshyn's view, the important thing about an image is the propositions that it is derived from, rather than any "pictorial" properties. The opposing point of view is that images can convey "appearance" information better than propositions. The obtained patterns of reaction times to tasks that would appear to involve image comparing, rotating and scanning have been taken as supporting this latter view (Kosslyn and Pomerantz, 1977). But interpretations in propositional terms always seem possible and since it is not clear at this stage which position is correct (Pylyshyn, 1981; Kosslyn, 1981) or even whether the question is empirically decidable, (Anderson, 1978), the issue will be left open in this text.

B. Characterizing problems

Given the strong emphasis on problem-solving in this text and in the general literature on thinking, the question arises "what is a problem?" The definition offered by the Gestalt psychologist Karl Duncker (1945) is still serviceable. He wrote that "a problem arises when a living organism has a goal but does not know how this goal is to be reached".

This is a useful initial formulation that signals a number of points. First, that a "task" set by an experimenter, is not necessarily a problem for a given individual. Whether it is a problem or not, depends on the subject's knowledge and on his ability to locate relevant knowledge, should he have it. Second, a problem may vanish or be dissolved if the person changes his goals. A third point is that a problem does not effectively exist until the person detects some discrepancy between his goals and the situation he finds himself in.

Most psychological studies of problem-solving (especially, as we shall see, those within the information processing framework) have dealt with *well-defined* problems. If we accept Reitman's (1965) useful proposal that problems in general can be viewed as having 3 components (viz. a starting state, a goal state and a set of processes that may be used to reach the goal from the starting state) then a problem is well defined if all 3 components are completely specified. Problems in mathematics, in logic and in various board games tend to be well defined. Although well defined, such problems can be very difficult and the psychologist is faced with the task of explaining how we humans, with our various limitations, manage to solve geometry, chess and similar scale problems in reasonable times. Of course, it will be still more difficult to explain how we tackle those *ill-defined* problems that are more typical of real life than the well-defined variety.

Ill-defined problems leave one or more components of the problem statement vague and unspecified. Problems can vary in degree of definedness (Reitman, 1965, Chapter 5); for example, from "make a silk purse out of a sow's ear", (which leaves possible methods unspecified), to "make something useful from a sow's ear", (which has a vague goal and unspecified methods), to "make something useful from some part of a pig" (which leaves vague the goal, the starting state and the methods available).

It seems a reasonable strategy for psychologists to start with people's ways of handling apparently well-defined problems and then move on to consider ill-defined tasks. Perhaps people tackle ill-defined tasks by seeking a well-defined version of the problem, which they then work within until the problem is solved or a new definition is tried. If this is so, then studies with well-defined problems will be relevant to part of the process of solving ill-defined problems. Indeed, processes of defining, or interpreting, the problem are also important in well-defined tasks and some attention has recently been given to task interpretation processes that must play a role in both well- and ill-defined tasks (Kochen and Badre, 1974; Simon and Hayes, 1976). Some studies relating to task interpretation processes will be discussed in later sections.

A further distinction can be made between *adversary* and *non-adversary* problems. In an adversary problem the person is competing with a thinking opponent. While in non-adversary problems the struggle is with inert problem materials (real or symbolic) that are not reacting to what the person does with a view to defeating him (despite what the problem solver may feel!) Both these sorts of problems will be dealt with in future Chapters.

II. APPROACHES TO THINKING

Historically a number of theoretical approaches have been taken to the topic of thinking. The principal early approaches were those of classical introspectionism, behaviourism, Gestalt theory and neobehaviourism. More recent work has been dominated by the information processing approach. Although this text is written largely from the point of view of the currently dominant information processing approach, a brief historical overview will now be given to help set recent developments in perspective.

A. Early approaches

1 Introspectionism

In the late 19th and early 20th century the classical introspectionists, such as Wundt and Titchener, took conscious experience to be their subject matter and attempted to analyse consciousness into elementary sensations. A good analogy for the introspectionist endeavour is with chemistry. As chemists analyse complex compounds into chemical elements, so the introspectionists sought to analyse complex experiences into elementary sensations. Such analyses were to be made by means of the classical introspective report. To produce a classical introspective report the subject was required to adopt a special attitude or "set" such that the "meaning" of the experience was to be ignored in favour of the component sensations. So, instead of a report, for instance, that one saw "a large red book", a report of "an experience of a red coloured slightly trapezoidal shape" was expected. At this point, it is worth distinguishing between "classical introspectionism", with its emphasis on reporting in the language of sensations, and "ordinary" introspective reporting in everyday terms. The latter form of introspection is still used quite widely in the study of thought, as will be seen in future Chapters. Classical introspectionism, by contrast, has fallen into disuse. One reason for the decline of the method of classical introspection was that it led to conflicting reports which could not be easily reconciled. In particular, the question of thinking without images aroused considerable controversy between the introspectionists of Wurzburg (who reported imageless thought under certain circumstances) and those of Leipzig and Cornell who adamantly insisted that thought was always accompanied by imagery even although it might be very faint.

As well as the difficulty of resolving conflicts on such basic matters as imageless thought, the introspectionist approach was, in any case, limited in its scope to the consciousness of specially trained, sane, adult human subjects. To tackle unconscious thought processes or those of children, the insane, untrained subjects or animals would require very different approaches (Miller, 1960). The early behaviourists offered a radical alternative to classical introspectionism and this alternative was eagerly adopted by many psychologists.

2 Behaviourism

The early behaviourists (e.g. Watson, 1913) changed the focus of psychology from conscious experience to observable behaviour. Their dominant theoretical notion was the "stimulus–response link" and as a topic of study, "thought" was displaced from its centre stage position by "learning". Thorndike, an important precursor of Watson, had paved the way for this development through his (1898) studies of trial and error behaviour during problem-solving in cats. Cats placed in puzzle boxes displayed considerable trial and error behaviour before escaping, and on being returned to the boxes after each trial, they were only a little faster at escaping on each successive trial. There was no sign of "insight" leading to sudden solutions that could then be repeated without error when the cats returned to the puzzle boxes. Ruger (1910) found similar patterns of results in studies of humans working with manipulation puzzles. Thorndike and Ruger suggested that thought in problem-solving could be described as *covert* trial and error similar to the *overt* trial and error observable in their subjects' behaviour. Notions of "insight" or "understanding" were felt to be unnecessary.

3 Gestalt

A contrasting view was put forward by the Gestalt psychologists who objected to the different forms of "elementarism" represented by the classical introspectionists and the early behaviourists. Gestalt theory focussed especially on perception, rather than on thinking or learning, and the importance of perceptual organization was particularly stressed. Thus, in dealing with thinking and problem-solving, the Gestalt theorists emphasized the way in which the problem was perceived as a determining factor in task difficulty. The solving process was described as one of perceptual restructuring in which the problem comes to be seen in such a way that the solution is obvious. Examples of purely perceptual restructuring would include suddenly seeing the alternative interpretation of an ambiguous drawing or coming to see a face hidden in a puzzle painting. In the problem-solving area, "restructuring" may be illustrated by the following anecdotal example (discussed by Wertheimer, 1945, Chapter 4). When the famous mathematician Gauss was a 6 year old schoolboy he amazed his teacher by being able to give immediate answers to problems requiring the sum of successive whole numbers from 1 to N. Gauss was able to do this, not by rapid addition, but by restructuring the task. In the case of adding the following series of numbers (1, 2, 3, 4, 5, 6, 7, 8, 9, 10), Gauss noticed that each number from the left increases by one and each number from the right decreases by one. Thus the numbers can be regrouped into pairs that all have the same sum ((1, 10), (2, 9), (3, 8), (4, 7), (5, 6)). There are 5 pairs in this example, each of which sums to 11, and so the answer to the original question is 55. In general, the number of pairs will be $N/2$ and the sum of each pair will be $N + 1$; hence the formula that the sum of such a series ending in an even number is given by $(N/2) \times (N + 1)$.

For the Gestalt theorists, then, problem-solving involved "insight", which was an appreciation of how the solution was necessitated by the nature of the problem, and this insight would come through a restructuring of the subject's perception of the problem. Some important early Gestalt research on problem-solving was carried out with animal subjects. Presumably, if insight could be convincingly demonstrated with animals then its occurrence in humans could scarcely be denied. So, Kohler (1925), on the basis of his famous series of studies with apes, claimed that his animal subjects suddenly solved manipulation problems, after periods of overt inactivity (interpreted as periods of thought).

Behaviourist critics argued that trial and error was evident in Kohler's behavioural records and that the results could be explained simply by trial and error. They also pointed out that prior experience with the tools (sticks) used in the tasks was necessary for solution (Birch, 1945). Gestalt replied that, even if trial and error had occurred, it was not blind or random; the behaviourist retort was that *random* trial and error had never been postulated, but rather trial and error biased by prior learning. The issue of trial and error *v.* insight was also taken up within the more constrained area of discrimination learning. Krechevsky (1935) reported data apparently showing sudden solutions by rats of discrimination learning tasks together with response patterns that could be interpreted as evidence of hypothesis testing. The response patterns in question showed consistent responding to some irrelevant cue, such as position or size of the stimulus when brightness was the relevant cue. However, Spence (1936) showed that these response patterns could be produced by gradual accretions and reductions of response strength to the cues in the task and so could be explained in simpler, less mentalistic terms than those proposed by Krechevsky.

Studies of human problem-solving were not neglected by the Gestalt school. Karl Duncker (1945) examined in detail solution attempts to a range of problems involving mathematical or practical contents. The task known as the "X-ray" or "radiation" problem was particularly closely studied by Duncker.

The radiation problem was posed as follows (Duncker), "Given a human being with an inoperable stomach tumour, and rays which destroy organic tissue at sufficient intensity, by what procedure can one free him of the tumour by these rays and at the same time avoid destroying the healthy tissue which surrounds it". The subject was usually also given a sketch (*see* Fig. 1.1) and told that someone had visualized the situation in that way, but that this simple approach of sending a beam of rays straight through to destroy the tumour would not do, since the rays would destroy healthy tissue on the way to the tumour.

Subjects were asked to think aloud as they worked on the problem and the resulting records or protocols indicated a tendency to work backwards from the overall goal to subgoals which if achieved would lead to solution.

So, for instance, the major goal of "treating the tumour by rays without destroying healthy tissue" could be achieved if the subgoal of "avoiding contact between rays and healthy tissue" could be attained. In the most thoroughly discussed protocol, this particular subgoal governed much of the subjects' efforts. However, solution was not obtained until an alternative subgoal was set up of "lowering the intensity of the rays on their way through healthy tissue". This subgoal led to the solution of using a lens to focus weak rays on the tumour so that lethal intensity is only reached at the focal point.

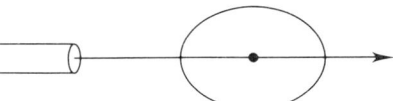

Fig. 1.1. Sketch similar to that given to subjects working on the X-ray problem (Duncker, 1945). The oval represents a cross-section through the body, with the tumour in the centre. The radiation apparatus is on the left, sending a beam through the tumour.

While Duncker investigated the development of insight, the opposite phenomenon of problem "blindness" (or "misleading sets") was studied by the Luchins (1942) in a series of experiments using water jug problems. In these tasks the subject was asked to say how one could get exactly a specified amount of water using jugs of fixed capacity and an unlimited source of water, e.g. given 3 jugs (A, B, C) of capacities 18, 43 and 10 units respectively, how could you obtain exactly 5 units of water? The solution may be expressed as B−A−2C. After a series of problems with that same general solution, subjects had great difficulty with the following problem. Given 3 jugs (A, B, and C) of capacities 28, 76 and 3 units respectively, how could you obtain exactly 25 units of water? In fact, the solution to this problem is very simple (i.e. A−C) but when it comes after a series of problems involving the long solution (B−A−2C) many subjects fail to solve or are greatly slowed down compared to control subjects.

A related block to effective problem-solving, known as "functional fixity", was also identified by work in the Gestalt tradition. Functional fixity tends to arise when an object has to be used in a new way in order to solve some problem. The classic study of functional fixity was carried out by Duncker (1945) using the "box" (or "candle" problem). In this task subjects were presented with tacks, matches, three small boxes and three candles. The problem was to put the candles side by side on a door, in such a way that they could burn in a stable fashion. For one group of subjects the boxes were empty but for the other group (experimental group) the boxes were used as containers and held the matches, tacks and candles. The solution is to use the boxes as platforms and fix them to the door using the tacks. It was found that the solving rate was much higher in the control group than in the experimental group. Duncker explained this result in terms of a failure to perceive the possible platform function of the boxes when they were presented as containers. Functional fixity has been independently demonstrated and further investigated in a number of later studies (e.g. Birch and Rabinowitz, 1951; Adamson and Taylor, 1954; Glucksberg and Weisberg, 1966; Glucksberg and Danks, 1968). Glucksberg has proposed an alternative interpretation of the effect, in terms of failure to notice the boxes as separate units when they are presented as containers. Whatever the detailed explanation, the phenomenon appears to be a robust one and is doubtless one source of difficulty in real life problem-solving.

4 Neo-behaviourism

The Gestalt investigators helped keep the study of thought processes alive in the 1920s and '30s while behaviourists focussed on associative learning in man and white rat. In the face of studies such as Duncker's on the X-ray problem, the simple Stimulus-Response (S-R) approach to extended chains of thought appears quite inadequate. Even in the case of maze problem-solving by rats, it was becoming evident that richer internal processes would have to be postulated within behaviourist theory. Thus the notion of a "mediating response" (r_m) was introduced into neo-behaviourist analyses. "Mediating responses" are seen as implicit, covert responses that generate "mediating stimuli" (s_m) which can elicit further mediating responses or overt behaviour. Chains of mediating stimuli and responses are taken to represent thought sequences. In many problems, various alternative sequences of actions might lead to the desired goal and such alternatives could be explored via mediational chains without overt trial and error. To take Berlyne's (1965) example, a resident of Boston may have many possible ways of travelling to New York involving different routes and different forms of transport. In thinking of how to make this journey the Bostonian subject would, on the neo-behaviourist analysis, "embark" (covertly) on one mediational chain out of those available. The alternative chains may be assumed to vary in strength of association to the problem stimulus i.e. they form a hierarchy, ordered from strongly associated to weakly associated chains. If the person is told that his dominant chain (air route, say) is blocked (e.g. airport closed), the next most dominant chain would tend to be evoked. Such a hierarchy of mediational response sequences is an example of a *habit-family hierarchy* (Hull, 1934).

Maltzman (1955) proposed an extension of the habit-family hierarchy notion which would permit hierarchies of habit-family hierarchies. Thus a problem stimulus could be associated in varying degrees of strength with a number of different habit-family hierarchies. Furthermore, the "nesting" of hierarchies within hierarchies could continue to many levels. These elaborate structures of mediating stimuli and responses are known as *compound* habit-family hierarchies. As Berlyne (1965) points out, when stimulus–response associations are organized in this way, the actual course of action followed will result from selection of a hierarchy at the highest level then from selection of a sub-hierarchy within the first hierarchy and so on. At each stage, "selections" would be made automatically on the basis of habit strength. This kind of scheme could, albeit in a cumbersome way, represent results such as those of Duncker on the X-ray problem, that show subjects following one general direction (corresponding to a selection at a high level of the compound hierarchy) down to a fair degree of detail (corresponding to selections at lower levels). Duncker's subjects abandoned directions and selected different ones when success was not obtained. In neo-behaviourist terms, continued failures within a given hierarchy of responses would reduce the relevant habit strengths and thus increase the probability of alternative hierarchies being evoked. Berlyne (1965) developed such ideas in an ambitious book (*Structure and Direction of Thinking*) that attempted to demonstrate how neo-behaviourist theory could account for directed thought. However by the time Berlyne's work appeared, the information processing "revolution" that still dominates cognitive psychology had begun (*see*, for instance, Miller, Galanter and Pribram's (1960) *Plans and the Structure of Behavior* for an important early manifesto of the new approach), and Berlyne's neo-behaviourist notions had little impact.

Although precursors of the modern information processing approach can be identified in researchers active before the Second World War such as Selz (*see* De Groot, 1965; and Frijda and De Groot, 1981), it appears to have taken developments in cybernetics and computer technology before psychologists in general felt secure in ascribing "goal directedness" and complex internal processes to man. Such concepts were felt to be open to charges of "mentalism", until implemented on machines such as guided missiles and computers. The information processing approach that has been dominant in cognitive psychology, will be discussed in the next section.

B. The information processing approach

1 Basic ideas

The main stimulus for the development of the *information processing* approach to thinking was the arrival of the computer. The basic idea of the information processing approach is that in his cognitive aspects, man can be regarded as a computer-like system that codes, stores, retrieves and transforms information. Computers work by following *programs* of step by step instructions. The instructions can be conditional, that is, can involve simple decisions so that the computer can be instructed to jump from one part of the program to another, depending on the outcome of intermediate operations—thus making the system very flexible. Furthermore, complete groups of instructions (sub-routines) can be given labels and activated by those names. This facility for creating and using sub-routines increases greatly the ease and flexibility of programming. Since both computers and humans flexibly manipulate symbols it is tempting to seek computer analogies and metaphors for human processes. Such analogies span a continuum of detail from vague verbal similarities between man and machine at one end to working computer programs that are intended to simulate (i.e. mimic) human processes at the other end. At an intermediate level of detail are flow charts or outlines of the organization and sequencing of major processing steps and decisions. Many information processing analyses are at this level.

Broad verbal analogies between man and computer provide an orientation to thinking about human processes. Within the loose constraints of this orientation, models of greater specificity can be constructed. If a model is at the flowchart level, then at least a definite sequence of broad steps has been specified and it may be possible to derive predictions from the flowchart itself. Furthermore the flowchart may be used to guide construction of a model at the most detailed and completely specified level, viz. that of a running program. Thus, the flowchart is a useful summary of the main features of the program. Indeed, it can be argued that the flowchart level is the most fruitful one (not too vague and not too detailed) for making comparisons between human and computer processes. However, having a running program corresponding to a given flowchart is a reassuring guarantee that the flowchart describes something that works.

2 Simulation

The virtues and problems of simulation level models will now be considered in more detail. Computer simulation is a general method that can be applied in all fields that involve the study of complex processes. For instance, the economy could be theoretically represented by a large number of variables (wages, prices, employment levels, balance of payments, exchange rates, etc.) which are all related to one another. An economist might speculate that a particular pattern of relationships holds among the main economic variables and this hunch could be tested by programming a computer to behave in accord with the economist's model. Many predictions could then be generated and checked against subsequent events (or degree of fit to past events could be assessed) and the simulation model could be revised to improve its predictions and ultimately provide a better understanding of the process being modelled.

In a similar way simulation can be used to explore and test ideas about human information processing. If we thought humans solved, say logic problems, by going through a certain sequence of decisions and operations, we could program a computer to go through the same sequence on a number of such problems and compare the computer's performance with that of a sample of human subjects. If the computer tended to take more steps on the problems that humans found more difficult or to make the same patterns of mistaken conclusions as humans, then the theory would gain support from such results. Furthermore, the computer could be made to print out every operation and decision that it makes and the resulting record could then be compared with the records produced by humans "thinking aloud" as they work on the problems. Comparison of human "thinking aloud" records and the computer's self report can be used to assess the degree of detailed match between computer and human processes —though, in practice, there are many difficulties in assessing the degree of match between two such multi-dimensional records.

3 *Capacity limitations*

Whatever process is to be simulated, a clear and unambiguous model is required since a computer program cannot work unless it is completely specified. So, one benefit of simulation is that it forces the theorist to be clear and unambiguous—properties that have sometimes been felt lacking in psychological models! Of course, a simulation model should not invoke processes that exceed human capabilities. Knowledge of human limitations is derived from studies of basic information processing tasks (e.g. recognizing familiar symbols, comparing symbols, reproducing previously presented symbols and so on). The following broad picture seems to emerge from such studies. Humans have a vast *long-term memory* capacity which is so organized as to permit generally rapid recognition of familiar symbols and retrieval of information associated with recognized symbols. Familiar symbols representing both presented information and associated, retrieved information, can be held temporarily in a small capacity *working memory*. Memory span studies suggest a capacity of about 5-9 symbols for this system (Miller, 1956). Many studies in the memory literature have focussed on the transfer of information from temporary storage in working memory to permanent storage in a long-term memory. From the point of view of problem-solving studies, the reverse traffic is more relevant. Problem-solving may often be seen as involving the application of retrieval rules which take inputs from working memory, locate appropriate symbols in long term memory and place those symbols in working memory, displacing old symbols if working memory capacity is exceeded.

In addition to storage capacity limitations, an important processing limitation is also generally acknowledged on the number of operations that can be carried out simultaneously. The human information processing system is assumed by most workers in the field to be *serial* at the level of problem-solving, i.e. only one operation is carried out at a time. This is a convenient assumption for computer simulation, since computers are serial devices. Also, there is little solid empirical evidence that humans can explore more than one line of problem development at a time. However, the notion of unconscious work progressing in parallel with the single conscious main stream of thought has been invoked (e.g. Neisser, 1963b), especially in connection with creativity, and the possibility cannot be ruled out *a priori*. Further discussion of this issue will be found in Chapter 7 on creative processes and in the final overview in Chapter 8.

The assumptions of *(a)* separate long-term and short-term working memories, and *(b)* of serial symbol processing, jointly serve to define a model of thinking that has been widely accepted within the information processing approach. Following Murdock on memory (1971), I will refer to this as the *modal model* of thinking. Although the modal model for thinking may well ultimately prove insufficient to cover all aspects of the topic, performance in a number of task areas has been successfuly analysed within its confines and many examples will be found in the following Chapters of research based on its assumptions.

4 Artificial intelligence
Before going on to discuss applications of the information processing approach, it should be pointed out that simulation programs are by no means the only ones that tackle problems hitherto the preserve of humans. Within the area of computer science there is a thriving sub-discipline known as *artificial intelligence* (AI) that attempts to construct programs capable of such achievements as playing master level chess, interpreting pictures and understanding natural language, among other undoubtedly intelligent activities. However, unlike simulation programs, AI programs are not restricted to processes that humans might conceivably use. Many chess programs, for example, are greatly superior to humans in their ability to look ahead exhaustively for a number of moves and cannot be considered to be simulations.

However, AI research has been a very useful source of ideas about possible human processes and of terminology for describing problems and methods. For example, in the field of memory, Quillian's (1968) program for natural language comprehension has led to some very fruitful notions about human semantic memory (Collins and Quillian, 1969; Collins and Loftus, 1975), while the General Problem Solver program (Newell and Simon, 1972) has been a valuable source of ideas about human methods in problem-solving (e.g. Egan and Greeno, 1974) and Winograd's (1972) language understanding program has helped underline interactions between grammatical, semantic and world knowledge in comprehension processes.

III. SUMMARY AND CONCLUDING COMMENTS

In this Chapter thinking has been characterized as an internal symbolic activity. This activity may be tightly directed to specific goals, as in problem-solving, or it may be free-floating, as in daydreaming. Thinking directed towards problem-solving involves exploring a symbolic model of the task to determine a useful course of action without overt and possibly costiy trial and error. Following Duncker, problems were defined as arising when an organism has a goal which it does not know how to reach.

Problems can vary in the degree to which they are well or ill defined. Most research has focussed on well-defined problems (drawn from puzzles, games, logic, maths) but it is hoped that results from these studies will be relevant to ill-defined problem-solving to the extent that people tackle such problems by first converting them into well-defined variants.

A variety of approaches have been taken to the topic of thinking in the history of psychology; the principal approaches having been those of classical introspectionism, early behaviourism, Gestalt, neobehaviourism and information processing. Although the field has been dominated by the information processing approach since the early 1960's, the earlier approaches were reviewed above in order to give some historical perspective. To summarize, the introspectionists focussed on the analysis of consciousness into elementary sensations, while the early behaviourists stressed observable behaviour and the importance of learning. The Gestalt school emphasized organization in thought and perception and argued strongly for the role of insight and restructuring in problem-solving. The neo-behaviourists attempted to explain the internal processes of thought in terms of covert chains of mediating responses and (response-produced) mediating stimuli. The resulting analyses could be stretched to deal with extended problem-solving, as in Duncker's X-ray problem, but only in a rather cumbersome fashion.

The currently dominant information processing approach takes the computer as its key metaphor for the mind. In their cognitive aspects, this approach sees people as computer-like systems that code, store, retrieve and transform information. Within this approach, models for thinking in particular tasks have been proposed in greatly varying degrees of detail. An intermediate level of analysis in terms of broad steps and decisions (flow chart level) has probably been the most prevalent and useful.

Most information processing models for various tasks accept certain limitations on cognitive capacities. More specifically, it is generally accepted that processing is serial at the problem-solving level and that while long-term memory is vast, working memory is very limited. These memory and processing limitations are key elements of what may be referred to as the "modal model" for thinking. According to this modal model, thinking involve serial symbol manipulations between long-term and working memory, in accord with rules or programs stored in the long-term memory. Throughout this text, and particularly in the final Chapter, the modal model assumptions will be considered against the data resulting from recent psychological research on thinking.

IV. FURTHER READING

Simon, H. A. (1981). Cognitive science: the newest science of the artificial. *In* "Perspectives on Cognitive Science" (*Ed.* D. A. Norman), pp 13–26. Ablex Publishing Corp., New Jersey.

This paper provides a historical and conceptual introduction to the information processing approach to cognition by one of the pioneers in the field.

Newell, A. (1981). Physical symbol systems. *In* "Perspectives on Cognitive Science" (*Ed.* D. A. Norman), pp 37–86. Ablex Publishing Corp., New Jersey.

In this difficult, but worthwhile, paper, Newell explores in considerable detail the basic notion of a "symbol system" as realized in minds and machines.

For recent contributions to the continuing debate on the functional role of imagery, the following may be consulted.

Pylyshyn, Z. W. (1981). The imagery debate: analogue media versus tacit knowledge. *Psychological Review* **88**, 16–45.

(Pylyshyn argues against imagery having a functional role in this very difficult paper.)

Kosslyn, S. M. (1981). The medium and the message in mental imagery: a theory. *Psychological Review* **88**, 46–66.

(Kosslyn offers a readable presentation of his "pro imagery" position without, however, emerging as the clear "winner" of the debate.)

2
Solving non-adversary problems

What mental processes are involved in solving, or attempting to solve problems? Since there are indefinitely many problems, varying greatly in content and form, the question, as it stands, is too broad and needs to be divided up into more specific questions to be manageable. This "splitting up" has been reflected in research practice, and efforts have been directed at mental processes involved in tackling *particular* problems, or *classes* of problems. It is, of course, hoped that similar processing limits will emerge over a variety of task areas. In the previous Chapter distinctions were drawn between well- and ill-defined problems and between adversary and non-adversary problems and these distinctions will help organize the discussion of research in this and following Chapters.

Within the field of problem-solving, certain methodological tendencies are quite marked and deserve some consideration at this point, before going on to deal with studies of particular topics. For instance, most research has focussed on well-defined problems in which the goal, starting state and permissible actions are all clearly specified. A major reason for using such problems is to increase the chances that all subjects will interpret the tasks concerned in the same way. Such unanimity would be useful in that it would simplify the theoretical task of explaining problem-solving behaviour if all subjects could be assumed to start with a similar model of the task which is to be worked on. Even if there is some variation in interpretation, the degree of variation is likely to be less for well-defined than for ill-defined tasks. A further tendency is for studies of non-adversary tasks to be limited to unfamiliar and rather artificial puzzles. The main reason for using artificial material has been to equate degree of familiarity with the task over subjects. The effects of familiarity (or expertise) in the task area have largely been studied in connection with adversary problems, such as chess, in which people vary widely in skill levels. An additional tendency has been to use small scale tasks that are usually solvable within an hour or less. This tendency has probably grown up for the very practical reason that subjects often cannot spare longer times to take part in experiments. Thus, studies of non-adversary problem-solving have generally focussed on puzzles that are well defined, small scale, artificial and unfamiliar. As indicated already, there are some advantages in using such materials, but there are also drawbacks, particularly in that generalization to problems not fitting the typical description (well-defined, small scale, etc.) must be somewhat uncertain. However, even within the typical methodological constraints, problem content and structure vary widely. So, it is not obvious, in advance, whether similar processes and limitations will show up across the various different, but typical, laboratory tasks. The current Chapter includes consideration of this issue.

The contents of the remainder of this Chapter will now be indicated. First, I will introduce some terminology and approaches, (largely from outwith psychology), that have proved useful in describing well-defined problems and solving processes. In broad terms, on one approach (state-action representation), the possible manipulations of the problem material are seen as generating an often vast network of possible paths leading to numerous intermediate states, and the solver is regarded as searching the resulting mental "maze" or "tree" of possibilities for a path to the goal. A second approach, (problem reduction) involves attempting to divide problems up into more manageable sub-problems. Again, this leads to a "tree" of possible divisions of the problem. How these notions have been used in the analysis of human problem solving will be discussed with reference to a range of laboratory tasks ranging from very well-defined examples (e.g. missionaries-and-cannibals puzzles) to less well-defined cases (e.g. cryptarithmetic). The issue of task interpretation processes will then be addressed. Finally, the Chapter closes with a brief summary and some concluding comments.

I. STATE-ACTION REPRESENTATIONS

A. Graphs and trees

Many well-defined problems can be represented as involving a search for a suitable series of operations that will transform the starting state of the problem into a state that meets the goal requirements. In general, the possible sequences of actions and intermediate states can often be represented by diagrams composed of points (or "nodes"), representing the states of the problem, connected by lines ("arcs") which represent the actions that transform one state into another. Such structures of "nodes and arcs" are known in mathematics as "graphs" and can be used to represent many phenomena. A clear application to problem representation comes from "travelling salesman" problems (*see* Fig. 2.1). In such problems the task is to find the shortest route around a number of cities (nodes) given the interconnections available amongst them in the form of road routes (arcs). This is an important class of problem in real life, and no mechanical solution is available which guarantees to find the shortest route, apart from generating all possible routes and selecting the shortest. But, since the number of possible routes grows very quickly as the number of cities increases, an exhaustive listing of all possible routes soon becomes impractical. Thus, heuristic methods are required; that is, methods that although not guaranteed to work, usually produce useful answers without too much searching.

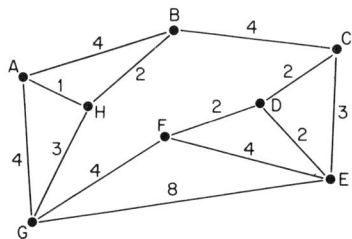

Fig. 2.1. The travelling salesman problem. Find the shortest route that visits all the cities and returns to the starting point (A).

A special form of graph which is frequently useful is the *tree*. In a tree graph the connections are directional and there are no loops or returns to earlier nodes. The appearance of such graphs is reminiscent of an upside down tree with the starting node at the top of the page and its descendants branching out down the page. The possible sequences of actions and intermediate states in well-defined problems can often be represented by this special form of graph and the resulting diagrams are known as *state-action trees* (Wickelgren, 1974). Take, for example, the 8-puzzle (Nilsson, 1971) as shown in Fig. 2.2. The numbers are on tiles in a 3 × 3 frame. One cell of the frame is always empty, so that an adjacent tile can be moved

Fig. 2.2. An example 8-puzzle. The tiles are to be moved so that the goal state is reached from the given starting configuration.

into the empty cell, thus moving the empty cell also. The possible sequences of moves in this 8-puzzle can be represented by a state-action tree (Fig. 2.3) in which states of the puzzle generated by making the possible moves are depicted. The first 3 levels of the tree are shown in Fig. 2.3 (assuming that no move is immediately "undone"). There are over 100,000 states that can be reached from the start. One of these is the goal. You may find it instructive to seek the solution path for the puzzle shown in Fig. 2.3.

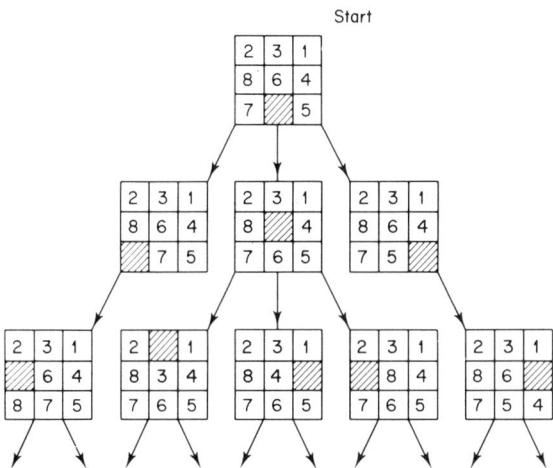

Fig. 2.3. First three levels of the state-action tree for the example 8-puzzle.

A major characteristic of state-action trees is the rapid way in which they grow. If there are m alternative actions per state, then there will be m^n possible sequences of n actions; in other words, with n actions one could reach any one of m^n states. (So, for example, with 4 alternative actions (moves) available from each state, one could reach any of 1,024 ($= 4^5$) different states in just 5 steps.) The difficulty is in finding a short path to a goal state with little search of the state-action tree.

In the fields of AI and operations research, ideas have been developed about searching state-action trees that are useful for discussing problem-solving both by man and by machine and a sample of these notions will be outlined in the following sections.

B. Basic search methods

In principle, paths from starting states to goal states can often be found by systematic searches. The two main search schemes are known as *"depth first"* and *"breadth first"* searching. Depth first searching follows up just one state from each state examined until either the goal or a dead end in reached. (A "dead end" would be a state which could not be developed further.) On encountering a dead end, depth first search would "back up" to the preceding state and follow up another hitherto unexplored branch. In terms of the 8-puzzle example a depth first search could develop as indicated in Fig. 2.4.

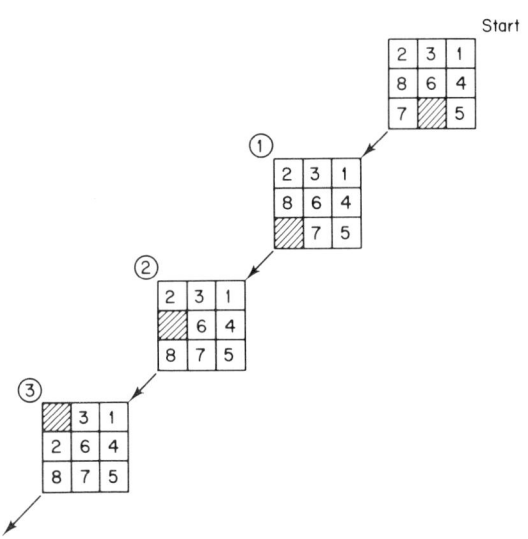

Fig. 2.4. A depth first search of the 8-puzzle state-action tree. The circled numbers indicate the order in which states are examined.

There are no dead ends in the 8-puzzle search tree and so the depth first search would never back up, but would continue indefinitely or until the goal was reached. Order of examination of the states is indicated by the circled numbers in Fig. 2.4.

As depth first search procedes, the memory load grows relatively slowly, just by one intermediate state per level of depth. Breadth first search is much more stressful in terms of memory load.

In breadth first search, all states at a given level are examined before using the moves from each state to check all the next level states. The resulting pattern of search is illustrated for the 8-puzzle example in Fig. 2.5. The circled numbers in the figure indicate the order in which states would be examined in a breadth first search.

Breadth first searches involve ever increasing memory loads as search progresses downwards through ever expanding trees of possibilities. In return for high memory loads, breadth first search is *algorithmic,* that is, it will always find a goal state and furthermore it will be a goal state that is a minimum number of moves from the start. (An algorithm is a procedure, possibly inefficient, that is guaranteed to solve all members of a given class of problems.) By contrast, depth first searches will not necessarily find the goal. They can be diverted down infinitely long byways and so fail to solve. Also, any solutions reached by depth first are not necessarily the best ones in terms of number of moves from the start to the goal.

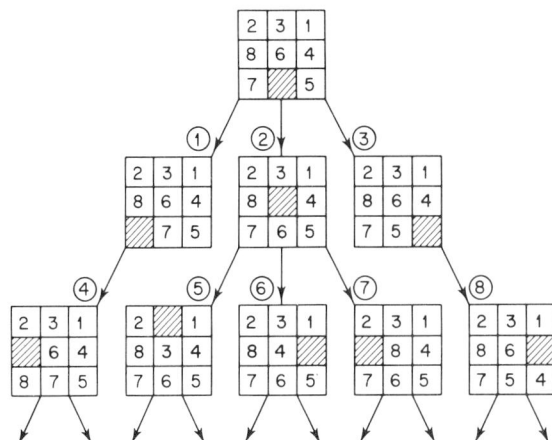

Fig. 2.5. A breadth first search of the 8-puzzle state-action tree. The circled numbers indicate the order in which states are examined.

A compromise form of search that mixes depth and breadth first methods is known as *"progressive deepening".* This method consists of searching depth first up to some limit, then backing up and continuing search down all branches up to the depth limit until the entire tree has been searched to the depth limit or the goal has been located. If the goal has not been found within the first depth limit, the limit is increased by some fixed amount and search continues in the same way until the new depth limits are encountered or a goal state is located. This method is of additional interest because rather similar strategies have emerged from studies of human search processes in chess (Charness, 1981b; De Groot, 1965; Newell and Simon, 1972; Wagner and Scurragh, 1971; *see* Chapter 3 for further details).

C. Selective search

Search of a state-action tree can often be made more efficient by selecting promising states for further development on the basis of an evaluation of how close the states are to the goal.

In the classical "hill climbing" method, the exact value of the goal state is not known and the solver tries to find the best state in the state-action tree. The task is rather like that of a real climber in thick fog, who wishes to reach the highest spot in the area. He or she can certainly find a peak by first testing out one pace in the four main directions and taking a pace in the direction that moves to the highest spot of the four tested, and then repeating this process until a spot is reached from which no move yields an improvement. This method is sure to find a peak, but there is no guarantee that it will be the highest peak, if there are foothills around. If the climber has an altimeter and knows the height of the highest peak then he or she could backtrack from any mistakenly climbed foothills and keep trying until the desired peak is reached.

Hill climbing can be useful but it does have hazards. Apart from the "foothill" problem just alluded to, there are also, the "plateau problem" and the "ridge problem". If a plateau is reached then no steps (actions) lead to any marked improvement and much wandering results. On a ridge, it might be that none of the four principal directions lead to improvement although some other intermediate direction might (Winston, 1977, Chapter 4).

A better procedure than hill climbing is known as *"best first"*. In this method, forward motion is from the best state encountered so far, no matter where in the search tree. For such a procedure to work the solver must remember the evaluations that have been made of previously encountered states.

For any selective search method to work, a useful *"evaluation function"* must be developed which expresses the "promise" of an intermediate state as a function of its characteristics, e.g. in attempting the 8-puzzle, a simple evaluation function would be to calculate the average distance of the pieces from their target positions. This should be better than nothing, though certainly sub-optimal and poorer than those functions that Doran and Michie (1966) developed for their Graph Traverser program that successfully tackles 8- and 15-puzzle tasks.

II. PROBLEM REDUCTION APPROACH

State-action approaches to problem-solving involve direct attempts to manipulate the problem materials (mentally or in reality) in worthwhile directions. A more roundabout, but often more useful approach, is known as *"problem reduction"*. The basic idea is to convert a single complex problem into a number of (easily) solved sub-problems. "Factoring" or dividing a problem into sub-problems, each of which can be solved separately, is generally a very useful procedure when it can be applied. Newell, Shaw and Simon (1962) give the example of safecracking. If 10 dials each with 2 possible positions have to be all set correctly before a safe will open then one try in 2^{10} (i.e. 1024) will be correct and on average you would need around 500 trials to find the correct combination, (assuming sampling without replacement from the possibilities). If, however, each dial clicked when it was in its own correct position, one would need on average only 1.5 trials per dial i.e. around 15 trials for the whole set. So when this problem is reduced from a single task to ten small ones the savings in terms of expected search effort are dramatic (a 97 per cent reduction in the number of trials required).

Of course, problems do not always yield to such a simple "factoring" approach. In the 8-puzzle, for example, one would not get far by trying to set the 8 pieces separately because getting one piece correct may disrupt those that have been previously set. Also, a more complex problem–subproblem structure may be required in which the subproblems themselves need further reduction.

A rather general method for developing subproblem structures is *"means-end"* analysis. In this, the solver compares the goal with the starting state and selects one of the ways in which they differ as a goal for the first subproblem. The solver then selects from memory an action or "operator" relevant to reducing this difference. If the first selected operator cannot be applied, because its preconditions are not met, then a new subproblem is generated viz. to reduce the difference between the current state and the operator's preconditions. This new subgoal causes a relevant operator to be selected and so on. The "means-end" process develops a tree of subproblems and, as in state action trees, some backing up will often be necessary.

Making travel plans provides a real life example of means-end analysis. If the problem is to travel from London to New York, the difference between the starting state and the goal is a large distance. Large distances can be reduced by using aeroplanes (the first operator). But to use a plane one needs to have a ticket and to be at the airport. That is, the preconditions of the first operator have to be met. These preconditions define two subproblems. The "ticket" problem may be solved by using a travel agent, but to use a travel agent the would-be traveller must be in communication with one and so a new "communication" subproblem arises . . . and so on, until the solving of the subsidiary problems resolves the overall problem.

Means-end analysis is especially useful when the number of alternative actions is very large—because it offers rules for selecting actions for further exploration. Only actions relevant to approaching closer to the goal are selected on this method.

The usefulness of the means-end approach was demonstrated by the successes of Newell and Simon's General Problem Solver (GPS) program. This program incorporated means-end analysis and achieved a fair measure of success with a range of problems including integral calculus, symbolic logic, missionary-and-cannibal puzzles and the Tower of Hanoi (Ernst and Newell, 1969). Comparison of the steps taken by the GPS program and the thinking aloud record of a human subject when both tackled a symbolic logic task, indicated a promising degree of match between the problem-solving processes of humans and GPS. Other evidence for means-end analysis in human problem-solving may be found in Duncker's (1945) thinking aloud records from subjects attempting the X-ray problem (discussed in Chapter 1).

III. EXPERIMENTAL STUDIES

In this section I will review some recent experimental studies of human problem-solving in which there is no element of competition or conflict with another rational being. We will consider first of all tasks, such as "missionaries-and-cannibals" and water jar problems, to which the state-action approach can be applied quite directly, next a task that lends itself to a problem reduction approach (the Tower of Hanoi), then an example of a task in which the "space" that the solver works in is less obvious (i.e. crypt-arithmetic) and, finally, studies of how task representations are constructed from problem descriptions.

While considering the experimental studies discussed in this and in the following Chapter, it might be useful to keep the following questions in mind:

(1) Under what conditions do humans adopt state-action as against problem reduction approaches? What factors of problem structure or prior experience are relevant?

(2) Both state-action and problem reduction methods require search. What factors shape human search patterns? What affects the depth and breadth of search? Can limits of working memory be related to the search strategies adopted in various tasks? What factors of problem structure or prior experience are relevant?

A. Move problems

The two main examples of problems that can be easily described in state-action terms and that have been studied recently, are the "missionaries-and-cannibals" and "water jars" tasks. These are also referred to as "move" problems, in which movements of units or materials are required to transform the starting state into the goal state.

1 Missionaries-and-cannibals tasks

The first study of the "missionaries-and-cannibals" problem that used a state-action approach seems to have been carried out by Thomas (1974). He used a variant of the task in which "hobbits" replaced the missionaries and "orcs" the cannibals. The "hobbits-and-orcs" problem requires that the solver produce a sequence of moves to transport 3 hobbits and 3 orcs across a river. The only way to cross the river is by use of a boat and the boat can carry one or at most two creatures. At least one creature must be in the boat for it to cross. The major constraint in the problem is to avoid having the hobbits ever outnumbered by orcs on the same side of the river, since as is well known (Tolkien, 1966), the orcs will gang up and devour the hobbits at the slightest opportunity.

This problem can be readily represented as a "state-action" graph in which states of the problem are specified by *(a)* the numbers of hobbits and orcs on the starting (left) side and *(b)* the position of the boat (on right or left bank). Actions consist of moving one or two creatures from where the boat is to the opposite bank. At each state a number of actions are conceivable; some are "illegal", i.e. result in consumption of hobbits; some take the subject backwards to a state already visited and one or at most two, advance toward the solution state. The "legal" search space is represented in Fig. 2.6 and the solution can be read from the diagram. Each state is specified by a three digit code: *(1)* the number of hobbits on the starting side; *(2)* the number of orcs on the starting side; *(3)* the location of the boat — "1" if on the starting side, "0" if on the other side.

The transitions are labelled to represent corresponding actions, e.g. 1H1O means that one hobbit and one orc were transported on the move.

In Thomas's study subjects tackled the problem on a computer display which showed the current state of the problem. The computer changed the display in accord with the subject's decisions about moves if the moves were legal, otherwise the computer informed the subject of the error and invited another try.

The relative difficulties of decisions are indicated by graphs of times to

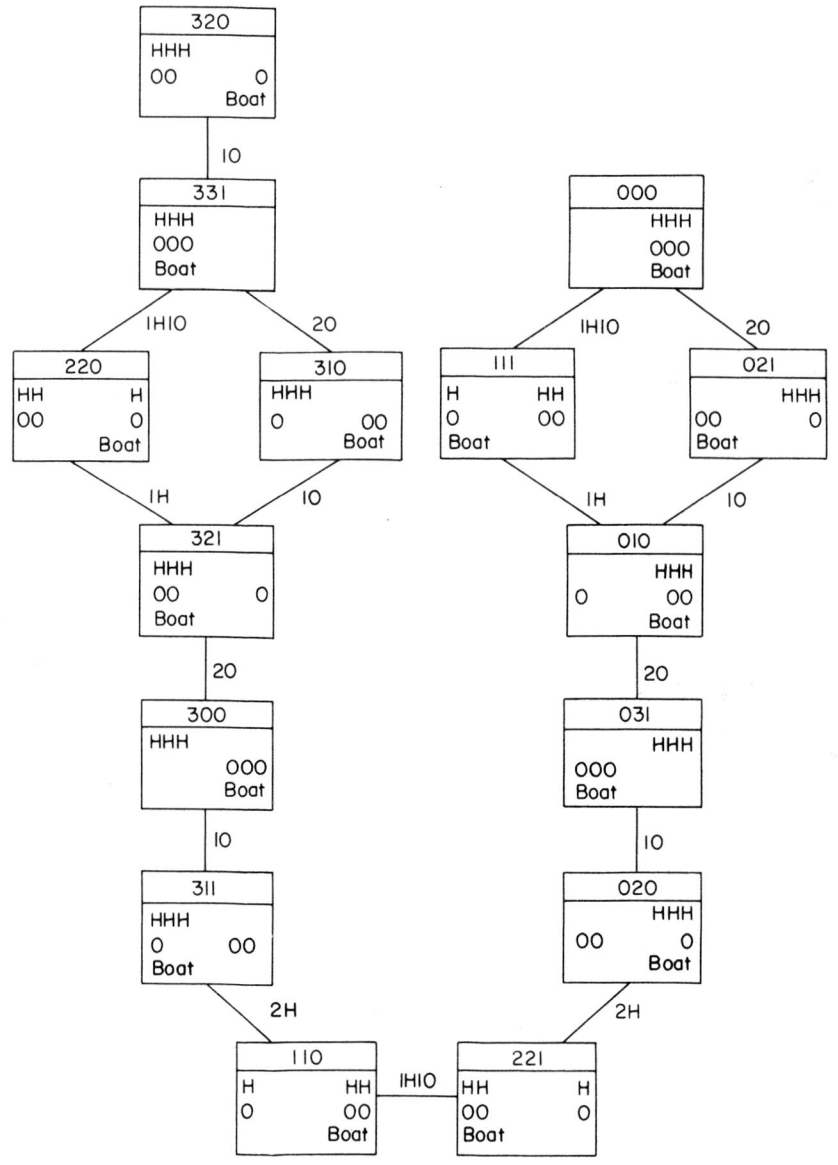

Fig. 2.6. State-action graph of hobbits-orcs problem. See text for further explanation. *(Reproduced with permission from Thomas, J. C. (1974). An analysis of behavior in the hobbits-orcs problem.* Cognitive Psychology **6**, *257–269.)*

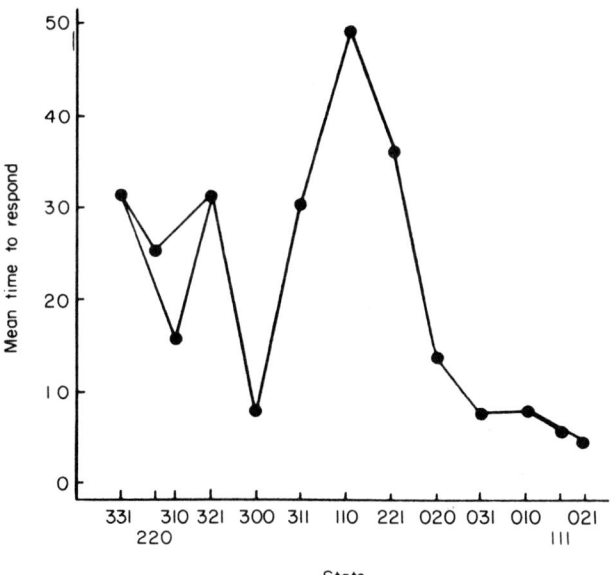

Fig. 2.7. Mean time to respond at each state. *(Reproduced with permission from Thomas, J. C. (1974). An analysis of behavior in the hobbits-orcs problem.* Cognitive Psychology *6, 257–269.)*

Fig. 2.8. Proportion of errors at each state. *(Reproduced with permission from Thomas, J. C. (1974). An analysis of behavior in the hobbits-orcs problem.* Cognitive Psychology *6, 257–269.)*

choose and error rates per state (Figs. 2.7 and 2.8). The greatest difficulties were experienced in states 321 and 110.

Thomas notes that these states may be difficult for different reasons. It may be pointed out that state 321 does have three legal moves, of which one is helpful. There are also two illegal moves possible in this state. Furthermore, at state 321 there is the possibility of "cycling" going from 321—310—331—220—321. So there are more alternative responses at 321 than at other states. The difficulty at 110 however, may be due to the apparent reversal of progress that is required at that point. This conflicts with the general "hill climbing" approach of moving to ever closer approximations to the goal. In going from 110 to 221 the solver actually appears to be getting further from the goal rather than closer. Wickelgren (1974) puts this problem into a general class of "detour" problems that pose difficulties for "hill climbing" methods.

As well as a (control) group of subjects who worked through the problem from the normal starting state, a part-whole group first solved the problem from the halfway state, 110 to 000. Then the part-whole group were given the whole problem from the normal starting state (331).

Table 2.1. Average moves in each half of hobbits-orcs problem (Thomas, 1974).

The part-whole group had prior experience of the second half and then tackled the whole problem. The control group worked through the whole problem in the normal way, without prior training.

	First half of task	Second half of task
Control group (n = 71)	13.0	15.5
Part-whole group (n = 44)	10.8	14.3
		(First attempt = 12.0)

The results (Table 2.1) indicate that the part group learned something from doing the second half that helped in tackling the first half. Interestingly the control group do not appear to have benefitted from the first half when they tackled the second half, furthermore, when the part group repeat the second half while attempting the whole problem, they do *worse* than on the first time through. Apparently, a strong context effect occurred when subjects reached state 110 while solving the whole problem. This seems to support the idea, based on Wickelgren's analysis, that people tackling the whole problem, are reluctant to reverse the apparent flow of moves in the direction of the solution, but the "detour" is less apparent without the background of progress through the earlier states.

Finally, from an analysis of the distributions of total items to solve, using a statistical technique devised by Restle and Davis (1962), Thomas inferred that some three or four major cognitive steps were involved in solving.

These steps would be decisions about whole blocks of moves, blocks that were then run off with increasing speed. At the end of each preplanned block of moves a longer pause would be evident while the next major decision was taken. The plot of latencies over states was consistent with about 3 such major decisions points (Fig. 2.7). However, more recent studies, some of which will be described next, suggest that subjects tackle this problem by making only very "local" move-by-move decisions, rather than higher order strategic decisions.

Simon and Reed (1976) examined a more complex version of the hobbits-orcs or missionaries-cannibals task than that studied by Thomas. In the Simon and Reed study, subjects were required to solve a problem involving five missionaries and five cannibals (known as the 5MC task from now on). In this problem the boat can hold up to three people. The state-action graph for this problem is shown in Fig. 2.9. There are 27 legal states and although there are only a few possible moves per state, subjects find the task quite difficult. For example, although it can be solved in 11 moves, one of Simon and Reed's naive groups averaged 30.6 legal moves to solution.

Simon and Reed put forward a model involving *strategy shift* during solving. According to their model, people start out with a "balancing" strategy that leads them to try to have equal numbers of missionaries and cannibals on each side, but then they switch at some point to a "means-end" strategy in which legal moves that maximize the number of people on the target side are preferred (as long as missionaries are not outnumbered). Additionally, the model assumed that subjects performed a local "anti-looping" test to avoid reversing the move made on the immediately previous trial. This was suggested because at each step it is possible to go back to the preceding state. Some randomness was built into the model by an assumption that people would sometimes make random moves and would not always check for loops.

The model was tested against data from two experiments. In experiment 1 a control group tackled the problem without any special hints while an experimental "subgoal" group were told that on the way to solution, a state would be reached in which three cannibals were on the target side, on their own, and without the boat (state L in Fig. 2.9). In experiment 2, subjects solved the same problem twice, thus producing data on training effects.

In each condition, estimates were made of the model's five parameters. These parameters were the probabilities of *(1)* shifting strategy; *(2)* checking

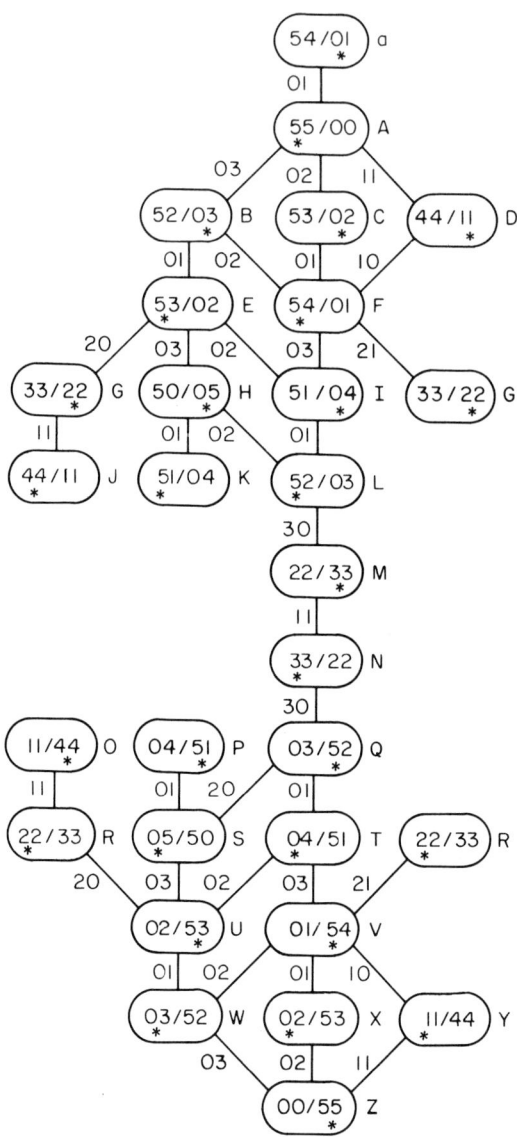

Fig. 2.9. State-action space for the five missionary-five cannibal (5MC) problem. The four digit code for each state represents the number of missionaries and cannibals on the left and right banks. The position of the boat at each state is marked with a small star. *(Reproduced with permission from Simon, H. A. and Reed, S. K. (1976). Modelling strategy shifts in a problem solving task.* Cognitive Psychology **8**, 86–97.)

for loops; *(3)* making a random move; *(4)* the rate of increase in the probability of loop checking; *(5)* the rate of decrease in the probability of moving at random. It was found that providing a subgoal (experiment 1) facilitated performance of the experimental subjects and this was reflected in an increase in the probability of shifting strategy from "balance" to "means-end" in the experimental group as compared with the control group.

Similarly a second attempt at the task (experiment 2) led to an improved performance which was reflected in a larger estimated strategy shift parameter on the second attempt than on the first. Furthermore, the model predicted quite closely the average number of times, within each condition, that subjects made each possible move. Thus, the data can be interpreted reasonably well within the framework of this model; a model that involves only local decisions with no extensive forward planning or look ahead beyond the immediate alternatives. It may be that this is the case for the 5MC problem while the 3MC problem, that Thomas (1974) studied, may permit more strategic planning; or it may be that Simon and Reed's analysis was not sensitive enough to uncover features of performance not consistent with their model. Thomas used latency and error data in his analysis while Simon and Reed ignored error trials (which were approximately 20% of all trials), and did not use latencies.

2 Water jug tasks

A somewhat similar style of model exploration is found in Atwood *et al.*'s studies of water jug and missionaries-and-cannibals tasks, to which we now turn.

Atwood and Polson (1976) have developed a model for solving the following sort of water jug problems. Given three jugs, A, B, C, where A can hold 8 units, B, 5 units and C, 3 units; A is initially full, and B and C are empty. The subject's task is to find a sequence of pourings which would divide the contents of the largest jug evenly between the largest and the middle size jug. In pouring, water is transferred until the jug the subject is pouring from is empty or the jug being poured into is full. Water cannot be added or flung away during the course of solving the problem. Such problems can be succinctly represented by state-action graphs, as in Fig. 2.10.

As can be seen from the state-action graph there is ample scope for "looping". Of course, the subject only sees the current state at any one time and has to envisage the successor dates and evaluate them mentally. Under such conditions these problems are generally found to be difficult, (e.g. the (8, 5, 3) problem can be solved in seven moves yet it took a naive group 26 moves on average).

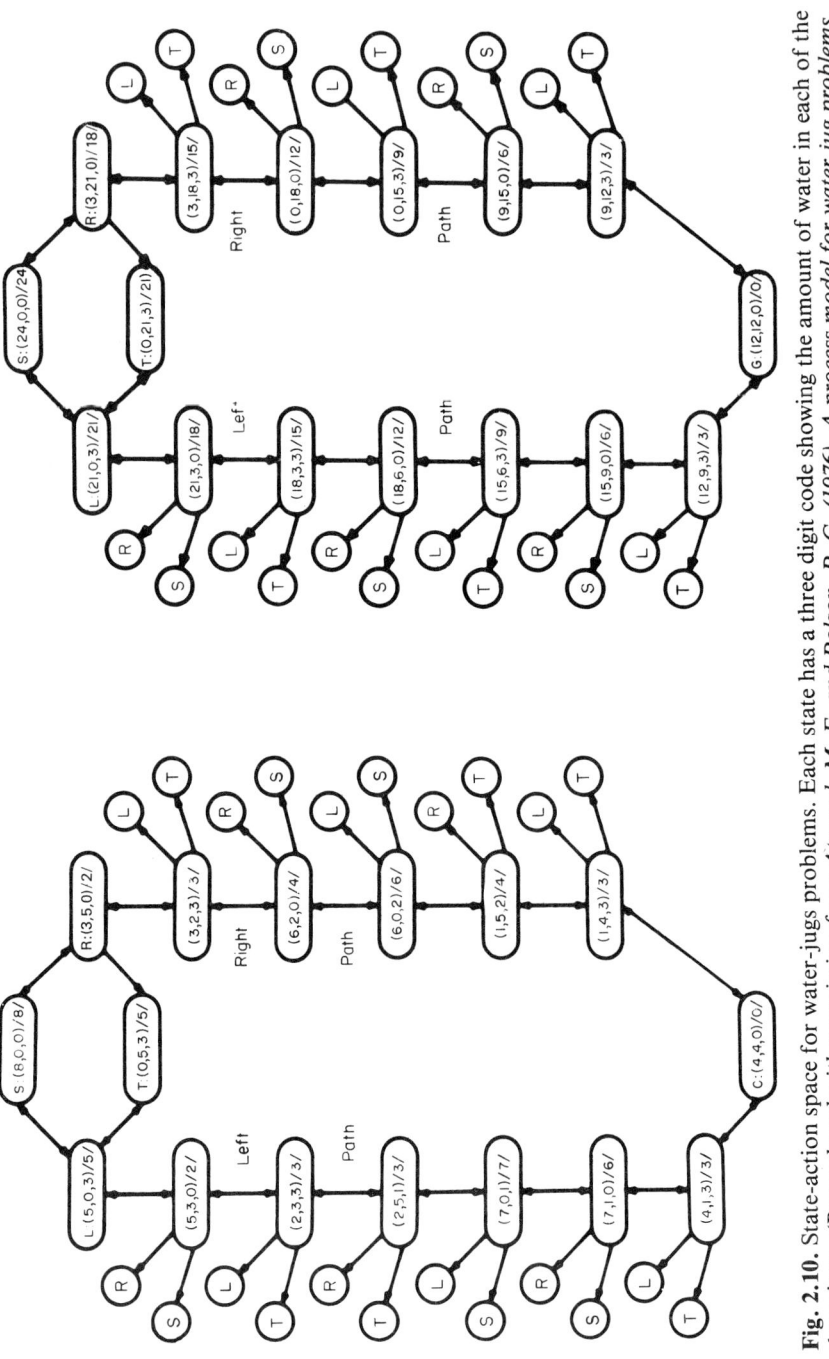

Fig. 2.10. State-action space for water-jugs problems. Each state has a three digit code showing the amount of water in each of the three jugs. (Reproduced with permission from Atwood, M. E. and Polson, P. G. (1976). *A process model for water jug problems.* Cognitive Psychology **8**, 191–216.)

The Atwood and Polson model combines assumptions about state evaluation, look ahead and memory processes. It assumes that subjects only look ahead to a depth of one step and that they evaluate the immediate successors of the current state by means of an evaluation function that sums the discrepancies between the target (goal) quantities in jugs A and B and the quantities in each successor state considered.

The actual evaluation function is:

$$e_i = c_i(A) - G(A) + c_i(B) - G(B)$$

where $c_i(A)$ is the number of units in jug A in state i and $G(A)$ is the number of units in jug A in the goal state. The smaller e_i is, the more the evaluated state is like the goal state. It is assumed that short-term memory can hold information on up to some small number, r, of possible moves. At the beginning of the problem all moves are *new* and the one with the best evaluation will be selected. Information about that move is stored in long term memory with some probability s. In future decisions, "old" moves tend to be avoided, unless there are no "new" moves.

Experiment 1 involved two conditions. In condition 1, subjects solved a practice problem (6, 4, 1) then the (8, 5, 3), the (24, 21, 3) and the (8, 5, 3) task. The (24, 21, 3) problem could be solved by applying the "means-end" evaluation heuristic already outlined while (8, 5, 3) requires a "detour" (i.e. a move to an "Unacceptable" state with a much poorer evaluation than the current state). It was predicted that tackling the (24, 21, 3) problem first would strengthen reliance on the means-end strategy, and so make the (8, 5, 3) problem more difficult, and that the (8, 5, 3) would be harder than (24, 21, 3) problem. In experiment 2 all subjects did the practice problem (6, 4, 1) followed by one of (8, 5, 3), (4, 9, 5), (12, 7, 4) or (16, 10, 3) problems.

As the model predicted, (8, 5, 3) was considerably more difficult than (24, 21, 3), but there was no order effect, in that doing (24, 21, 3) first did not hinder performance on (8, 5, 3). Analysis of both experiments indicated that the *number of acceptable looping moves* was the main determinant of problem difficulty.

The numbers of visits per problem state were quite well predicted by the model when the parameters were set such that information about 3 possible moves could be held in short-term memory and information about a visited state entered long-term memory with probability 9.

3 A general model?

Jeffries, Polson, Razran and Atwood (1977) described and tested an extension of Atwood and Polson's water jug model that can handle missionaries-and-cannibals problems. The extended model assumes that moves are selected on the basis of state evaluation processes and memory processes. Possible moves are evaluated in terms of how close they come to the goal state. The following general evaluation function is proposed:

$$e_i = aM_i + bC_i = cP_i$$

where M = number of missionaries, C = number of cannibals and P = number of MC pairs, on the target side in all cases.

By varying the parameters (a, b and c), pure means-end, balancing, cannibals- or missionaries-first strategies can be represented, as can mixed strategies. The proposed memory processes are the same as in the water jug model. Information about a small number of moves (r) being currently considered is stored in short-term memory. Information about actually visited states is stored in long-term memory with some probability (s).

It is assumed that move selection may involve up to three stages. First, all "acceptable" moves are considered. These are moves that do not lead to "worse" states than that already occupied.

Moves to new "acceptable" states are more likely to be taken than moves to "old" states (i.e. states recognized as having been already entered). If a move is not selected at this stage, the subject then seeks any moves leading to new states ("acceptable" or not). If all immediate successor states are "old", the next stage begins and the subject simply selects the best one of the r states that he is considering. Finally, once a move is selected it may or may not be screened for *illegality*. If illegality is detected the selected move is dropped and the process returns to the point where the illegal move was selected and continues from that point. So, this model permits illegal moves as well as legal ones.

Twenty-five to 35 subjects tackled four variants of the missionaries-and-cannibals problem. These variants had the same structure but were couched in terms of *(1)* hobbits-and-orcs, *(2)* elves-and-men I, (elves disappear if outnumbered by men), *(3)* elves-and-men II, (custom requires elves and men to be paired or for 3 elves to be together), *(4)* silver-and-gold (a monk must convey 6 talismans through a forest. Gold talismans must never outnumber silver talismans on either side of forest).

Quite good fits to the state to state transition frequencies were obtained using the following parameter values over all problems.

$$\alpha = .70, \beta = .15, s = .85, r = 2$$

where α = probability of picking a new move at stage 1, β = probability of picking an old move at stage 2, s = probability of storing information

about a visited state in long term memory and r = number of successor states about which information is held in short term memory.
The evaluation function was

$$e_i = 3M_i + C_i + 2P_i$$

(Note: A wide variety of functions would lead to similar results.)

The illegal move detection parameters varied across problems. However, the general pattern of results was very similar over task variants.

The model was supported by reasonable fits between its predictions and the data, including illegal move data over all conditions. It is an attractive model in that it relates missionaries-and-cannibals tasks to water jug tasks and thus helps to reduce the fragmentation so prevalent in the problem-solving area. On the negative side however, the number of free parameters to be fitted is rather large, (nine, in fact, if we count the three evaluation function parameters). The model has so far only been applied to the three missionaries-and-cannibals task; it would be interesting to see an extension to the five missionaries-and-cannibals task, in which it could be compared directly with Simon and Reed's "strategy shift" model. Also, the model deals only with the move data and not at present with latencies (cf. Thomas, 1974). Again, it would be interesting to see extensions in that direction. Finally, the model does not seem to offer a ready explanation for the effects of hints and prior experience—effects which are dealt with by Simon and Reed's model.

A more recent study (Atwood, Masson and Polson, 1980) focussed on the question of the degree of planning used by subjects in the water jug task. The Jeffries *et al.* model proposes that people only look one move ahead. Subjects were given a number of water jug problems under different memory aiding conditions. For some subjects the immediately available successor states were presented on each trial, for others the successor states were shown and were also marked to indicate whether they had been visited before. This manipulation should help reduce looping moves. Control subjects worked under the normal conditions of problem presentation. Analysis indicated that very good fits to the move data could be obtained without assuming any look ahead beyond one level. These data then support the Jeffries *et al.* model. However, we must note that a large number of free parameters are involved and that the subjects were naive with respect to the task.

4 Tower of Hanoi problem

In the classic Tower of Hanoi (or Tower of Brahma) problem the subject is presented with three vertical pegs on one of which are n discs piled up in order of size, with the largest on the bottom. The task is to transfer the entire stack of discs from the starting peg to a target peg, moving only one disc at a time and never placing a larger disc on top of a smaller disc. The spare peg may be used as a temporary holding place. If there are n discs then the minimum number of moves required is 2^n-1. Thus the four disc version in Fig. 2.11 below would require a minimum of 15 moves.

Fig. 2.11. A Tower of Hanoi problem. The stack of discs is to be moved from the starting peg to the target peg, moving only one disc at a time and never placing a larger disc on a smaller one.

According to legend (Raphael, 1976) some monks near Hanoi are working on a 64-disc puzzle, and when they complete it the world will end. However, even if they make no mistakes or wasted moves it will still take them nearly a trillion years to finish, at one move per second!

Research with small versions of this puzzle suggests that subjects come to impose a goal-subgoal (or problem-subproblem) structure on the task (Egan and Greeno, 1974; Luger, 1976). For example, the four-disc task may be structured as follows:

(1) Solve the 3-disc puzzle of moving the top 3 discs from peg 1 to peg 2, so that disc 4 can be moved to the target peg 3. (8 moves)
(2) Now solve the 2-disc puzzle of moving the top 2 discs from peg 2 to peg 1 so that disc 3 can be moved to the target peg 3. (4 moves)
(3) Now solve the 1-disc puzzle of moving the top disc on peg 1 to peg 2 so that disc 2 can be moved to peg 3. (2 moves)
(4) Finally move disc 1 from peg 1 to peg 3 (1 move)

Following the above structure the problem is solved in the minimum of 15 moves — and the solution was guided by splitting up (reducing) the task into subproblems. The 3-disc subproblem can be tackled by reducing it to a 2 disc and a 1 disc subproblem. A possible "problem reduction" tree for the 4 disc task is shown in Fig. 2.12.

Egan and Greeno (1974) report a study in which some subjects had prior experience with 3-disc problems before tackling 5- or 6-disc puzzles. Other subjects attempted the difficult tasks without prior experience. The error profiles for all groups indicated that they performed better as important goals were near accomplishment. Also, they tended to perform worse (i.e. make more moves off the best solution path) when they were at points in the task that were remote from satisfying important goals.

Further evidence that a goal–subgoal structure is commonly induced by this problem comes from studies by Luger (1976). The state-action graph

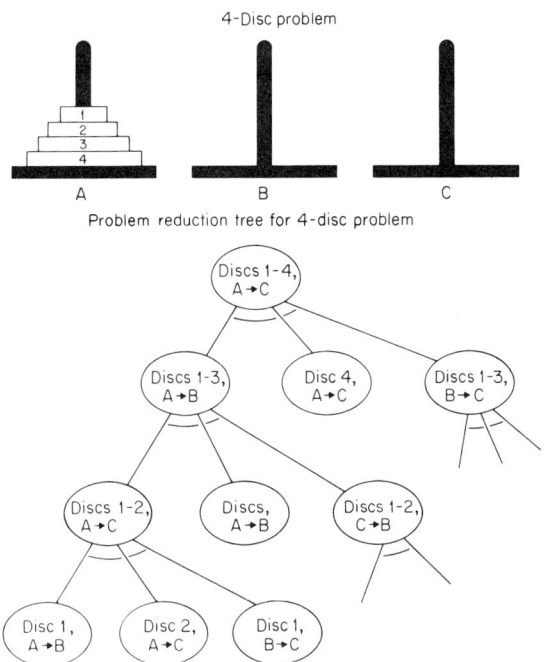

Fig. 2.12. Part of problem reduction tree for 4-disc Tower of Hanoi problem. The overall task is successively reduced into subproblems until subproblems soluble in one move are reached.

for Tower of Hanoi problems clearly shows subspaces corresponding to the subproblems. (*See* Fig. 2.13).

By tracing subjects' paths through such state-action graphs, Luger has found that subjects generally, *(1)* follow goal directed paths, in that each successive step tends to approach a goal or subgoal and *(2)* whenever a subgoal state is reached the preferred path exits from the space of the just completed subproblem to enter a new subproblem space. However, Luger's analysis is not conclusive regarding strategies since as Simon (1975) has shown, a number of rather different strategies could produce minimum solution paths.

Simon considers three main alternative strategies. The first, "goal recursion", is essentially the one already outlined. As he points out, this

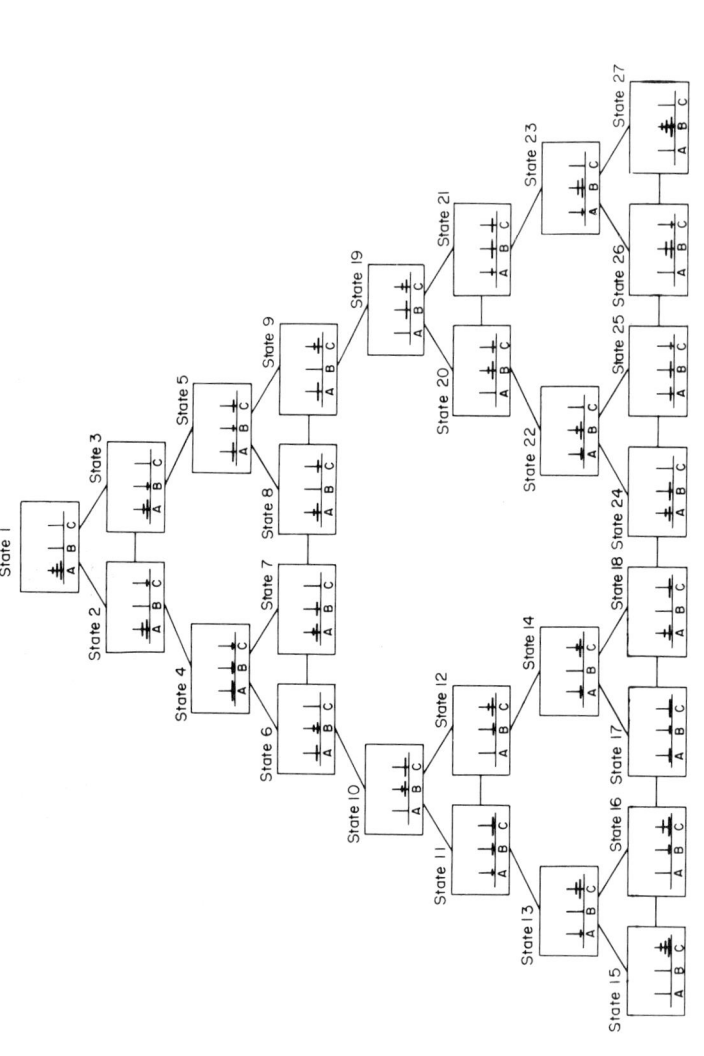

Fig. 2.13. State action graph for a 3-disc Tower of Hanoi problem. The upper 9 states correspond to 2-disc problems (the left hand side to one such subproblem and the right hand side to another). On leaving the upper 9 states further 2-disc subproblem spaces are entered. *(Reproduced with permission from Cognitive Psychology: Learning and Problem Solving (Part 3), Unit 28, D303. The Open University Press, Milton Keynes.)*

strategy requires a list of goals and subgoals to be kept in working memory and the list grows with the number of discs so that by the time 10 discs are tackled, the list would be completely unwieldy. For large numbers of discs at least, a different strategy is needed. The second strategy, the "perceptual" strategy, is much less demanding on memory. The main steps are *(a)* identifying the largest disc (label it k) not yet on the target peg; *(b)* identify the largest disc obstructing movement of k to the target peg; *(c)* if there is no obstructor, make the move; *(d)* if there is an obstructor, establish the goal of moving the obstructor to the other peg (neither source not target of k), then recurse, for the obstructor, through steps *(b)* and *(c)*. This strategy involves perceptual tests but much more limited load on memory—only one goal need be in working memory at any one time no matter how large the stack.

Finally, Simon describes a "move pattern" strategy that also involves very little memory load, that could be used with large versions of the Tower of Hanoi problem, but whose rationale is obscure. This strategy can be described as follows:

(1) On odd numbered moves, move the smallest disc.
(2) On even numbered moves, move the next smallest disc that is exposed.
(3) If peg S is the initial source, peg T the target peg and O the other peg, then if the total number of discs is odd, the smallest disc is always moved from S to T to O to S and so on, while if the total number of discs is even, the smallest disc is always moved in the opposite cycle; from S to O to T to S, and so on.

While people can follow such a strategy, if they are told about it, it seems unlikely that it would be discovered spontaneously. The strategy makes very small demands upon either pattern recognition or on working memory and can be applied to any number of discs.

Simon's analysis alerts us to the existence of alternative strategies (even within this very well structured task) that can produce identical patterns of moves but involve very different demands on memory and perceptual processes. Clearly, further data on reactions to task variants (increasing numbers of discs, for instance), further response measures (e.g. latencies) and verbal protocols would be useful in determining which strategies actually tend to be followed under which conditions.

One factor that has been examined recently is the degree of experience that the solver has with the task. Anzai and Simon (1979) allowed a single subject four attempts at a 5-disc version of the Tower of Hanoi problem. The instructions urged the subject to seek a good solution procedure. Over the four attempts, distinct strategies evolved. The earliest was a form of forward search from the starting state, with a check against repetitions of previously obtained positions. Thus, a form of state-action representation seems to have been used initially. Subsequently, a strategy similar to Simon's (1975) "perceptual" strategy was evolved and this in turn gave way to a "pyramid" strategy in which the subject saw the task as one of moving sets and subsets of discs. This final strategy is essentially the same as Simon's (1975) "goal recursion" strategy. These results are suggestive of an order of acquisition of alternative strategies with task experience. Anzai and Simon propose some plausible mechanisms for strategy improvement; for example, if a short sequence of moves leads to a desired subgoal, then remember that subgoal-sequence association and use it next time the same subgoal is sought. However, since this experiment involved but a single subject, the results are suggestive only and do not allow confident generalization. The study does serve as a reminder that strategy change within subjects exists, and indicates how it might be examined further.

B. Cryptarithmetic

The missionaries-and-cannibals, the water jugs and the Tower of Hanoi tasks have clear, simple structures. In such tasks subjects were successfully represented as working with state-action or problem reduction representations that followed, quite directly, from the problem statements. In the case of *cryptarithmetic* tasks, the permissible actions and the problem states are relatively more open to differing definitions (and so such problems represent a step toward less well defined types of problem).

Newell and Simon (1972) attempted a detailed analysis of behaviour on the following cryptarithmetic task. (The solution is on page 42. You may find it instructive to attempt the task at this point.)

DONALD
+ GERALD
= ROBERT

Given D = 5. Each letter stands for a different digit from 0 to 9. Find the assignment of digits to letters that makes the sum correct.

This problem could, in principle, be tackled by trying out all possible mappings of 9 digits to 9 letters in a pure trial and error manner. However there are 9! (= 362,880) such mappings and so a serial processor testing five mappings per minute would require about a month to solve.

Since human subjects can solve in 15–20 minutes, we can rule out pure trial and error on their part.

Whatever human subjects do, Newell and Simon claim that they work within some definite *problem space* and that attempts to solve can be seen as searches through the problem space. A "problem space" is the set of possible states of knowledge that a solver can be in with respect to the problem. The problem space is essentially defined by the distinctions and relationships that the solver uses while working on the task. Clues about the problem space used by a particular subject can be gained by examining thinking aloud records or protocols obtained while the problem is worked through.

The beginning of a thinking aloud protocol from this task is shown in Fig. 2.14. The subject concerned here (S3) makes use of information he has inferred about inequalities, parity (i.e. oddness or evenness of numbers) and whether there are carries or not from column to column. He also makes assignments by calculation and later on, by hypothesis. Hypothesized assignments are rejected if they lead to contradictions. Newell and Simon conclude that S3 is working within what they call the "augmented problem space" for cryptarithmetic. This may be contrasted with a "basic space" that deals only in assignments and contradictions and does not use information about parities and carries.

> There are ten different letters and each of them has one numerical value.
> Therefore, I can, looking at the 2D's — each D is 5; therefore, T is zero. So I think I'll start by writing that problem here. I'll write 5, 5 is zero.
> Now, do I have any other T's? No, but I have another D. That means I have a 5 over the other side.
> Now I have 2 A's and 2 L's that are each — somewhere — and this R — 3 R's. Two L's equal an R. Of course, I'm carrying a 1 which will mean that R has to be an odd number because the 2 L's — any two numbers added together has to be an even number and 1 will be an odd number. So R can be 1, 3, not 5, 7 or 9.
> (The experimenter asks at this point, "What are you thinking now?")
> Now G — since R is going to be an odd number and D is 5, G has to be an even number.
> I'm looking at the left side of this problem here where it says D + G. Oh, plus possibly another number, if I have to carry 1 from the E + O. I think I'll forget about that for a minute.

Fig. 2.14. Beginning of thinking aloud record (protocol) from subject working on the DONALD + GERALD problem. *(Reproduced with permission from Newell, A. and Simon H. (1972). Human Problem Solving, pp.230–231. Prentice-Hall Inc., Englewood Cliffs, New Jersey.)*

Newell and Simon propose that a person's movement through the problem space can be represented by a *Problem Behaviour Graph* (PBG). The subject is envisaged as moving through a series of "states of knowledge" (some of the knowledge may be of provisional assignments or hypotheses). Movement from state to state is mediated by operations that modify the current knowledge state into a different knowledge state. It is possible to return to previously visited knowledge states (though the subject may not realize that this has happened). Four broad operations were distinguished in S3's protocol:

(1) *Process column* (PC). Extract whatever information can be inferred from a given column in view of other information available in current knowledge state.
(2) *Assign value* (AV). Assign a digit to a letter.
(3) *Generate* (GN). Generate possible values for a given letter, in view of available information in current knowledge state.
(4) *Test digit* (TD). Check whether a particular digit could be assigned to a given letter, in view of information available in current knowledge state.

Part of the PBG for S3 is shown in Fig. 2.15. The PBG for the complete protocol involved 238 states. Note that there is no automatic procedure for producing a PBG for a given protocol, despite some preliminary proposals (Bhaskhar and Simon, 1977). Deriving PBGs from such protocols is largely a matter of judgment at present. The major pitfalls in PBG construction are that the graph will be (*a*) too superficial (will miss important details); (*b*) too disaggregated (over detailed) or (*c*) be epiphenomenal (will be in terms of the wrong problem space).

At the various states in the PBG, alternative operations would often be possible and the question arises of the strategy by which operations are chosen. The order in which letters are solved provides a clue to strategy. Newell and Simon report that those subjects who solve tend to substitute numbers for letters in approximately the same sequence, i.e., first, T = Ø then E = 9, R = 7, then A = 4 and L = 8, then G = 1, then N = 6, B = 3 and finally O = 2.

Fig. 2.15. Part of the Problem (Behavior Graph (PBG) for S3. The boxes represent states of knowledge and the arrows represent operations that move the subject from state to state. *(Reproduced with permission from Newell, A. and Simon, H. (1972). Human Problem Solving, p.174. Prentice-Hall Inc., Englewood Cliffs, New Jersey.)*

The structure of the task allows subjects to concentrate on the column whose entries are most constrained by virtue of previous information or by the nature of the column, e.g. O + E = Ø is constrained and very informative. Processing the most constrained columns first in this way greatly cuts down the amount of trial and error and leads to the observed order of solving.

Newell and Simon propose a fine grain analysis that is intended to account for the state to state transitions in the PBG and to be a specific implementation of the general strategy of "focussing on the most constrained columns". Their analysis is in terms of *"production rules"*. A production rule is of the form, "if condition C applies, take action A". A collection of such rules forms a production system. Computer programs can be written in the form of such systems and a number of researchers (e.g. Young, 1974; Baylor and Gascon, 1974) have found production systems to offer a useful way of building models. Production rules are reminiscent of S-R links, but are more flexible. The conditions may refer to memory contents, goals or observed states of the world; the actions may be overt or internal. Each action leads to a new state of affairs which in turn triggers a new rule and so on.

Newell and Simon were able to account for around 90% of state to state transitions in the PBG with just 13 production rules. It should be noted, however, that the rules were not sufficient to form a complete running production system, and the analysis appears to have been carried out by hand rather than by computer.

Finally, Newell and Simon extended their analysis to other related problems and to new subjects. Broadly similar results were obtained, but some novel problem spaces were tried out by at least one of the subjects (S8). For instance, there was a "typographical space" in which similarities in appearance between letters and digits were sought as a guide to the answer. There was also a "cryptogram space" in which rules were sought to associate digits to letters on the basis of letter position in the alphabet. Solution is unlikely within these spaces. Evidently, the initial phase of developing an understanding of the task (i.e. a problem space) is crucial to later action. So, we now turn to some studies directed at task comprehension or problem space construction.

C. Understanding task instructions

In a typical laboratory study of problem-solving the subject is presented with written or spoken instructions from which he must develop a representation of the task. Despite the evident importance of the task interpretation stage relatively little work has been carried out on it.

Simon and Hayes have reported some studies that indicate how the topic can be tackled within the information processing framework. They propose that understanding instructions involves two subprocesses (Hayes and Simon, 1974), that they label the *language process* and the *construction process*. The language process deals with the basic interpretation of the sentences in the instructions and draws on the subject's knowledge of syntax and semantics. After every sentence or two, the construction process tries to build up an internal model of the task and the operators available to deal with the task. It is assumed that the internal model can be represented by list processing notions, i.e. the internal representation involves symbols, lists of symbols and operations that change symbols on lists or transfer symbols from list to list.

A computer model (called Understand) incorporating these ideas was developed and compared (albeit loosely) with human protocol data obtained using the Tea Ceremony problem (Hayes and Simon, 1974). The Tea Ceremony (TC) problem is an isomorph of the Tower of Hanoi (TOH) i.e. it has the same abstract structure but differs in content. In the TC problem there are five tasks of varying "nobility" and there are three participants. Initially all tasks are the responsibility of one participant (host) and the goal is to transfer all the tasks to a specified other participant (the most senior guest). The major constraints are that only the least noble task that a person is performing can be transferred and it can only be transferred to someone who does not already have a less noble task. A TC task can be translated into a TOH task and vice versa by using the correspondences below.

Tea Ceremony	*Tower of Hanoi*
3 participants	3 pegs
5 tasks	5 discs
Nobility of tasks	Size of discs

The Understand program incorporated sufficient methods to produce from the problem text a list processing representation of the task that could, in theory, serve as input to a GPS-like program for solving the problem. However, some differences emerged between the program and human protocol data. For instance, the program alternated between language and construction processes but never returned to earlier parts of the text to reanalyse them for possible misunderstandings. The human subjects, in contrast, went back, re-read and reinterpreted certain portions when they realized that their first interpretation of the task was leading to difficulties.

Also when the problem was attempted subjects often went back to the instructions and modified earlier mistaken attempts at understanding. The program thus requires extra flexibility to make it a closer simulation.

Hayes and Simon's (1974) analysis suggests that list processing operations are used in the task representation that is finally constructed as a result of the understanding process. An interesting check on this idea was reported on in a study (Simon and Hayes, 1976) involving further isomorphs of the Tower of Hanoi. Subjects were presented with "monster" problems e.g. in which three monsters of different sizes each hold a different sized globe and have to transfer globes so that the monsters end up holding globes proportional to their sizes. Variants of the problem required that the globes be shrunk or expanded to attain the desired consistency of monster to globe assignments. Despite differences in the surface descriptions, all problems could be represented by a common abstract structure. Simon and Hayes (1976) argued however that the Understand program and human subjects would reach different representations for problems of *transferring* items as compared to problems of *changing* items. In list processing terms, if each monster is represented by a list of globe names (i.e. the globes he is holding) then a "transfer" task requires symbols to be shifted from list to list while a "change" problem involves replacing symbols on lists. In both cases the moves must be in accord with the task constraints. It happens that the change representation requires a more complex testing procedure to ensure that proposed moves are legal than does the transfer representation and so, it was predicted that change problems would take longer. Consistent with this analysis, Hayes and Simon (1977) found that the change tasks took almost twice as long (28.1 min) as the transfer tasks (16.9 min).

Human subjects' comments showed a tendency to modify the names or labels that they used with certain of the problems as they continued to work on them. This was the case where the monsters were referred to by variable names (e.g. the monster with the small name) that would not be directly appropriate later on (e.g. in a task that involved name swapping). Subjects would replace variable names by shorter permanent ones (e.g. "the first monster", "the left-most monster"). These changes presumably helped to reduce demands on short term memory.

To sum up, it appears that people are more flexible in constructing and revising problem representations than the Understand program but that like the program they interpret the instructions in terms of list structures and general purpose operators, presumably, drawn from long-term memory.

IV. SUMMARY AND CONCLUDING COMMENTS

The following picture seems to emerge from the studies reviewed above of processes involved in solving well-defined non-adversary problems. The person faced with a novel laboratory puzzle spends some time building up a symbolic model of the task materials, the available operations and the desired goal (Simon and Hayes, 1976). The person's model of the task determines the problem space within which he or she will work and explore consequences of possible actions. Two kinds of problem representation that could be used in modelling a problem were distinguished viz., state-action and problem reduction. With a state-action representation, the solver explores the consequences of alternative actions forwards from the starting state while the problem reduction representation involves breaking the overall problem into more manageable sub- and sub-sub-problems. Models of the solving process that postulated state-action representations and heuristic searches of the resulting state-action graphs, gave reasonable fits to data from missionaries-and-cannibals, and water jug problems (Jeffries *et al.*, 1977). These models proposed only a small degree of mental look-ahead, involving two or three immediate successor states, thus reflecting working memory limitations as proposed by the "modal" model of human information processing. Problem reduction approaches were implicated in cryptarithmetic (Newell and Simon, 1972) and Tower of Hanoi problems (Luger, 1976). In the case of the latter task, preliminary evidence (Anzai and Simon, 1979) suggests that degree of acquaintance with the problem may be influential in determining the adoption of one approach or the other. On initial exposure to a Tower of Hanoi task, Anzai and Simon's subject adopted a state-action representation but switched to a problem reduction representation when more experience of the task had been gained.

On the question of when and why, in general, people adopt state-action or problem reduction approaches, it does not seem possible to give definite answers at present, because few, if any, studies have been carried out with this question in mind. Intuitively, a problem reduction approach seems more likely in tasks that permit a large number of possible actions. After all, problem reduction offers a useful way of cutting down on the number of actions to be considered at each step. Within a given task area, it may well be that a problem reduction approach is more likely with subjects experienced in that area than with naive subjects. Some experience with the task area is probably required to enable subjects to learn which differences between starting states and goal states are relevant and in what order these differences are best dealt with. The results of Anzai and Simon are consistent with this view. Further studies are needed, especially of problem formulation and interpretation as a function of task structures and subject experience, to help answer this question.

Finally, it may be noted that the tasks considered in this Chapter have been unfamiliar puzzles and solution processes could not draw heavily on expertise stored in long-term memory. The unfamiliarity of the puzzles is useful from the point of view of controlling for level of prior experience among the subjects but it also must be seen as a limitation on the problem-solving conditions being studied. It is quite possible that when working in more familiar domains, people can usefully structure a task more rapidly and look ahead further than they can with unfamiliar types of task. The next Chapter concerns an area in which this possibility can be checked, viz., the area of board games, in which fresh problems can be readily generated within frameworks which vary greatly in familiarity for players ranging from novice to master levels.

V. FURTHER READING

Boden, M. A. (1977). Artificial intelligence and natural man. The Harvester Press. Hassocks.

Chapter 12 provides a very readable discussion of computer methods of problem-solving.

Simon, H. A. (1979). Information processing models of cognition. *Annual Review of Psychology* **30**, 363–396.

This review paper includes a concise discussion of work on problem-solving in the information processing mould during the 1970's.

Wickelgren, W. A. (1974). How to solve problems. W. H. Freeman and Co., San Francisco.

A fascinating text by a leading cognitive psychologist in which various strategies for dealing with well-defined problems are explained.

3
Solving adversary problems

In tackling adversary problems solvers must consider not only their own possible sequences of actions but also those of an opponent. The games chess, GO, bridge and poker provide good examples of adversary problems and have been studied from psychological, AI and normative points of view. (The normative approach is concerned with how best to play the games concerned.) Psychologists have found it helpful to use some of the terminology and concepts that have been developed in the normative Theory of Games (e.g. Von Neumann and Morgenstern, 1944) and in studies of machine game playing. Accordingly, I will first outline the basic notions of "game tree" and "minimax" and then briefly describe AI developments in chess before going on to studies of human game playing.

I. GAME TREES AND THE MINIMAX PRINCIPLE

In board games the possible sequences of moves and counter-moves from a given position can be represented by state-action trees known as "game trees". If it is possible to look ahead from the start to all the possible endings of the game then the best starting move can be chosen by application of the "minimax" principle. This principle was illustrated by Newell and Simon (1972) for the artificially simple 2 move game shown in Fig. 3.1. White determines his best move by *looking ahead* to the possible endings and then works backwards, applying the *minimax* principle of minimizing one's maximum loss. This is a conservative policy which expects the opponent will do his worst to you. Working backwards, minimaxing would label W3 as (—), W2 as (—) and W1 as (O), and recommend W1 as the best starting move since it is found to lead to a draw whereas the other moves must lead to losses.

The problem with a simple application of this approach to many games, including chess, is that in order to determine the value of a move the player must consider the opponent's possible replies and then his own replies to each of his opponent's replies to those, and so on. In theory, a "brute force" program could generate such information and select the best move on each trial. Unfortunately, the tree of possibilities is just too big — approximately 10^{120} possible sequences of moves in chess and only 10^{16} micro seconds per century to explore them all.

The cognitive effort required to explore all the possible chess games is just too much for any present or likely future machine, or for any human. Computers and humans can only investigate and keep track of the consequences of relatively few moves, and then only to a limited extent. So, in order for humans or computers to play reasonable chess some strategies or heuristics must be available to restrict search to plausible moves and to evaluate lines of development in the absence of complete information about their remote consequences.

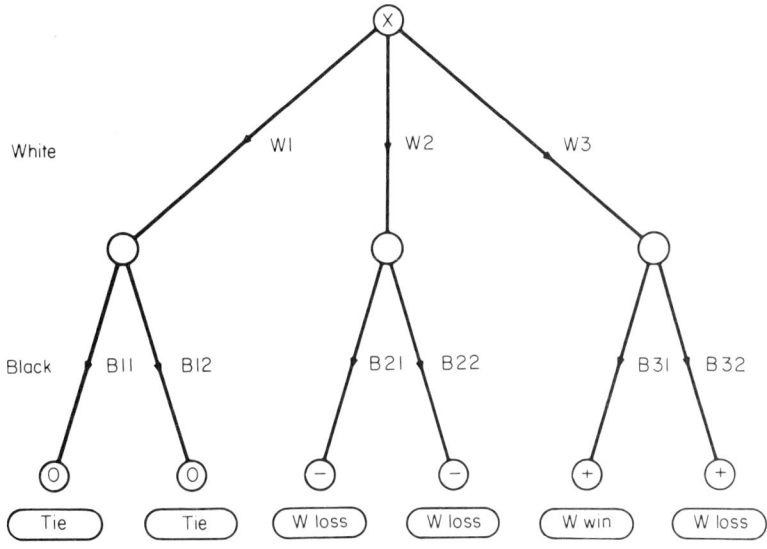

Fig. 3.1. Minimaxing in a game tree. See text for full explanation. *(Reproduced with permission from Newell, A. and Simon, H. (1972). Human Problem Solving, p.669. Prentice-Hall Inc., Englewood Cliffs, New Jersey.)*

II. ARTIFICIAL INTELLIGENCE AND CHESS

Some of the early chess programs are worth a brief consideration. In 1956 and 1958 a computer called Maniac at Los Alamos was programmed to play chess using the following methods. At each turn the machine looked ahead to a depth of 4 turns and considered *all* legal moves on each turn. In other words, given a starting position of the board all of the average 30 moves were generated, then all the opponents replies, then all machine replies and finally all the opponents replies to those replies. On average, $30^4 \simeq 800{,}000$ continuations were generated. Each of the near million possible states of the board after 4 moves was then *evaluated* by adding a measure of material advantage and piece mobility. A minimaxing procedure was then followed to work back up the tree of possibilities to find the best first move. This program is near the brute force end of a sophistication continuum and could not be regarded as a simulation. According to Newell and Simon (1972) the program played rather weak chess and was susceptible to serious blunders, even though close to a million possibilities were considered! Presumably a lot of the possible moves were not really worth looking at and the evaluation of possibilities may have been too crude to select good moves.

Additional sophistication was introduced into a program devised by an IBM programmer named Bernstein in 1958. Instead of considering *all* legal moves at each step, Bernstein's program considered only 7, which cut the size of the tree at depth 4, from near 1,000,000 branches to around 2,500 branches.

The program incorporated about 8 so-called "plausible move generators", each of which was related to some feature of the game, such as king safety, development, defence, attack, etc. When the program had to select a move it generated 7 alternatives by applying the generators in a priority order. For each of those 7 alternative moves, 7 opponent moves were generated and so on to a depth of 4 moves.* So, this program searched the tree of possibilities very selectively. The end positions, 4 moves ahead, were evaluated by numerical measures of material strength, defence area controlled and mobility of pieces. The program then minimaxed back up the tree to select its "best" move. The program's play is reported to have been rather uneven — sometimes it played well for a series of moves, and then displayed glaring blind spots. Although not a great deal of evidence is available about the program's performance, it appears to have been an improvement over the less selective Maniac program in method and in end results. Further details on early chess programs can be found in Newell and Simon (1972) and Bell (1978).

The 1977 world champion computer chess program (Chess 4.6) exploited the speed and storage space of modern machines and examined an average of 400,000 successor positions per move. It looked ahead about 4 or 5 moves and could beat 99.5% of rated human players although it was

---

*In some discussions a single move by one player is referred to as one *ply* and a move-countermove sequence is described as two *plies*, while a "move" is taken to be *two* plies (i.e. a move-countermove sequence). In this text, however, a "move" is taken to be simply a single move by one player, i.e. one ply. Thus my references to "4 moves deep" for example, mean the same as "4 plies deep" in some other treatments of this topic.

relatively weak in the end-game. Chess 4.6 is clearly not human-like in its methods (Levy, 1978).

Although a number of advances have been made in computer chess playing since the late 1950's, almost all the programs seem to possess the same kind of structure. They all search ahead through a tree of possibilities with some heuristic restrictions on the search, evaluate positions at the end of the search, and minimax. (This general structure was anticipated by Shannon, one of the founders of information theory, in a 1950 paper.) Essentially all of the programs choose moves in given chess positions, rather than play a chess game with an overall plan, although the end product may look quite planned.

The effort to develop chess playing programs helps underline the difficulties faced by any system that deals effectively with complex adversary problems. How do humans tackle such difficulties? This question is addressed in the following sections.

III. EXPERIMENTAL STUDIES OF HUMAN ADVERSARY PROBLEM SOLVING

A. Human chess play

1 Search in chess

Perhaps the most direct way to try to find out about thought processes during chess play is to present subjects with a chess problem and ask them to think aloud as they decide which move should be made next by one of the players (usually white). This method has been followed by De Groot (1965), Wagner and Scurrah (1971), Newell and Simon (1972, Chapter 12) and Charness (1981b).

De Groot was particularly interested in possible differences between players of differing degrees of expertise. Five grand masters and 5 expert players were given the same position (*see* Fig. 3.2) and thought aloud while choosing a move. The search trees that they developed could be abstracted from their protocols and De Groot reported the summary statistics shown in Table 3.1.

A number of points emerge from these data. First, there was little or no difference in the quantitative aspects of the search patterns of the grand masters and the experts. The only major difference was in the quality of the move finally chosen. (Move quality was rated by independent experts.) Both groups looked ahead to similar maximum depths (about 6-7 moves), considered a similar number of possible first moves (about 4) and a similar total number of first moves and subsequent replies and counter-replies

Table 3.1. Average protocol statistics for De Groot's position A.
(Reprinted by permission from De Groot (1965). Thought and Choice in Chess, p.319. Mouton Publishers, The Hague.)

Variable	Grand masters (n = 5)	Experts (n = 5)
Time to choose move	9.6 min.	12.8 min.
No. of different first moves considered	4.2	3.4
Maximum depth of search (moves)	6.8	6.6
Total no. of moves considered	35.0	30.8
Rated value of move selected	8.2 (max = 9)	5.2

(30-35). Although, as Hearst (1977) suggested, the grand masters might be able to search deeper and broader if they were sufficiently motivated (e.g. in competition) it is still noteworthy that they consistently reached a better conclusion without any more search than the weaker players. Also, of course, the amount of sheer search is very small compared to that of the best computer chess programs. (According to Levy (1978), the program Chess 4.6 sometimes examined around 3 *million* possible positions that could be reached from the current position before choosing a move, while De Groot's players were averaging around 35 possible positions).

As well as being more selective in search than most chess programs, the way in which human chess searches developed was also different from the way program searches usually develop. De Groot's players and those of Scurrah and Wagner followed a *progressive deepening* method in which the same small number of alternative first moves were returned to repeatedly and generally followed up in greater depth on each occasion that they are re-examined. Re-examinations to greater depth were quite often immediate, but delayed re-examinations were also fairly frequent. Progressive deepening offers a way of gradually building up in long-term memory a representation of a long sequence of moves which would overload working memory. Also, the method permits repeated checks of apparently promising lines, in case some danger has been overlooked.

Finally we note that human players do not search to a fixed depth but to a "quiet" position where no immediate exchanges are possible. Such positions appear then to be evaluated on the basis of some salient feature or "general impression" (e.g. "awkward for black") rather than in terms of some explicit combinatorial weighting of many features (which is how the programs tend to make evaluations).

How is it that expert human chess players can be so selective to such good effect when they search for a next move? The answer may well lie in the extensive repertoire of chess patterns and schemas that could be built up over many years of study of the game. These patterns help the master structure his perceptions of the board appropriately and could be attached to recommendations for possible actions in a production system organization. Clues as to this possible explanation were obtained from a task that De Groot found was much easier for master players than for amateurs. This was the chess memory task to be described in the next section.

2 Chess memory and perception

De Groot (1965) put chess positions—taken from actual games—in front of subjects for 5 seconds (e.g. Fig. 3.2); then he removed the positions and asked subjects to reconstruct them. Chess masters could reconstruct the positions almost without error, 91% correct, while poor players made many errors, 41% correct. (There were 20/24 pieces on board.)

Fig. 3.2. Position A, used in De Groot's (1965) studies of chess thinking and memory. *(Reproduced by permission of Mouton Publishers, The Hague.)*

A clue to the chess masters' performance is given by another of De Groot's findings. When good and poor players were shown boards with the 20 or so pieces *arranged at random*, both groups did equally poorly. This corroborates some early Russian results that showed chess masters not to have superior visual memory *in general*. Chase and Simon (1973a, b) argued that the chess memory data are consistent with the view that perceivers of the chess board store about 7 familiar units or "chunks" (Miller, 1956) in short-term memory during the inspection period irrespective of their skill level. However the chess masters' 7 chunks of information are much richer than the novices' i.e. they are larger units. Similarly if you have learned to read in a given language you could reproduce about 7 words after brief exposure to a set of random words, whereas a non-reader of the language might only manage to reproduce about 7 letters (especially if the words were difficult for the non-reader of the language to pronounce).

Chase and Simon (1973a, b) were able to demonstrate quite directly the proposed superiority of master player's chunks compared to those of weaker players. In their study, three players varying in skill were given chess perception and memory tasks. The perception task required the subjects to reconstruct on one board a chess position which remained in view on another board. The main variables of interest were the numbers of pieces placed following each glance at the stimulus board, the times between piece placements and the nature of the relationships between the pieces placed between one glance and the next. For all players the average number of pieces placed after a glance was similar (2-3). However the master's glances were significantly shorter, indicating more rapid encoding. The chess recall tasks were similar to those of De Groot and involved 5 seconds presentation followed by board reconstruction. Times between placements of pieces were recorded and intervals of 2 seconds or more were taken to correspond to boundaries between chunks in recall. On this basis, the number of pieces per chunk varied systematically (if not dramatically) with skill level from 2.5 to 1.9 pieces per chunk from strongest to weakest player. Pieces within a single chunk tended to have relations of defence and attack, be close together and be of common colour and type. Thus, Chase and Simon's studies indicate that, compared to weaker players, the stronger player encodes chess information more rapidly when perceiving the board and encodes a given position in larger chunks when recall is required.

Research on chess perception and memory is relevant to chess playing in that players seek to structure the board in terms of familiar patterns before trying to choose a move. De Groot and others have found that when a chess position is given and the player must select a move, the first 15 to 30 seconds are occupied with gathering information about the situation in order to build up an internal representation of the position. Players do not begin to explore possible moves until an initial perceptual preparatory phase is complete. Indeed it is sometimes suggested that the initial perception or structuring of a problem is what is really important in problem solving in general. The early chess simulation programs did not take account of this perceptual phase (nor do most current AI programs). However, Simon and Barenfeld (1969) have reported a program labelled Perceiver which can simulate eye movements in the first 5 seconds of examining a chess board for the next move.

Perceiver begins with a central fixation point and follows lines of "attack" or "defence" as they are noticed and stores relationships of attack/defence between pairs of pieces. In this way it builds up a representation of the board position. Very little data on eye movements in chess are available, but Perceiver's successive fixations on a particular board have been compared with Russian eye movement data for a single expert subject. Both program and subject tended to focus on the same squares, and the overall patterns look similar. Further data would be useful to refine the program—but Simon and Barenfeld were mainly concerned to demonstrate the *possibility* of simulating the initial perceptual phase and succeeded in that aim.

To sum up on the evidence so far, the expert chess player probably detects and stores about as many "chunks" as a poor player but the better player's "chunks" or units are much larger. Thus a good player "structures" a given situation differently from a poor player and, in a sense, "sees" the same problem quite differently from a poor player. The advanced coding scheme of the expert is, of course, bought with many years study. The extended study required is consistent with Simon's suggestion that a slow serial device with limited short term memory, equipped with a discrimination learning program could build up a sufficiently complex discrimination net to recognize many thousands of chess patterns over a lifetime's play.

3 The memory-aided pattern perceiver (MAPP) model

Simon and Gilmartin (1973) converted the general notions sketched by Simon and Barenfeld (1969), into a working computer model for the chess memory task. This model, known as the Memory-Aided Pattern Perceiver (MAPP), assumed that a position is encoded as a set of chunks (pattern labels) that occupy a limited capacity short-term memory. The pattern labels are then decoded during the position reconstruction phase. The chunks or pattern labels are produced by a pattern recognizer that seeks to match board configurations to known patterns permanently stored in a long-term memory. The pattern recognizing component consists of a discrimination net that is organized around salient pieces. It is assumed that the skilled player has a large discrimination net that incorporates a great many different patterns while the weaker player has fewer patterns available with which to describe any given position. The program can thus simulate different levels of expertise by varying the number of patterns in its long-term store.

Two versions of MAPP were explored. One had available 894 patterns and the other 1144 patterns. Given the same board positions, the more "knowledgeable" version was able to encode the positions more efficiently into its short-term memory and thus scored better on position reconstruction than the less knowledgeable version. The "knowledgeable" version's performance seems to be intermediate between that of a master player and a class A (good amateur) player according to comparisons between the program and human data on positions used by Chase and Simon (1973a). See Table 3.2.

Table 3.2. Percentage of pieces placed correctly by MAPP (with 1144 patterns in long term memory) and Chase and Simon's (1973) Ss after 10 secs. exposure. *(Reprinted by permission from Simon, H. A. and Gilmartin, K. (1973). A simulation of memory for chess positions.* Cognitive Psychology *5 29–46.)*

		Master (%)	MAPP (%)	Good amateur (%)
Positions	Set 1	62	43	34
	Set 2	81	54	49

Simon and Gilmartin estimate that a MAPP-like system could replicate master level performance on the chess memory task with somewhere between 10,000 and 100,000 patterns in LTM. Assuming the model has some validity, similar estimates would apply to the store of patterns available to the human master. Acquisition of this order of patterns is certainly possible over many years study, since a well educated person's vocabulary, for instance, has been estimated at around 75,000 words (Oldfield, 1966).

Some of MAPP's assumptions have been tested independently by Frey and Adesman (1976) and Charness (1976). Frey and Adesman confirmed the importance of chunking by showing that recall of a position, the development of which had been shown from the start in a sequence of two seconds "snapshots", was better than recall of the same position shown without its development. Presumably the chess patterns were more evident when their build ups were known. The effect was present for three levels of players and tended to be stronger for the more expert players. Also, memory performance was better for positions that had been built up in a meaningful order than for positions that had been built up in a random order. Again, skill level was an important factor in performance in both order conditions. However, when Frey and Adesman examined the assumption that the chess chunks are stored in a limited capacity short-term memory the results were contrary to expectations based on MAPP. Subjects were presented with chess positions for 8 seconds and then required to count backwards from a 3 digit number for either 3 seconds or 30 seconds before attempting to reconstruct the position. The counting backward procedure is usually assumed to "clear" short-term memory by preventing rehearsal and/or displacing the contents of short-term memory (Brown, 1958; Peterson and Peterson, 1959). This manipulation had only a very slight effect. Correct recall after 3 seconds interpolated activity was 13.1 pieces and after 30 seconds was 11.6 pieces. These data cast doubts on the assumption that chunks are held in short-term memory. Further strong evidence against the "short-term memory assumption" was reported by Charness (1976). He carried out a number of studies using 5 second presentation and Brown-Peterson interference paradigms. The 30 second interpolated tasks varied in complexity and modality (shadowing digits, summing digits, copying symbols, rotating and then copying symbols, studying other chess problems, naming pieces on a chess board). Recall of chess positions was only reduced by about 6-8% by the most effective of these manipulations. (Control conditions indicated that recall of trigrams was affected by some of the interpolated tasks.) As usual, the skilled players performed better across all the memory task conditions than the weak players. One interesting effect was a marked increase in time to place the first piece as a function of interpolated processing. It appears that the interpolated tasks did have some effect on *ease* of retrieval but not such as to reduce *accuracy* of retrieval. The degree to which memory for briefly presented chess positions resists interference, strongly suggests that the information is stored in long-term memory rather than short-term memory. Charness and Frey and Adesman suggest a "depth of processing" interpretation whereby the skilled player can encode to a deeper level, more rapidly, than the less skilled player. However, even the least skilled groups used in the experiments discussed here appear to have encoded sufficiently deeply to be little affected by interpolated processing tasks of the type found very effective by Brown and the Petersons in recall of verbal materials.

4 Age and skill in chess
The studies of chess perception, memory and play discussed so far, have focussed on individual differences in skill and have proposed that strong and weak players differ in the efficiency of their chess encoding schemes. Charness (1981a, b) has recently also investigated possible player-age effects additional to skill effects. Ageing is generally thought to affect memory operations, particularly those of retrieval, and so Charness hypothesized that players of equivalent skill, but widely differing ages, might differ in the underlying processes that yielded similar molar results (i.e. similar skill ratings).

Charness (1981a) assembled a sample of 34 chess players who varied independently in age (16-64 years) and skill level (skill ratings ranged from 1283 to 2004). The players were presented with four positions in which they had to choose a move while thinking aloud. Next, they were asked to rapidly evaluate end game positions as being wins, draws or losses for white. After this task, the players were asked unexpectedly to recall the four initial positions by reconstructing them. Finally a recognition task was administered in which the subjects attempted to identify the first four problem conditions among a set of 26. Only skill level was predictive of performance in the move choosing task and in the end game evaluation task. Skill level was positively related and age was negatively related to chess recall scores. Measures of chunk size in recall were obtained using a procedure similar to that of Chase and Simon (1973a, b) described above. This indicated that chunk size was positively related to skill and negatively related to age. That is to say, the older subjects made use of more but smaller chunks in recall than did younger subjects of similar skill levels. These results then suggest that differences in encoding efficiency may not be sufficient to explain differences in skill levels. It should be noted however that Charness's memory task was a delayed one, while the usual chess memory study has involved immediate memory.

Charness (1981b) followed up the question of possible differences in the processes underlying move selection between older and younger players by analysing thinking aloud records produced in his 1981a study. Analysis of these records indicated that the more skilled players searched more extensively and deeply than the less skilled. This result departs from De Groot's (1965) finding based on fewer subjects (see Table 3.1), that skill level was independent of search depth or breadth. The discrepancy is probably due to the wider range of skills sampled by Charness. The average maximum depth reported by Charness (5.7) is of a similar order of magnitude to that reported by De Groot (6.7). Also Charness found that the older players searched less extensively, though as deeply as younger players and did not differ in quality of move finally chosen.

So, given similar skill levels the older player searches less extensively than the younger player, yet reaches conclusions of similar value. Perhaps older players can evaluate possible positions more accurately and dispense with the prolonged checking and verifying more typical of the younger players. More sensitive "evaluation functions" could compensate for the poorer encoding of chess positions by older players indicated both by Charness's delayed memory study (1981a) and by further results showing age effects on *immediate* recall of chess positions (Charness, 1981c).

B. Memory, perception and play in GO

A number of the basic findings reported by De Groot and others for chess have now been replicated in other games. Judith Reitman (1976) showed superior GO board reconstruction, after brief exposure, by a master level player as compared with a beginner. A typical GO board position is shown in Fig. 3.3. As with chess, the master's recall superiority only held for positions that were meaningful and not for random positions. She was also able to show that the way in which the master structured meaningful positions was rather complex, and involved perception in terms of overlapping clusters of pieces rather than simply as independent chunks or as hierarchically nested chunks and subchunks.

Further aspects of internal representation and perceptual scanning in board games have been examined in the contexts of both GO and GO-moku. Both these games use the same board and the same black and white "stones" or counters; but GO is the more complex game.

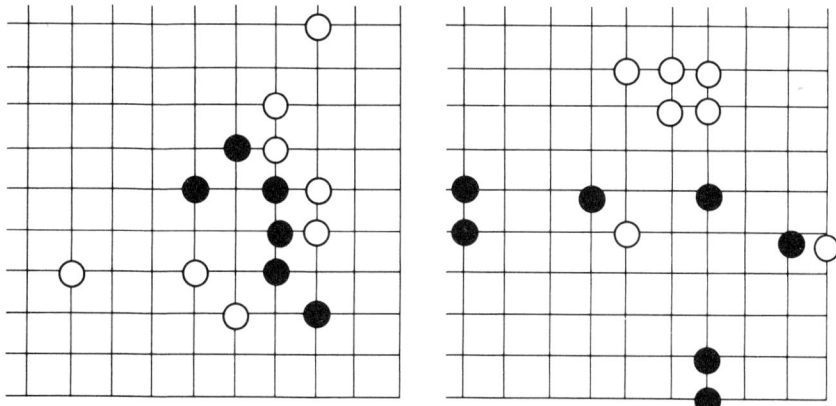

Fig. 3.3. An example of meaningful (left panel) and random (right panel) GO board patterns. *(Reproduced with permission from Reitman, J. S. (1976). Skilled perception in GO. Deducing memory structures from inter-response times.* Cognitive Psychology *8, 336–356.*

First, Eisenstadt and Kareev (1977) were able to show that subjects represented the same board configurations differently, depending on whether the configurations were presented as coming from a GO game or a GO-moku game. Subjects were shown positions and told either that the positions were from a GO game or GO-moku and asked to decide what the best move would be for one of the players. After they had done this and an intervening task, they were unexpectedly asked to reconstruct the position that they had originally worked with. Different pieces were of critical importance for the GO and GO-moku interpretations and the accuracy of the reconstructions of the positions of the critical pieces varied in line with the interpretations. So, it can be concluded that people encode the board position in a manner relevant to the game they are playing.

This result suggests that people look for patterns typical of (or important to) the game in which they are engaged. Scanning the board may then be guided by expectations about types of patterns to be found. Indeed, Simon and Barenfeld's simulation of scanning in chess successfully assumed that scanning followed lines of attack and defence. Eisenstadt and Kareev suggest that Gestalt principles of similarity, proximity and continuity might also play a role, especially in GO-moku since its basic game-specific patterns are straight lines.

In particular they examined the extent to which players detected an important type of configuration known as an "open-three". This pattern has two forms, continuous and noncontinuous, as shown below.

      X/X/X   /X/X/ /X/
     continuous   non-continuous

If the player does not notice that his opponent has constructed an open three and so *fails to block it*, he will lose the game. The winner is the first to establish a row of 5 pieces in his colour and an unblocked open three is bound to lead to a winning line.

Additionally, open threes can be either non-diagonal (high proximity) or diagonal (low proximity).

Subjects played against a computer program and the proportions of trials on which they failed to respond to open threes were recorded. As would be predicted from the Gestalt principles, probability of responding was greater for open threes on non-diagonals as against diagonals, and for continuous as against non-continuous patterns. These results indicate that Gestalt principles had a strong effect on scanning with this material.

Scanning was examined more directly in a further study in which subjects were only able to examine 1 square of the board at a time. Taking into consideration the patterns of scanning and verbal protocols, Eisenstadt and Kareev distinguished 4 major types of scanning:
    (1) *Confirmatory scans.* S has a hypothesis about the contents of certain squares and examines them to check his hypothesis.
    (2) *Exploratory scans.* S has no particular hypothesis but simply looks to see what is present.
    (3) *Revival scans.* S looks again at a square which he has recently

examined, and whose contents he must be fairly certain of. This type of scan serves to "rehearse" what is already known.

(4) *Imaginary scans.* While planning a move, S points to one of the squares where he is considering placing a piece as part of his planning.

Eisenstadt and Kareev constructed a computer model that generated quite realistic scanning data. The model consists of 3 parts: a "fovea", a working memory and a long-term memory. The fovea is a "window" which indicates the square on the board at which the model is currently "looking". Working memory lists processes waiting to be executed and data waiting for processing. Long-term memory consists of a set of pattern rules, which show how large configurations are made up of smaller ones (e.g. Trios from Pairs and Pairs from individual pieces).

"Top down" scanning occurs to check if important patterns are present (e.g. Trios). "Bottom up" discovery occurs if new patterns are recognized during scanning. "Bottom up" suggestion may occur if parts of familiar patterns are detected. If no high priority processing is waiting, then a general exploration begins in which the fovea moves around squares adjacent to the current fixation point.

The model does incorporate ideas derived from studying human scanning and encoding and its scanning patterns appear reasonable. However, no detailed comparisons with human data are presented, nor are there novel predictions of future (independent) data from the model. Also the model is a restricted one—for scanning in "window" GO-moku. It would be interesting to see it extended and incorporated into a more complex model for scanning and play in full-vision GO-moku.

C. Bridge

Expertise in a third game, bridge, has also now begun to be studied. Successful bridge play involves memory demands that are not present in chess or GO. A bridge player benefits if he can remember what cards have already been played in the preceding rounds as well as what the bidding was at the initial auction stage. So, in addition to a working memory load involved in planning which sequence of plays to attempt at a given point, a player also has to remember which cards have already been played. Thus, accurate memory is essential for good play. As with chess and GO, we might expect skilled players to demonstrate superior memory for bridge information, based on a large repertoire of familiar patterns in long term storage. Evidence recently reported by Engle and Bukstel (1978) and Charness (1979) bears out this expectation.

Engle and Bukstel (1978) gave 4 subjects (an expert, a life master, an average player and a novice) three tasks. First the subjects played 10 hands of bridge and were then given an unexpected memory test for the cards in the 10 hands. An intentional memory task required subjects to reconstruct 4 bridge hands from one deal where the cards within each hand were either arranged systematically or at random. Finally, a perception task required subjects to reconstruct stimuli similar to those used in the memory task after brief glances at the stimulus. The higher the level of bridge expertise of the subject the better his or her performance on the structured tasks but no effect of expertise on the unstructured tasks was found.

Charness (1979) confirmed these results in a study that had a firmer empirical basis, since it used 20 subjects of varying degrees of bridge ability. The subjects were given the following tasks: planning the play of a contract, rapid bidding, incidental learning and recall memory for structured or unstructured bridge hands. Performance on all tasks, except memory for randomly arranged hands, was strongly positively related to bridge expertise level.

An incidental result was that memory performance declined with age of the player, independently of level of expertise (though it may be noted that age had no effect on recall of randomly arranged hands). To sum up, it appears that in bridge, as in chess and in GO (and probably in most areas of expertise), the expert has a vast repertoire of familiar patterns in terms of which he can efficiently encode most situations he meets within his area. Furthermore, it is reasonable to suppose that these patterns are linked with appropriate action possibilities, so that the master player often directly accesses an appropriate action once he has classified the situation, whereas the weaker player has to conduct an effortful search through various possible actions.

D. Poker

Chess and GO are games of complete information in which the opponents' material strengths and weaknesses are available to inspection. In many real life cases of adversary problem-solving such complete information is not available and partial information must be relied on, thus introducing probabilistic considerations. Bridge clearly involves some uncertainty, about where particular cards lie, and poker even more so. Thus poker playing has been studied as a microcosm of problem solving in uncertain conditions.

Lopes (1976) reported experiments on how poker players' internal models of the game and of their opponents' styles of play influence decision making in a modified version of five-card stud poker. In stud poker, players initially receive one card face down and one card face up. Normally a round of betting follows in which some players might drop out. A further card is dealt face up to the remaining players and another round of betting ensues. This procedure continues until 5 cards have been dealt (or until only one player remains active). Final rounds of betting are then held between those players left in the game. Lopes used a simplified task in which subjects saw two hands (4 cards face up, 1 face down) together with the amounts bet on those hands and had then to make various judgments and side bets. They rated the likelihood that a pair of 7s could beat both opposing hands and then bet on the pair of 7s. The results supported the view that the subjective probability of beating both hands was a multiplicative function of the probabilities of beating each of the individual hands. The subjective probability estimates were generally accurate reflections of the objective probabilities. The more likely the players judged that they would win, the larger the bet they would make. Interestingly, when in further conditions, subjects were told that some hands and bets were from "conservative" (low bluffing) players and others from "average" players they varied their bets to take into account the different bluffing tendencies of their imaginary opponents. As Lopes concluded, this series of studies showed that performance was affected by the players' model of the probabilities of having the winning hand and by the players' model of the opponents' bluffing tendencies.

Findler (1978) has explored computer models of processes underlying play in the related game of five-card draw poker. In draw poker all cards are hidden from the players except their own. Five cards are dealt initially and a first betting round is followed by the discarding of up to 4 or 5 cards and drawing of replacements. All a given player knows is his or her own cards, the number of cards drawn by the other players and the bets made. Thus, draw poker involves even more uncertainty than stud poker. Findler has developed a number of programs to play draw poker that incorporate both fixed, static, strategies and adaptive, learning, routines. The "simplest" strategy is that of the *mathematically fair player* who decides when and what to bet in accord with the objective odds of winning—taking no regard of the other players' styles of betting. This strategy serves well against unsophisticated opposition but is vulnerable to bluffers who bet enough to make the perceived risk of losing unacceptable to the mathematically fair player. A more useful static strategy uses the objective odds and incorporates an index of the desirability of staying in the game at a particular juncture. This index takes into account the number of other players left in the game, how long they have remained in and how much extra must be bet to stay in the game. Programs embodying this strategy do well in competition with the mathematically fair player. A number of learning programs have also been devised that attempt to take account of their opponents' playing styles as relevant evidence accumulates through a game session. Such programs that update models of their opponents were the most successful investigated, and it seems likely that good human players also use similar processes. Indeed, Findler reports that human players usually cannot tell whether they are competing with other humans or with an adaptive program when the game is played over computer terminals.

IV. SUMMARY AND CONCLUDING COMMENTS

In this Chapter recent studies of processes involved in adversary problem-solving have been reviewed. From the game theory literature on how best to tackle such problems, came the useful notions of game trees and minimaxing. These ideas have been taken up both in analysing human play of board games, and in developing AI programs capable of high level performance in chess and other games. Board games provide a useful focus for studying thought because they permit the generation of an indefinite number of fresh problems within tight frameworks.

This is very useful from the AI point of view since the basic rules of such games can be readily programmed. From the point of view of studying human processes an extra benefit of games as research tools, is that people's experience of particular games varies widely, and so studies of the effects of varying familiarity with the task area can be readily carried out.

In comparison with studies of non-adversary problems then, a strong emphasis on effects of experience is found in the study of human game playing. As De Groot (1965) showed, there is little difference between good and excellent players in depth of look ahead or breadth of search or other easily quantified aspects of the mental search process and yet the excellent (master level) players almost always choose a better move. It may be noted in passing, also, that the depth of look ahead (5-6) reported by De Groot and Charness (1981b) is markedly larger than that assumed by the successful models for water jug and missionary-cannibal problems discussed in the previous Chapter. This difference may be due to the complete unfamiliarity of these non-adversary problems as against the relative familiarity of the chess task to the subjects concerned. One would very likely obtain quantifiable differences in search patterns between novices and good players (and Charness's results point in that direction). However, this comment does not detract from the basic point that master players can select better moves with no more searching than (merely) good players.

The explanation for this difference was suggested by data on memory for chess positions after brief exposures. Master level players could reconstruct complete board positions much better than weaker players. This difference only held up if the board position made "chess sense". Level of playing skill made no difference to recall of positions constructed by arranging pieces at random on the board. Similar results have now been reported for GO (Reitman, 1976) and bridge (Charness, 1979; Engle and Bukstel, 1978).

Simon and Gilmartin (1973) put forward an explanation for the chess memory results in terms of "chunking" (Miller, 1956) in working (or short-term) memory. The master level player was assumed to have a larger store of patterns in long-term memory with which to label board configurations and thus could find pattern labels that encoded the position more economically than the weaker player. Support for this view came from a successful simulation program, MAPP. The notion that the "chunks" are held in short term memory until recall, is no longer plausible following Charness (1976) and Frey and Adesman's (1976) reports of little or no effects from interpolated tasks on chess memory. These results suggest, rather, rapid encoding in long-term memory. They do not, however, damage the major assumption that master level players have a more advanced coding scheme than lesser players.

Some of these conclusions may require modification when subject age is taken into consideration. According to Charness's results (1981a, b, c) older players may encode a board position less efficiently than younger players but apparently compensate by using better evaluation functions to cut down on search.

The game position memory tasks have thrown light on the coding schemes built up over many years of practice, but how are these schemes involved in actual play? First of all, they are involved in the initial structuring of the task, i.e. in developing an internal model of the problem materials, goals and methods. Secondly, in deciding what to do, it has been suggested (Chase and Simon, 1973b) that familiar patterns will be linked to recommendations for action in a production system-like fashion (condition ⟶ action). The "actions" may be to explore internally in certain directions or to set particular goals for achievement, rather than overt actions.

Both the artificial intelligence (Findler, 1978) and the human experimental studies (Lopes, 1976) of poker playing underline the need to consider players' internal models of their adversaries as well as of the task materials.

Overall, then, the implications of the studies of adversary problem solving are quite consistent with those of investigations of non-adversary problem solving. Both lines of research indicate the role of internal models in problem-solving and are consistent with the view that the human subject searches trees of possibilities in a serial fashion, with a small capacity working memory backed up by an extensive long-term memory. The role of long-term memory comes out more clearly in studies of adversary problem solving, because skill (or experience) levels have been investigated more fully in games than in non-adversary tasks.

V. FURTHER READING

Newborn, M. M. (1979). Recent progress in computer chess. *In* "Advances in Computers" (*Eds* M. C. Yovits), vol. 18, pp.59-118. Academic Press, London and New York.

Provides a readable overview of computer chess methods. Comparisons may be made with the evidence on human methods that emerges from studies such as those of Charness, e.g.

Charness, N. (1981a). Aging and skilled problem solving. *Journal of Experimental Psychology: General* **110**, 21-38.

Charness, N. (1981b). Search in chess: age and skill differences. *Journal of Experimental Psychology: Human Perception and Performance* **7**, 467-476.

4
Deductive reasoning

This chapter and the next deal with reasoning and continue the theme of considering how people "go beyond the information given". The preceding two Chapters concerned studies of how people tackle problems that involve extensive mental searches, or, in the case of games, an extensive long-term memory of relevant patterns. By contrast, the reasoning tasks to be considered here would not appear to require extensive mental searches or extensive prior knowledge structures. Nevertheless, the tasks to be dealt with are frequently found to be very difficult despite their apparent simplicity.

The reasoning problems discussed in this Chapter and in the next may conveniently be labelled "deductive" and "inductive" respectively. In deductive tasks, people are required to determine what conclusion, if any, necessarily follows when certain statements are assumed to be true. In the case of inductive reasoning, people are required to determine the implications, if any, of some particular observation(s) for the truth of possible generalizations (hypotheses). The topics of deductive and inductive reasoning are very closely related and both have been extensively studied in recent years. To keep the text to a manageable length, I will largely deal with selected "prototypical" instances of the two types of inference.

I. SYLLOGISTIC REASONING

A fairly common type of deductive problem in everyday thinking, is to determine what conclusion, if any, must follow from certain assumptions about category membership.

Because the classical argument form of the *syllogism* provides small-scale instances of such deductive problems, it has been widely used in laboratory studies of reasoning. The main features of syllogistic arguments may be conveyed by a few examples. Consider the following:
All mammals have backbones.
All dogs are mammals.
Therefore, all dogs have backbones.

Since the third statement (the conclusion) follows necessarily from the first two (the premises) this is a *valid* syllogistic argument and may be compared with:

All cats are mammals.
All dogs are mammals.
Therefore, all dogs are cats.

In this case the conclusion plainly does not follow from the premises and the argument is *invalid*. It should be noted that the validity of an argument is independent of the truth of the premises. So, for example, the following is a deductively valid argument.

All cats have nine lives.
All dogs are cats.
Therefore, all dogs have nine lives.

A valid argument is simply one in which, if the premises are true, then the conclusion is also, necessarily, true.

In addition to validity, syllogisms can be varied in many other ways for experimental purposes. For example they may be varied by changing the *quantifiers* ("some", "all") used in the argument; the *terms* may be abstract or concrete; the premises and conclusion may be *negative* or *affirmative*; the *propositions* in the argument may be empirically true or false, . . . and so on. Clearly, many features of the task can be readily manipulated. A number of variations are also possible in the response requirements. Subjects can be asked to *produce* valid inferences from given conclusions; to *judge* a possible conclusion as valid or not; or to *select* a valid conclusion from a set of possibilities.

Early studies (e.g. Wilkins, 1928) established some of the main factors associated with the difficulty of syllogisms, such as concreteness. Intuitively, the invalidity of an argument seems less clear when the terms are abstract, e.g.

All Ps are Ms.
All Ss are Ms.
Therefore, all Ss are Ps.

This abstract argument may well be accepted, even although it exhibits the same invalid pattern as a previous concrete example that led from true premises to the conclusion that "all dogs are cats".

The role of concreteness in facilitating syllogistic reasoning was experimentally established by Wilkins. She found that syllogisms which employed concrete terms resulted in more correct deductions than syllogisms in abstract form. 81 subjects were given a series of problems like the following.

All good ballet dancers have many years of training. Some of the dancers in this musical comedy have many years of training. Therefore:

(1) Some of the dancers in this musical comedy are good ballet dancers.
(2) All good ballet dancers are in this musical comedy.
(3) Some of the dancers in this musical comedy are not good ballet dancers.

Or, the same thing in symbols: all A's are B's; some C's are B's. Therefore:
(1) Some C's are A's.
(2) All A's are C's.
(3) Some C's are not A's.

the instructions were "to put a plus sign before every conclusion which you are sure follows necessarily from the given statements . . . a minus sign before every conclusion that does not necessarily follow from the given statements . . .". The average score was 76% correct for the letter terms and 84% for the syllogisms expressed in familiar words.

Why, even in the case of concrete syllogisms, did the subjects accept so many invalid conclusions? Misunderstanding of the use of the term "some" could have caused errors. In logic, "some" means "at least one and possibly all" while in normal usage it means "not all but at least one". Thus, in logic, it is *not* valid to infer from "some X are Y" that "some X are not Y".

An additional proposal has been that there is an "atmosphere effect" which leads subjects to accept invalid conclusions. This proposal has generated a long-lasting controversy which will now be surveyed.

A. The "atmosphere effect" controversy

1 Basic results
All Cs are Ms.
All Ds are Ms.
Therefore, all Ds are Cs.

The above argument is invalid. (In logic it is known as the "fallacy of the undistributed middle"). To account for this common form of error, Woodworth and Sells (1935) hypothesized an "atmosphere" effect which predicted that the form of the premises would influence people's expectations about the form of the conclusion. They proposed that if both premises involve the universal ("all"), people are disposed to accept an "all" conclusion. Similarly, if both premises are particular ("some"), people will be disposed to a "particular" conclusion. Similar predictions apply if both premises are negatively particular or universal; in such cases, the preferred conclusion is predicted to be negatively particular or universal respectively. With mixed premises it is proposed that *(1)* a negative premise creates a negative atmosphere even when the other premise is affirmative,

(2) a particular premise creates a particular atmosphere, even when the other premise is universal.

To test the atmosphere hypothesis, Sells (1936) presented 65 subjects with 180 syllogisms, using abstract material, e.g.

If all Zs and Ys
and all Xs are Ys
are all Xs then Zs? True, probably true, false or indeterminate? (Correct answer—indeterminate).

The meaning of "some" in logic was explained in advance.

Of the 180 syllogisms 52 were valid and 128 invalid. With the invalid syllogisms the conclusions that accorded to the atmosphere of the premises were predominantly accepted as true/valid conclusions, in accord with the hypothesis.

Sells and Koob (1937) report a similar result in a study that required subjects to draw their own conclusions from premises rather than merely judging already set out conclusions. This study required subjects to "work quickly" which would probably favour an atmosphere effect.

How might atmosphere operate? The suggestion is that one becomes quickly set or adjusted to the total impression of the presented situation and responds accordingly. This would lead to fast responses—some of which would be correct. Accurate reasoning, on the other hand, surely requires analysis of the situation, and noting of relations—presumably a slower, more deliberate process than is suggested by the atmosphere hypothesis.

As a model, the atmosphere hypothesis proposes very superficial processing with minimal understanding—and it may be correct, when abstract problems are given to untrained subjects working under time pressure.

2 Conversion errors and probabilistic inference

More than 20 years after Woodworth and Sells proposed the atmosphere hypothesis, an alternative was put forward by Chapman and Chapman (1959). First, they collected from fresh data by giving subjects 42 syllogisms that had no valid conclusions, e.g.

Some Ls are Ks.
Some Ks are Ms.
Therefore:
(1) No Ms are Ls.
(2) Some Ms are Ls.
(3) Some Ms are not Ls.
(4) None of these.
(5) All Ms are Ls.

The correct conclusion is (4) "None of these". Subjects tended to be wrong on these items and the kind of error made depended on the form of syllogism. The study involved 14 main types of syllogism and the atmosphere effect predicted the preferred errors on many of these. But it failed on syllogisms that involved premises of the following type

(A) Some X are Y / No Y are Z   and   (B) Some X are not Y / No Y are Z

The predicted error (on atmosphere) is "Some Z are not X" but in fact subjects tended to choose "No Z are X", especially on (A) but split fairly evenly between the universal and the particular conclusions on (B).

Chapman and Chapman proposed that their results could be better explained by the operation of two reasoning errors that they called "conversion" and "probabilistic inference". There are 2 conversion errors. These are to assume *(1)* from "all X are Y" that "all Y are X" and *(2)* that "some As are not Bs" implies "some Bs are not As". That these are errors is shown clearly by concrete material. "All women are human" does *not* imply that "all humans are women". Again, "some humans are not politicians" does *not* imply that "some politicians are not human".

However, the Chapmans argue that conversions often happen to be correct with real materials (e.g. "all 3 sided figures are triangles") and they suggest that subjects tend to make conversions unless they have information to the contrary (which they do not have with abstract material).

Probabilistic inference involves "plausible reasoning" that is not strictly valid, *deductively* speaking, e.g. "Some cloudy days are wet", "Some wet days are unpleasant", therefore "Some cloudy days are unpleasant". The Chapmans report that the joint operation of illicit conversion and probabilistic inference accounts better for their obtained error patterns than does the atmosphere hypothesis. This is largely on the strength of improved predictions for the types of syllogism mentioned before. On other syllogisms the alternative hypotheses make the same predictions. It is notable that the Chapmans' results differ from those of Sells on the "crucial" syllogisms. (Sells's results favoured the atmosphere prediction.) To sum up, the Chapmans have presented a plausible alternative to the atmosphere hypothesis, an alternative that is congenial to a cognitive approach—however their data do *not* represent a complete demolition of the atmosphere hypothesis.

In 1969 Begg and Denny re-examined the atmosphere *v.* illicit conversion etc. controversy and provided a brief reformulation of atmosphere hypothesis, that covers most of the obtained effects. They proposed 2 principles. *(1)* Whenever at least 1 premise is negative, the conclusion is negative and otherwise it is positive. *(2)* Whenever at least 1 premise is particular (some), the conclusion will be particular, otherwise it is universal. These 2 principles can be combined for any pairs of premises to predict the preferred conclusion.

For most syllogisms these assumptions predict the same results as the conversion and probabilistic inference hypothesis. Begg and Denny analysed error patterns on 45 syllogisms, representing the main types and found that, again, atmosphere predicted the majority choices very well. They also re-analysed the data of Sells (1936) and the Chapmans (1959). There was great consistency among the 3 sets of data and on the average of the 3 studies, the atmosphere predictions were more often upheld than the conversion and probabilistic inference predictions.

Begg and Denny emphasize that their study is not informative about the processes that lead subjects to error; but their results do support the use of the atmosphere "formula" as a convenient predictor of error patterns, even if the underlying processes may not be as described by the atmosphere hypothesis.

Wason and Johnson-Laird (1972) bring out some other points which suggest that, at the least, the atmosphere hypothesis is inadequate as a *complete* explanation, e.g. from Sells's own data:

When subjects are given
All B are A
All C are B

they accept the correct conclusion "All C are A" twice as often as the incorrect conclusion "All A are C". Both are equally predicted by the atmosphere hypothesis. Again, Wilkins's (1928) data shows that the atmosphere effect is weaker with familiar as opposed to abstract or unfamiliar material and the atmosphere hypothesis does not explain this difference. Wason and Johnson-Laird ran a further informative study. This differed from most of previous experiments in that the subjects were simply given the premises and asked to draw a conclusion. They were not asked to evaluate given conclusions or to select one from a multiple choice list. Also, the premises they were given permitted *valid* inferences to be drawn (cf. Sells and the Chapmans).

Wason and Johnson-Laird found that there were reliably more errors *incompatible* with atmosphere (average of 3.9 per problem) than compatible with atmosphere (1.8 per problem). Further, the tendency to conform to atmosphere varied from one sort of problem to another. They concluded that the atmosphere explanation left something to be desired and in view of the "anti-atmosphere" evidence, go so far as to suggest that "Perhaps there is no atmosphere effect in syllogistic reasoning at all, but merely an amassed set of data which, when casually viewed, gives rise to the illusion of such a phenomenon".

Another attack on the atmosphere hypothesis that has led to some interesting work was developed by Henle (1962) and this will be discussed next.

3 Henle's defense of "rationality"

The atmosphere notion portrays people as non-logical and under the influence of non-rational sets; on the other hand, the Chapmans' hypothesis suggests that people are somewhat rational—but may misinterpret premises (leading to illicit conversion) and may draw plausible but not strictly warranted conclusions from premises (probabilistic inference). This second kind of approach is consistent with the views put forward by Mary Henle (1962) in a paper that argued for the essential logicality of everyday thinking.

Henle argues that many apparent instances of illogical thinking may involve the implicit introduction of additional premises, the ignoring of some of the given premises and the misinterpretation of still other premises —*but* she claims the *inferences* are generally rational, given the subject's real premises. Henle here harks back to the old view that logic and thinking are closely related—as against the more recent view that thinking is not intrinsically logical and only conforms to logical paths under special circumstances. She illustrates her points with typical responses given by a sample of graduate students to syllogisms that one might come across in everyday life, e.g.

It's important to talk about things that are in our minds.
We spend so much of our time in the kitchen that household problems are in our minds.
Therefore, it's important to talk about household problems.

Subjects were asked to assess the validity of the argument, and give their reasons. Some subjects failed to accept the task at all, and did not distinguish logical validity from factual truth, e.g. "No it's not important to talk about things in our minds unless they worry us". In a number of cases, subjects tacitly re-stated premises or the conclusion so that the intended meaning was changed. (Since Henle's syllogisms omitted quantifiers they were very open to changes of this sort. Indeed—to digress slightly—omission of quantifiers is a prime source of crooked and confused thinking according to Thouless, (1953)). Other examples showed that subjects sometimes omitted entire premises and sometimes introduced premises that had not been given.

Henle concludes "that when subjects arrive at apparently invalid conclusions, or when they fail to spot a fallacy, they often do so because they have worked with materials different from those intended or because they have undertaken a task different from one intended. In such cases, if we consider the materials and task as they were actually understood by individual subjects, we fail to find evidence of faulty reasoning. It must be concluded that the presence of error does not constitute evidence that the laws of logic are irrelevant to actual thinking. The data tend, rather, to support the older conception that these laws are widely discernible in the thinking process".

Although Henle's final conclusion from her informal study of a small, highly educated sample may be regarded as debatable, she has made a very sound point in stressing the need to consider the subjects' *interpretation* of the task materials and goals. It is easy to assume that subjects interpret a task exactly as the experimenter intends and then go on to make extraordinary blunders, that the experimenter is perplexed to explain. Consideration of possible interpretations may well make subjects' behaviour more intelligible.

4 Misinterpretation of premises: further evidence

The question of premise interpretation was again taken up by Ceraso and Provitera (1971) who examined the ambiguity of the traditional statements used in syllogistic tasks. There are 4 basic statements, obtained by combining universal or particular quantifiers, positively or negatively. These statements are as follows:

(A) All A are B
(I) Some A are B
(E) All A are not B
(O) Some A are not B

and are traditionally labelled A, I, E and O. These labels come from the initial vowels of the Latin words "affirmo" and "nego", meaning "I assert" and "I deny" respectively. An A statement can refer to two different situations, an I statement to four situations and an O statement to three, while an E statement is unambiguous and refer to only one state of affairs. These points should become clearer by reference to Venn diagrams. (*See* Fig. 4.1.) If, as seems likely, many subjects misinterpret the traditional, ambiguous premises, then apparently mistaken conclusions (e.g. those attributed to atmosphere effects) may be *valid* inferences based on misconstrued premises.

Cesaro and Provitera gave subjects syllogisms in which the premises were given a definite interpretation, e.g. instead of "Some As are Bs", subjects were told "Some of the As (but not all, are Bs, but all of the Bs are As". Another group of subjects were given the traditional syllogism statements. The subjects with the clarified premises performed much better (averaging 2.5 errors/13 syllogisms) compared to the traditional group (who averaged 5.5 errors/13). Also, the responses of the traditional syllogism subjects could largely be explained by proposing that they tended to interpret their premises in a more restricted way than was intended by logic.

Even with the modified premises, some difficulties still arose, which seem to be related to the multiple possibilities that could follow from certain premise combinations. Subjects do not seem to completely analyse all the possible consequences of such premise combinations. Rather they develop one *possible* consequence and adopt it as the conclusion. This leads to an overrestricted conclusion which is *consistent* with the premises but *not necessarily* true, e.g. from

All B are A
All B are C

Subjects tended to conclude "All A are C" rather than the more general and correct deduction "Some A are C".

Cesaro and Provitera dub this an example of "could be" reasoning. Wason and Johnson-Laird (1972) report other evidence supporting the notion of premise misinterpretation and incomplete analysis of consequences. They also suggest that when a subject has drawn a plausible, consistent conclusion he is reluctant to try to *falsify* it, by for example, checking whether the negative of his initial conclusion is also consistent with the premises.

B. Erickson's model

Erickson (1974, 1978) has also considered the problems of premise interpretation and inadequate analysis of proposed conclusions. He found

Fig. 4.1. Venn diagrams showing the possible interpretations of the traditional premises of syllogistic logic.

consistent patterns of interpretations that held over large student samples drawn from 4 different universities. When subjects were asked to draw Venn diagrams corresponding to the statement "All A are B", approximately 40% of responses were in terms of a set identity interpretation while 60% were in terms of a set inclusion interpretation (see Figure 4.2).

These different interpretations would logically lead to different conclusions if they were used in syllogistic reasoning. Erickson (1978) focussed his research on "AA" syllogisms, in which both premises are "A" statements, i.e. are affirmative universals. Since subjects were quite self-consistent and would tend to interpret all universal statements in the same way, he could then consider only identity-identity interpretations and inclusion-inclusion interpretations of the premises in AA syllogisms.

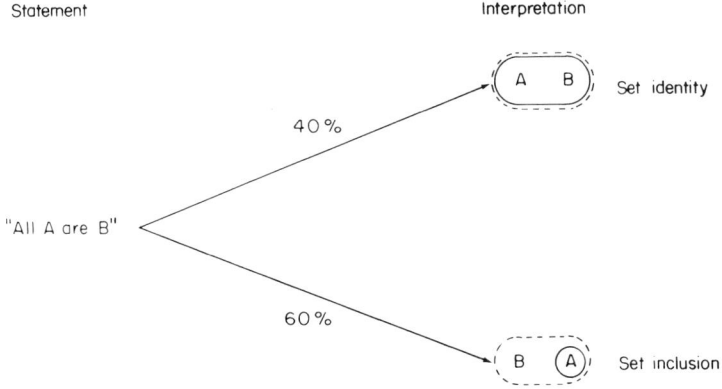

Fig. 4.2. Distribution of interpretations given to the universal affirmative premise by Erickson's subjects (1974).

At this point we must consider an aspect of the structure of syllogisms that it has been possible to ignore up to now. This aspect relates to the terms and their arrangement within the syllogism. A syllogism involves three terms (category or individual names). The premises state the relationships of one term (the middle term, M) to a predicate term (P) and to a subject term (S). A valid conclusion states the relationship that must hold between the S and the P terms. So, a typical example reads, "All M are P. All S are M. Therefore, all S are P". In accord with the tradition that the first statement relates M and P and the second relates S and M. Clearly, the order of the terms within each premise can be varied in two ways. Putting together the combinatorial possibilities for two premises yields four syllogistic patterns known as the four *figures. See* Table 4.1 below.

Erickson (1978) pointed out that the possible conclusions consistent with the premise interpretations of AA syllogisms differed over the four figures.

Figure 4.3 illustrates the conclusions consistent with the figures. Note that only one conclusion follows from the identity-identity interpretation over all figures. When subjects were given Venn diagrams representing the different AA premise interpretations, their drawn Venn diagrams conclusions were generally consistent with the premises and showed reliable (and different) distributions over the possible conclusions for the four argument figures.

Table 4.1. Possible syllogistic figures.

figure I	figure II	figure III	figure IV
M — P	P — M	M — P	P — M
S — M	S — M	M — S	M — S
S — P	S — P	S — P	S — P

On the basis of *(a)* the estimated proportions of subjects making identity-identity and inclusion-inclusion interpretations, and *(b)* of the estimated proportions who would produce each alternative conclusion from each premise-premise interpretation, Erickson was able to predict very accurately the proportions of subjects who would make each of the possible conclusions (A, E, I, O) to AA syllogisms in the 4 figures. The data from 5 independent studies were fitted very well by predictions based on the above analyses. Thus, there is a good measure of support for Erickson's model which proposes a three stage process of *(1)* premise interpretation, *(2)* combination of interpreted premises to yield a conclusion, and *(3)* response formation depending on the conclusion and on the task demands (e.g. draw a diagram; give a verbal statement; select one from a list of alternatives, etc.). This analysis is quite consistent with Ceraso and Provitera"s (1971) results which showed that disambiguated premises improve performance. Erickson's three stage model would explain Ceraso and Provitera's results by assuming that correct interpretations at stage 1 were made more likely by the clarified premises.

C. The analogical model

A recent series of studies (Johnson-Laird, 1975; Johnson-Laird and Steedman, 1978) has revealed an interesting effect due to the figure of the syllogism and this effect can be accounted for by a promising model of syllogistic inference developed by Johnson-Laird. In the experiments in question, subjects had to draw conclusions from syllogistic premises dealing

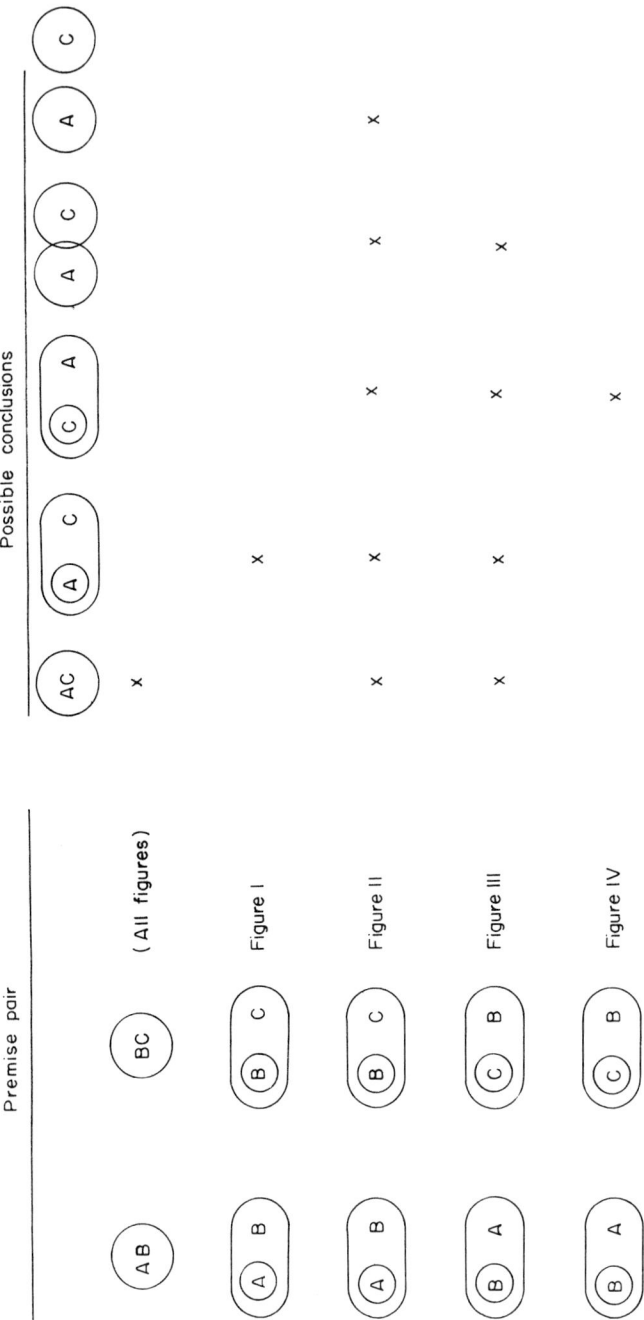

Fig. 4.3. Conclusions consistent with set identity and set inclusion interpretations of two universal affirmative premises. The consistent conclusions are marked "X" for each syllogistic figure. (Reprinted by permission from J. R. Erickson (1978). Models of formal reasoning. In "Human Reasoning" (Eds Revlin, R. and Mayer, R.), p. 43. V. H. Winston and Sons, Washington D.C.)

with concrete but uncontroversial matters, e.g. "Some of the parents are scientists; all of the scientists are drivers; therefore . . . ?". This particular form of syllogism (figure IV in Table 4.1) tended to elicit the conclusion "Some of the parents are drivers" rather than the equally valid "Some of the drivers are parents".

While, on the other hand, the premises "Some of the scientists are parents; all of the drivers are scientists" (Figure I in Table 4.1) would tend to elicit the conclusion "Some of the drivers are parents" rather than the also valid "Some of the parents are drivers". Indeed, throughout their experiments premises of the form "A — B; B — C" (i.e. Figure IV in Table 4.1) produced a bias towards conclusions of the form "A — C" ("C — A" conclusions being also valid). Whereas in the premises of the form "B — A; C — B" (figure I in Table 4.1), led to the bias towards "C — A" conclusions, ("A — C" conclusions being also valid). This strong "figural" effect had not been noticed hitherto, perhaps because of the widespread use of forced choice testing formats that would not include the unorthodox (from the classical point of view) conclusion "A — C" to the "A — B; B — C" syllogism. This conclusion, it should be explained, is unorthodox because it has taken the first premise as relating subject to middle term, while, traditionally, the first premise has related predicate to middle term. Johnson-Laird points out that traditionally 64 "moods" of syllogism were recognized since the 2 premises and the conclusion have to be chosen from the 4 sentence moods (A, E, I, O) giving $4^3 = 64$ possibilities. Combining the 64 moods with the 4 figures (explained in the previous section) yields $64 \times 4 = 256$ different syllogistic structures. While this number had been taken for granted by psychologists, Johnson-Laird observed that one could in fact generate twice as many. Logicians had decided to arrange their syllogisms so that the subject of the conclusion always appeared in the second premise, but the logic of the argument is not really affected if the subject term (S) happens to appear in the first premise as in:

$$\frac{\begin{array}{c}S-M\\M-P\end{array}}{S-P}$$

cf. traditional figure I in Table 4.1,

$$\frac{\begin{array}{c}M-P\\S-M\end{array}}{S-P}$$

It seems that the failure to consider all 512 possible syllogisms led to the figural bias effect remaining undiscovered until recently.

It is noteworthy that the figural bias effect is not predicted by previous approaches. The atmosphere hypothesis, the conversion and probabilistic inference hypothesis and Erickson's set theoretic approach are alike in failing to predict any effect of the order of occurrence of the major premise (relating middle term and predicate) and the minor premise (relating middle term and subject). In view of this and of other problems with the earlier approaches, Johnson-Laird and Steedman (1978) have put forward a new theory for syllogistic reasoning, known as the *analogical* theory. (A preliminary version was reported by Johnson-Laird, 1975.)

The broad stages proposed by the theory are mostly similar to those suggested by other recent analyses (e.g. Erickson, 1978). They are *(1)* interpretation of premises; *(2)* an initial *heuristic* combination of the representations of the two premises; *(3)* the formulation of a conclusion corresponding to the combination of premises and *(4)* a *logical test* (or series of tests) of the initial heuristic combination which may lead to the conclusion being modified or abandoned. In terms of broad stages, the main novelty is the provision of a final testing stage that can lead back to a changed combination of premises which in turn may be tested again. In terms of detail, an explicit information processing model has been developed that incorporates a number of distinctive ideas.

First, the premise representations are assumed to take the form of list structures. A clue to the possible use of list structure representations in this task came from one of the subjects' retrospections on how he had tackled the syllogisms. In connection with the premise "All the artists are bee keepers", he reported "I thought of all the little artists in the room and imagined that they all had bee keeper's hats on". This remark suggested the hypothesis that a class is represented by thinking of an arbitrary number of examples. So, to represent the above premise, the reasoner imagines an arbitrary number of artists and tags each of them as a bee keeper. Since the sets are not identical he should add an arbitrary number of beekeepers to the representation. The elements in the representation may be images, or verbal or abstract items; the important feature is the relationship between the elements, rather than the exact nature of the elements. The structure of the representation of the current example may be taken to have the form:

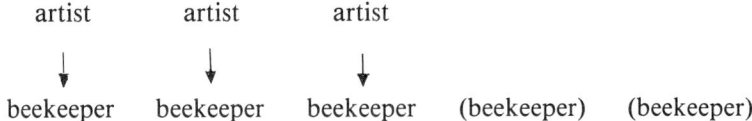

(The arrows represent the relationships "is a"). It is asserted that this representation is structurally analogous to what the reasoner thinks when he understands the sentence "All artists are beekeepers". The proposed representation is a list-structure and this has the advantage of being readily encodable in computer programming. In list-structure terms, each entry on the artist list has stored with it the address of a corresponding beekeeper on the beekeeper list and there are entries on the beekeeper list who are not connected to entries on the artist list. It is notable that such list-structure notions were also found useful by Simon and Hayes (1976) in their analyses of problem comprehension, discussed in Chapter 3.

Having fixed on a representation of the individual premises, the next step is to combine them in some way. Johnson-Laird proposes that there is a heuristic bias towards forming connections that link up all the classes if possible. So, given

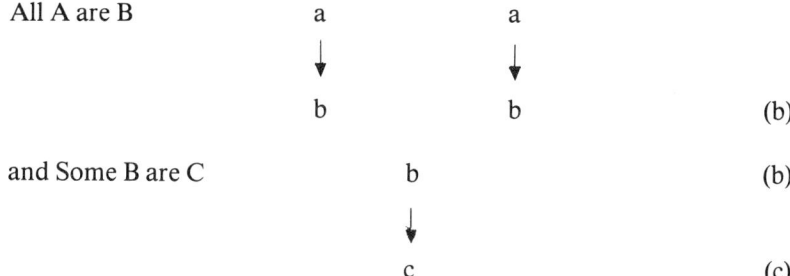

these would be combined to yield the structure:

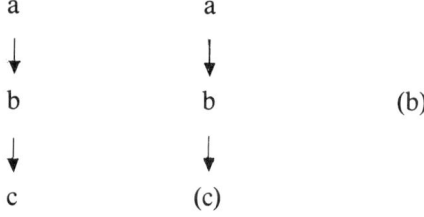

This structure readily suggests the invalid conclusion "Some As are Cs", (and this conclusion is often erroneously made).

To draw a conclusion the paths between end terms must be considered. Taking the structure resulting from the initial combination of "All A are B" and "Some B are C" the paths would be labelled:

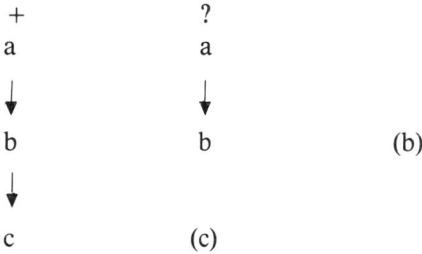

One path is positive and one indeterminate. (Negative paths can arise if the negative operators "no", "not" occur in the premises. For the sake of simplicity negatives will not be considered here). The path labelling of the above structure would lead to the (erroneous) conclusion "Some A are C", in accord with the principle that "where there is at least one positive path the conclusion is of the form "Some X are Y", unless there are only positive paths in which case it is of the form "All X are Y"; in any other case no valid conclusion can be drawn". To avoid invalid conclusions, it is proposed that logical tests are applied to the combined representation in an attempt to remove links between end items without damaging the correctness of the individual premise interpretations. In the example, "All the artists are beekeepers. Some of the beekeepers are chemists", the initial combined representation has an artist tagged as a beekeeper who in turn is tagged as a chemist. This particular beekeeper–chemist linkage can be broken without losing the initial meaning. The modified representation would not include any artist positively linked to any chemist. No conclusion could be drawn and the final overt answer would correctly so indicate.

The analogical theory, then, proposes a heuristic combination of premises to yield a tentative conclusion, followed by a logical testing process. Differences in persistence of testing preliminary conclusions could well lead to differences in the conclusions finally drawn by different individuals to the same premises.

The theory has been realized in the form of a computer program and its performance compared to that of human subjects on a set of 64 problems. With some syllogisms the process of testing does not lead to any modifications (hence thoroughness of testing does not matter). Such syllogisms were predicted to be easier than those to which the model would produce a modified conclusion after testing. This prediction was upheld, (80.4% correct on predicted "easy" problems *v.* 46.5% correct on others). Also, the model predicts the figural bias effect because the directionality of the linkages in the figures in question leads naturally to the particular ordering of terms most often observed in subjects' conclusions. Further support for the theory comes from responses to those premises that do not permit a valid conclusion to be drawn. Invalid syllogisms in Figures I and IV, (*see* Fig. 4.3), in which it is easy to form paths in the initial representation, are predicted to be more difficult than invalid syllogisms in the other figures. The predicted difference was upheld by 18 out of 20 subjects.

To sum up, the following positive comments may be made. This work has led to recognition of a previously undiscovered phenomenon in syllogistic reasoning i.e. the figural bias effect. The analogical model put forward by Johnson-Laird encompasses this effect (which previous approaches do not) and it is consistent with much of the fine grain data of the Johnson-Laird and Steedman (1978) paper. Furthermore, the theory is sufficiently well specified to be translated into a working computer program. On the negative side, only the data from one or two studies have been compared with the model. It should be noted that the instructions used by Johnson-Laird and Steedman may have induced a bias toward the type of representation that they propose as a general rule. Subjects were told that they would be given "pairs of statements about people whom they were to imagine as assembled in a room". These instructions could well suggest an analogical type of representation of the sort reported by their one retrospecting subject. The theory would be on firmer ground if compared with other data from subjects not given that representational suggestion. On the whole, though, the analogical approach seems very promising and relates nicely to other attempts to model representational processes using list structure notions (e.g. Simon and Hayes, 1976).

II. SUMMARY AND CONCLUDING COMMENTS

From the evidence reviewed in this Chapter, what answer can be given to the often raised question, "Do people think logically?". If the criterion of logical thinking is reaching conclusions consistent with those of formal logic then one must answer that people are not always logical reasoners. They do make errors. According to one authority (Erickson, 1978), "for *most* syllogisms the modal response is incorrect". However the errors do not appear to be random and various suggestions have been made regarding the processes underlying both errors and correct responses.

A proposal of completely non-logical processing is embodied in the atmosphere hypothesis. This hypothesis is consistent with many typical responses to syllogistic tasks; however, it is "over inclusive" and is thus consistent with many possibilities that tend not to happen. Furthermore it does not cope well with fine grain effects, such as, the figural bias effect or the often correct choice of "no conclusion" by Johnson-Laird's subjects. The atmosphere hypothesis always predicts that some conclusion can be drawn, but, at least some of the time, people can appreciate that certain syllogisms are inconclusive. An alternative proposal is that various "illogical" processes which have some plausibility may jointly produce many errors. In particular, illicit conversion of premises and probabilistic inference have been proposed by the Chapmans (1959). However, the empirical evidence distinguishing this suggestion from the atmosphere hypothesis is not strong (Begg and Denny, 1969). Again, the figural bias effect and many fine grain features of reasoning data are not dealt with by this hypothesis.

Henle (1962) put forward the very influential view that people *do* reason logically, but frequently misinterpret the premises or the task demands, thus producing overt errors. Indeed, Henle (1978) has gone so far as to say, "I have never found errors which could unambiguously be attributed to faulty reasoning". Unfortunately, this may reflect the difficulty, in principle, of obtaining falsifying evidence for the Henle position. No matter what response is given, a suitable interpretation of the premises (or task) can be inferred to make the response seem "logical". Clearly, some independent check on premise and task interpretation is required when considering individual examples. However most research has involved the more indirect methods of group analysis. For example, Ceraso and Provitera (1971) showed that clarified, unambiguous premises led to many fewer errors than traditional ambiguous premises. This is consistent with the Henle position. Erickson (1974, 1978) proposed a specific form of "Henle" model in which premise interpretation was assumed to take the form of mental Venn diagrams. Using the proportions of people in one group who interpreted universal affirmative (A) statements as set identity and as set inclusion, he was able to predict the obtained proportions of alternative conclusions to AA syllogisms, in the four different figures, for independent groups of subjects. Again, this result is consistent with the Henle approach. A stronger test would have been to compare the inferences of subjects classed as "set-identity interpreters" with those of subjects classed as "set-inclusion interpreters" of AA premises.

A different and more detailed proposal is contained in Johnson-Laird's (1975; Johnson-Laird and Steedman, 1978) analogical model for reasoning. In this model most of the individual variability in reasoning behaviour is not attributed to differences in the premise interpretation stage but to different degrees of thoroughness in checking initial conclusions. Differences in syllogism difficulty are explained in terms of the complexity of the list structures required to represent the premises.

The model is precise enough to be expressed as a computer program and handles much fine grain data. One possible reservation about this model is that it has only been tested against data from two studies, in both of which the instructions were suggestive of the analogical representation scheme proposed by the model. It would be desirable to have the model tested with groups not receiving such instructions and extension to abstract materials would also be useful. On the whole, though, the analogical model is the best specified, most broad-ranging and promising current model. Furthermore, it readily relates to other studies of comprehension processes (e.g. Simon and Hayes, 1976). By contrast, the other models tend to be isolated in the syllogism field and lack obvious ways of connecting with other topics in the thinking area.

How might syllogistic reasoning relate to the processes of problem solving discussed in Chapters 2 and 3? On the surface, syllogistic tasks are well defined and appear to require but one "move" from a given starting state (the premises) to a goal state (a valid conclusion). However, from the review in this Chapter a variety of processes seem to be involved. First, as in all problems, the starting state has to be defined by the subject. In dealing with syllogisms, this is the process of premise interpretation. Since premises are frequently ambiguous, alternative interpretations are often possible, though it would appear that only one interpretation is considered at a time, i.e. a serial search among interpretation possibilities is undertaken. Indeed, generally it seems that only one interpretation is derived (Erickson, 1974). Once an interpretation of the premises has been made, then by using general logical rules, presumably stored in long-term memory, more than one conclusion might often be drawn (e.g. "strong" or "weak" conclusions). According to Johnson-Laird's analysis, it seems that rather lax "evaluation functions" are often used to determine whether a possible conclusion is valid or not. There seems to be a tendency to accept conclusions that are consistent with the premises but which are not required by them. To the extent that there is a search among alternative conclusions, it seems to be a serial search. Frequently, however, it seems that if the first conclusion drawn is acceptable to the subject then alternatives are not generated.

There is nothing in the syllogistic reasoning data to counter the view that, when problem-solving, we work as limited capacity, slow, serial processors of information.

III. FURTHER READING

Henle, M. (1962). On the relation between logic and thinking. *Psychological Review* **69**, 366-378.

This very readable paper contains Mary Henle's classic statement in defense of human rationality. Much later research can be seen as amplifying or reacting against her position.

Thouless, R. (1978). Straight and crooked thinking. Pan Books, London.

An extremely useful and clearly written guide to many of the logical pitfalls which threaten everyday thinking. This book should help you to correct both your own reasoning and that of others with whom you may be debating.

Johnson-Laird, P. N. (1981). Mental models in cognitive science. *In* "Perspectives in cognitive science" (*Ed.* D. A. Norman), Ablex Publishing Corporation, New Jersey.

This paper considers the role of mental models in cognition, drawing heavily on Johnson-Laird's research on syllogistic reasoning.

5
Inductive reasoning

In the last Chapter we considered studies of deductive inference from statements (premises) that were to be taken as true. Somewhat different but related tasks arise when one has to test statements (hypotheses) for truth against external data. Detectives and scientists, for instance, constantly face the inductive problem of deciding whether certain hypotheses are true or false. A possible general approach is to follow the "hypothetico-deductive" method. In this technique, implications are deduced from the hypothesis and are then checked empirically for truth or falsity. If the implications of the hypothesis turn out to be true, then the hypothesis is supported, otherwise it can be rejected on the grounds that if validly drawn inferences from the hypothesis lead to empirically false conclusions then the hypothesis must be false. Whether the apparently simple prescription embodied in the hypothetico-deductive method is descriptive of behaviour in the face of inductive problems has been the topic of numerous studies, a selection of which will be considered in this chapter. Our review will start with tasks in which people are *given* both some particular hypothesis to test and sources of potentially relevant data. Next, we will discuss a range of more complicated tasks in which people are required to both *generate* and *test* their own hypotheses. The hypothesis testing behaviour of scientists in real life will be considered in the final, summing up section.

I. THE FOUR CARD SELECTION PROBLEM

Wason (1966, 1968) has devised the following deceptively simple paradigm in which to explore hypothetico-deductive reasoning.

Suppose you are given four cards showing:

$$\boxed{E} \quad \boxed{K} \quad \boxed{4} \quad \boxed{7}$$

Each card has a letter on one side and a number on the other. Your task is to name the cards which *need* to be turned over to test the following statement

5 Inductive reasoning

—"If a card has a vowel on one side, then it has an even number on the other side". You may find it instructive to pause here and decide on your answer before reading on.

By far the most common answers are wrong. Why they are wrong, and what the correct answer is, should become clearer with the aid of a more concrete example. Take the statement "Paper ignites at 481°F". If we had a furnace set at 481°F we could test this proposed rule by inserting samples of paper and noting whether they ignite or not. A difficulty arises, in that no matter how many different samples of paper conform to the rule there could always be as yet untried papers that would not. Thus, no matter how many "positives" are recorded, the rule can never be absolutely verified; but, it would be *falsified* if just one sample failed to ignite at 481°F. This is a general characteristic of such universal hypotheses and the example should alert us to the need to consider *potentially falsifying* data as well as potentially supporting data in testing proposed rules. Suppose now that a study was conducted on what sorts of things ignite at 481°F and that four cards are available representing four individual experiments. On one side of each card is listed the type of material put into the furnace and on the other side, whether it burned or not. Which of the four cards below would have to be turned over to test the hypothesis, "If it is paper, it will ignite at 481°F"?

| Paper | Plastic | Burned | Did not burn |

Clearly we must look at the "Paper" card to see if it burned or not. The "Plastic" card can be ignored as irrelevant. Surprisingly, perhaps, the "Burned" card need not be turned over. Once we know that the material burned, whether the material was paper or not does not affect the status of the hypothesis. No information regarding the hypothesis could be gained by turning over the "Burned" card and so it should be left untouched. The "Did not burn" card should definitely be turned over, since it would be falsifying if "Paper" were on the other side.

Similarly, in the abstract version i.e., "If vowel on one side, even number on the other side", the cards showing "E" and "7" should be examined because they are potentially falsifying. The "4" and the "K" cards may be left unturned since the truth of the hypothesis would not be affected no matter what is on their other sides.

The kind of rule involved in the four card task has been extensively used in studying hypothesis testing. Before reviewing the empirical studies, we should briefly examine the logic of such rules in a little more detail. The rules are of the abstract form "If p, then q" and are known as "conditionals" or "implication" rules. In propositional logic there are two main valid inference patterns involving such rules and two main fallacies. These are shown in Table 5.1. Note that a bar over a letter means "not", so that $\bar{q}$ is to be read as "not q".

Another way of thinking about the implication rule is to consider how its truth or falsity varies as a function of the truth of the component terms. The two terms in the rule can be independently true or false, yielding four combinations. The rule's status given these combinations is represented in Table 5.2 which shows the "truth table" for implication.

Table 5.1. Valid and fallacious inferences based on implication.

Valid inferences		Fallacious inferences	
1. (Modus ponens)	if p, then q p ∴ q	1. (Denying the antecedent)	if p, then q $\bar{p}$ ∴ $\bar{q}$
2. (Modus tollens)	if p, then q $\bar{q}$ ∴ $\bar{p}$	2. (Affirming the consequent)	if p, then q q ∴ p
			($\bar{p}$ = not p)

Table 5.2. Truth table for implication.

$$p \longrightarrow q$$
$$\begin{array}{ccc} T & T & T \\ T & F & F \\ F & T & T \\ F & T & F \end{array}$$

T = True, F = False, ⟶ = "implies", or "if . . . then"

A. Basic results

In testing a rule of the form "if p, then q", there are four possible cases that might arise viz. pq, p$\bar{q}$, $\bar{p}$q and $\bar{p}\bar{q}$. (Remember $\bar{q}$ is to be read as "not q".) In logic, only the second case (p$\bar{q}$) is inconsistent with the rule while the remainder are consistent (see Table 5.2).

When subjects are given a conditional rule to test and the opportunity to observe what is paired with cases of p, q, $\bar{p}$, $\bar{q}$ in the four card task, they almost always select the cards showing p and q, rather than the logically correct p and q̄ cards. The results of four typical studies by Wason *et al.* are given in Table 5.3. One way to describe these results is to say that subjects are "set" for verification and so choose the potentially verifying cards (p, q) and ignore the potentially falsifying card (q̄). (Note: p is potentially falsifying as well as verifying.)

Table 5.3. Results from four experiments on the four card selection task. (Reprinted by permission from Johnson-Laird, P.N. and Wason, P. C. (1970). A theoretical analysis of insight into a reasoning task. *Cognitive Psychology* **1** 134–148.)

Selection	Frequency
pq	59
p	42
pqq̄	9
pq̄	5
others	13
	N = 128

Subjects generally recognize that the q̄ card falsifies the rule if the q̄ card is turned over to reveal p—but rarely spontaneously examine it.

B. Procedural variations

Wason and others have examined a number of procedural variables in an attempt to locate the sources of difficulty in this task. For example, in one study (Wason, 1969), the task materials were made strictly binary—with only two possible letters and numbers—but this had no effect. Thus the source of the difficulty was not confusion induced by the sheer number of possibilities in the "Vowel/even number" cards.

It was suggested that subjects might have been confused by the expression "the other side of the card" and might have misinterpreted this to mean "the side face downward". Wason and Johnson-Laird (1970) therefore presented subjects with cards that had all the information on one side and used masks to hide the appropriate part of the card. Again, no facilitation occurred. Goodwin and Wason (1972) made a duplicate set of fully revealed cards available to subjects while they performed the task with equivalent partially masked cards. The fully revealed cards could serve as aids to memory or imagery in solving the problem. This had a slight but nonsignificant beneficial effect on choice of the q̄ card. But most subjects still chose the q card.

Perhaps the apparent "set" for verification could be broken by instructions which emphasize falsification? However, Wason (1968) found that instructions to pick cards which "could break the rule" did not enhance performance.

Perhaps more familiarity is required with the rule? Wason and Shapiro (1971) trained subjects to construct or evaluate instances of the four types of cards (pq, p$\bar{q}$, $\bar{p}$q, $\bar{p}\bar{q}$) for 24 trials in relation to a given rule. They were given the selection task with four more partially concealed cards in relation to the same rule. The "construction" group did a little better than normal, while the "evaluation" group showed averagely poor performance. However, the difference between the groups was not significant.

A more successful method of rule familiarization was devised by Legrenzi (1971). He first gave subjects instances of 4 types of cards. The cards had a triangle or a circle on their left and right half. The cards were clearly marked as "+" or "—" and the subjects had to express a rule in their own words to describe the cards' assignment to the "+" and "—" categories. They were given partially covered cards and asked which ones should be uncovered to test the rule. The "rule discovery" subjects were compared with "yoked" subjects presented with the discovered rules and the selection task. The "rule discovery" subjects were very significantly better than the controls.

Interestingly, the rules "induced" by the experimental subjects were rarely in the form of *conditional* sentences—but were more usually in terms of "either . . . or" e.g. "circle on right or 2 triangles together" instead of "if circles on left then circle on right". In a second study subjects were required to find a rule of the form "if . . . then" that fitted the figures. Again, rule discovery subjects did very much better on a selection task than control subjects simply given the rule.

Performance on reasoning tasks is often improved by concrete material. The conditional rule testing task does not seem to be an exception. Wason and Shapiro (1971) found considerable improvement when the task was presented in terms of 4 journeys. The four cards were said to represent journeys, with names of towns (destinations) on one side and modes of transport on the other. Subjects were given cards marked, face up, as follows:

| Manchester | Car | Train | Leeds |

and were told that the cards represented journeys made by the experimenter. The proposed rule to be tested was "Every time I go to Manchester, I go by train". (Answer: turn over "Manchester" and "Car" cards.)

Subsequent analyses of this thematic effect, by Gilhooly and Falconer (1974), and by Bracewell and Hidi (1974), indicated that the concreteness of the terms and the presence or absence of a concrete relationship contributed separately to improving performance on the task. (Despite this early accumulation of data in favour of the thematic effect, it should be noted that Manktelow and Evans (1979) failed to replicate many of the relevant results and thus cast some doubt on the strength of the effect.)

Further facilitation of performance was reported when the task was made still more lifelike and concrete by Johnson-Laird, Legrenzi and Legrenzi (1972). Subjects were asked to imagine that they worked in the Post Office, sorting letters. Their task was to discover whether the following rule had been violated.

"If a letter is sealed, then it has a 5d. stamp on it". Envelopes were provided either sealed or not and bearing either a 4d. stamp or a 5d. stamp on their showing side. A parallel abstract condition had the following rule.

"If an envelope has a D on one side, then it has a 5 on the other side". Again, suitable envelopes were provided to test the rule. Twenty-four subjects were given both tasks in a balanced order. 22 out of 24 were correct in the concrete condition; only 2 out of 24 were correct in the abstract condition. Surprisingly, perhaps, there was no transfer from the concrete to the abstract form of the task.

In the context of rules using realistic material, Van Duyne (1974) found a high success rate when the rule was known to be false (e.g. "If a student studies philosophy, then he is at Cambridge"). Further, in a later study (Van Duyne, 1976), more logical reasoning was obtained with rules that the subjects believed to be "sometimes true" as against "always true", (an example of the latter case is, "If it is glucose then it is sweet"). Pollard and Evans (1981) extended this to include rules thought to be "usually false" and "always false" and found that perceived falsity had a significant effect on response frequencies in the direction of better (i.e. falsifying) performance.

In sum, it appears that the main facilitating effects on selection task performance are those of *(a)* using realistic material, *(b)* allowing rule familiarization through discovery learning and *(c)* using rules of dubious truth value.

C. "Insight" model

Wason tried to induce "insight" into the task by means of post task discussions or "confrontations". When subjects made a wrong selection they were asked to consider the $\bar{q}$ card. Could it be relevant? Could it falsify? It was pointed out that it might have p on the other side. What then? Subjects were shown the reverse of the $\bar{q}$ card (p) and asked if the rule still held.

On the basis of such "dialogues", Johnson-Laird and Wason (1970) proposed a model for insight into the task. They proposed three levels of insight. First, there is the level of no insight, in which the person is fixated on verification and chooses p or p and q, (depending on whether he thinks the rule is reversible or not). The second level, partial insight, is obtained when it is realized that potentially falsifying cards should be examined as well as potentially verifying cards. This leads to a choice of p, q, q̄. The third level, complete insight, consists in realizing that only cards which could falsify should be selected, i.e. p and q̄.

Some evidence in support of the "insight" model was obtained from studies in which subjects wrote down their reasons for selecting or not selecting each card, (Goodwin and Wason, 1972). These results were claimed to provide independent support for the model in that the choices were justified by reasons consistent with the insight model.

The "insight" model explains errors partly in terms of misinterpretation of the rule as reversible, but mainly in terms of failure to appreciate the importance of potentially falsifying information in rule testing. Two main types of alternative explanations have subsequently been put forward. The first type focus on the ambiguities of the task and essentially follow a similar line to that taken by Henle *et al.* in connection with syllogistic reasoning. The second type propose an "atmosphere-like" explanation known as the "matching bias" hypothesis. This supposes that people have a tendency to simply select cards that match the terms mentioned in the rule. These alternatives will be discussed in the following sections.

D. Interpretation factors

A number of investigators have pointed to ambiguities in the standard four card task. Typical patterns of performance on the task might be explained in terms of people making interpretations different from that intended, but reasoning correctly on their interpretations.

Smalley (1974) distinguished 3 sources of ambiguity:
1. Is the rule "reversible" or not? i.e. does p → q also mean q → p or not?
2. Does the rule refer to both sides of the card or just to the showing side.
3. Is the task one of verification, falsification or both? Putting together these ambiguities leads to (2 × 2 × 3) = 12 possible interpretations of the task. These 12 interpretations logically require certain patterns of card selection. Smalley showed that such interpretations occurred and that his subjects' choices were consistent with their interpretations.

Bracewell (1974) gave some subjects a "clarified" statement of the task, (cf. Ceraso and Provitera's syllogism experiment discussed in Chapter 4). The rule was given as follows:

> "If either the showing face or the underside face of the card has a J on it then 2 is on the remaining face. This hypothesis should not be interpreted to mean that 2 only occurs with J.
> Please indicate the card or cards it is necessary to examine in order to see if the above hypothesis is false."

The success rate with clarified instructions (7/12) was much higher than that obtained with standard instructions (1/12).

The beneficial effects of realistic material would be attributed, on the "interpretation" view, to reductions in ambiguity with such material. A rule, such as "If I go to London, I go by car", is unlikely to be interpreted as reversible (i.e. as implying "If I go by car, I go to London) because the reversed version is implausible. No such plausibility checks would prevent reversal of an abstract rule. In the "Post Office" variant, the nature of task —to seek potentially falsifying information—fits the thematic structure and so makes the task less ambiguous.

The interpretation approach has been strongly criticized by Evans and his colleagues, and they have put forward a collection of interesting, if somewhat loosely linked, ideas that constitute a radical alternative to previous approaches. This work will be discussed in the following section.

E. Evans et al. on "matching bias"

Evans (Evans and Lynch, 1973; Wason and Evans, 1975) has put forward the view that, in the abstract version of the selection task, most people simply select the cards showing the symbols mentioned in the rule, i.e. the responses match the input and no "deeper" processing is involved. One main source of evidence for this view is the finding that with a negative form of the rule ("If B on one side, there will not be 3 on the other") the success rate is very high. Most subjects choose the "B" card and the "3" card. Wason and Johnson-Laird's "insight" model would predict selection of "B" and the "not 3" card by naive subjects working under a verification set.

Interestingly, when subjects are given both the negative form of rule and the affirmative form of rule in succession, they tend to be correct on the negative and wrong on the affirmative. Furthermore, they give "verification" reasons for choices in the affirmative case and "falsification" reasons in the negative case. Evans argues that the reasons given are often *post hoc* rationalizations and that behaviour in this task is actually determined by an unconscious matching bias. This proposal is clearly reminiscent of the "atmosphere" hypothesis in syllogistic reasoning.

It is not suggested that "matching" explains all the data. Evans proposes that there is also a tendency to interpret and respond logically. This "interpretation" tendency, as he calls it (Evans, 1972), is weak in the case of abstract material and relatively strong with thematic material. Assuming that the strengths of both tendencies, "matching" and "interpretation", can vary independently and jointly affect the selection probability of each card, Evans (1977) has devised a mathematical model that fits much of the detailed data from a number of experiments on card selection frequencies surprisingly well. The parameter reflecting the strength of the (logical) "interpretation" tendency is estimated to be high for thematic material and low for abstract material, while the reverse holds for the "matching bias" parameter.

In Evans (1980a), the "matching" and "interpretation" tendencies are tentatively linked to two parallel modes of thought that are labelled Type I and Type II. Type I processes are conceived to be non-verbal and non-introspectible (and it seems to be suggested, non-logical) while Type II processes are verbal and apparently "rational".

If responses are made on the basis of a Type I process, and the subjects are asked "why did you do that?", it is proposed that they will generate rationalizations, using Type II processes to do so. As Evans (1980a) points out, "The 'rationalization' itself is a form of reasoning: the subject asks, in effect, "Given the structure of the problem and the instructions, what reason could I have had for the response I made?" Consistent with this approach, Evans and Wason (1976) found that when subjects were asked to justify various answers presented to them as being "correct solutions" to the selection task, they confidently gave reasons for accepting all the answers, including wrong answers. Thus, it is possible in the normal selection task that responses are made on a basis unknown to the subjects, but that they can construct reasons (rationalizations) for their responses if asked. This Evans and Wason demonstration seriously undermines Goodwin and Wason's (1972) arguments, in favour of the "insight model, which were based on subjects' justifications of their choices. The Goodwin and Wason analysis assumed that "reasons" preceded and produced responses, while Evan's analysis and data suggest the reverse order.

The general notion of two types of process, rational and irrational, competing for control of behaviour is intriguing and is consistent with some suggestions made by previous authors, especially in connection with creative thinking (e.g. Neisser, 1963b; *see also* Chapters 7 and 8 of this book). However, such ideas are rather startling in the literature on reasoning and have met with considerable resistance. Although not very clearly defined at present, Evans's ideas have heuristic merit and may help relate studies of reasoning to other areas (such as creative thinking and daydreaming in which his Type I processes may also be involved).

Another connection suggested by recent research is with neuropsychology. Evans (1980b) has suggested that Type I processes may reflect mainly right hemisphere activity and Type II processes left hemisphere activity. This would be consistent with the otherwise difficult to explain finding that patients with right hemisphere brain lesions performed markedly better on the selection task than normal subjects (Golding, 1981). Similarly, patients in whom the right hemisphere had been temporarily "disabled" by means of electro-convulsive therapy (ECT) performed better on the selection task than control subjects (Golding, 1980). In terms of the dual process approach, the explanation would be that Type I processes were reduced in the right hemisphere lesion and right hemisphere ECT patients. Thus, the behaviour of these experimental subjects was more likely than that of the controls to be determined by Type II (logical) processes embodied in the left hemisphere. Type II processes would not, it is surmised, be affected by right hemisphere disablement, while Type I (non-logical) processes would be diminished by such a state of affairs.

II. GENERATING AND TESTING HYPOTHESES

In studies of conditional rule testing, such as those discussed above, subjects are *given* a rule and possible evidence which may or may not support or disconfirm the rule. Usually, in real life research one is not given a rule but must generate possible rules (hypotheses) which can then be tested.

The processes of generating and testing self-produced hypotheses have been subjected to laboratory investigation in a number of ways. The three main approaches have involved the study of *(1)* concept learning tasks, *(2)* Wason's "reversed 20 questions" task, and *(3)* most realistically, performance in simulated research environments. As we shall see, somewhat similar points seem to emerge from these different lines of research.

A. Concept learning

In a concept learning task, a collection of stimuli have been classified by the experimenter into two or more categories on the basis of some rule. It is the subject's task to induce the rule on the basis of information about the category membership of individual stimuli. Normally, the stimuli are constructed by combining values on a small number of dimensions (e.g. *colour:* red/blue, *shape:* square/triangle, *size:* large/small). Information can be made available to the subject in two main ways. Either the stimuli and their classifications are presented to the subject in an order determined by the experimenter (reception paradigm) or the whole stimulus array is available and the subject chooses the stimuli to be informed about (selection paradigm). As Bruner, Goodnow and Austin (1956) put it, in the reception paradigm the subject is in a similar position to that of a researcher on the effects of human brain damage on, say, language. He must wait for accident cases to turn up and these may not arrive in the "best" sequence. In the selection paradigm the subject is more in the position of a researcher on, say, brain areas underlying pattern vision in monkeys. Such a researcher can choose which areas to remove in each study and can devise an optimum sequence of tests. Similarly, the selection paradigm subject can choose an optimum sequence of stimuli about which to receive classification information.

Bruner *et al.* had their subjects write down their hypotheses after each trial (stimulus followed by feedback on the correct answer) in reception paradigm studies. They found that people had difficulty in handling correctly information that falsified their current hypotheses. This was true whether their initial hypotheses were complex (based on all attributes) or simple (based on one or two attributes). In the selection paradigm, two main types of strategy were identified viz. focussing or scanning. Focussers took a particular instance which was a positive example of the experimenter's rule and sought out stimuli that differed in just one attribute from the "focus". If the new stimulus was still "positive" then the changed attribute was irrelevant and could be ignored; if the new stimulus was "negative", then the changed attribute was at least part of the answer and should be held constant when choosing a further stimulus to test. The focusser could thus narrow down to the correct set of attributes with little strain on memory or inference. The scanning approach was less efficient and produced information relevant to the question of verification bias. Scanners essentially picked on a particular hypothesis (e.g. "2 squares") and sought to test it against instances until it was falsified, whereupon another hypothesis would be selected. It was noticeable that subjects tended to pick stimuli that could verify their hypothesis rather than stimuli that could falsify it. For example, if the subject's hypothesis was "red squares", he tended to enquire about red square stimuli—rather than checking green squares or red circles. (All red squares may be +, but the rule could be "red" alone or "square" alone or "red *or* square" rather than "red *and* square"). Further evidence of "verification bias" also came from the next task to be discussed below.

B. Wason's reversed 20 questions task

Wason devised a special task in which subjects tend to generate over restrictive hypotheses of the sort that would lead astray a scanner with verifying tendencies. Subjects were given three numbers, "2, 4, 6", and told that these conformed to a rule which they had to discover. The means of discovery was to be by generating other three-number series that might match the rule or not. The experimenter gave feedback on each triple produced by subject. Subjects were asked to announce their rule when they were highly confident that it was correct answer. The correct rule was "numbers in increasing order of magnitude". As you might expect, subjects stuck to more restrictive hypotheses e.g. "intervals of 2 between increasing numbers", "arithmetic series". However, the main interest lay in *how* subjects tested their hypotheses. The overwhelming tendency (Wason, 1960) was for subjects simply to generate series *consistent* with their particular hypothesis and to keep on doing so until they felt sufficiently confident to announce their hypothesis as correct. Few subjects either tried out series that ran counter to their own hypotheses or spontaneously varied their hypotheses. About 20% of subjects discovered the rule without any incorrect announcements, and these people had tended to vary their hypotheses spontaneously. Very little evidence was found for a falsification strategy.

A number of task variations have been attempted—with little effect. The material has been varied from "numbers" to a task in which the subject is given an instance of some very general class (e.g. "microphone" as an instance of the class "inanimate objects") and is instructed to find the class by trying out other possible instances.

This modification was ineffective in changing the prevalent "verifying" strategy. Instructions to discover all the rules which *could* be correct had no effect. Finally, imposing a charge of 12.5 pence for each incorrect rule announcement made subjects more cautious about claiming to know the answer but did not affect the bias toward verification.

C. Simulated research environments

Although philosophers of science tend to stress the importance of falsification (Popper, 1959) and of considering more than one hypothesis at a time (Platt, 1964), the results of Wason and of Bruner, Goodnow and Austin, discussed above, suggest that naive subjects tend neither to consider alternative hypotheses nor to seek out potentially falsifying data. Some recent studies by Mynatt, Doherty and Tweney (1977; 1978) have sought to investigate such tendencies in complex environments that are intended to simulate real life research.

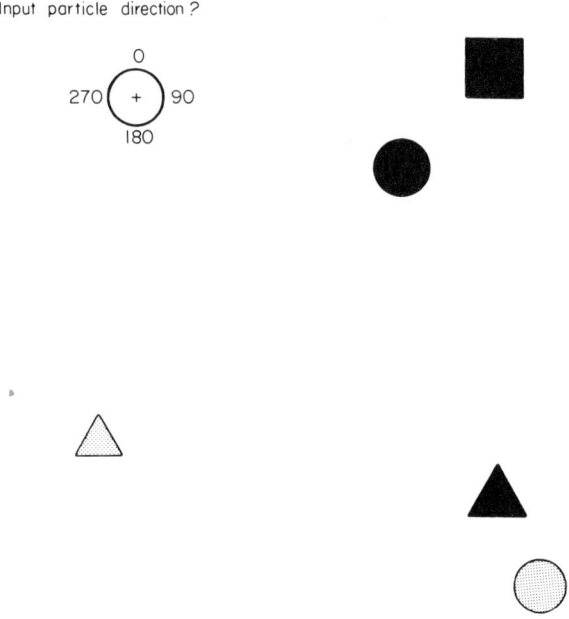

Fig. 5.1 Type of display used in study of confirmation bias. Textured features had 0.5 brightness levels. "Particles" were fired from the grid in the upper left of the screen. The subject controlled the direction of the particle's motion. *(Reprinted by permission from Mynatt, C. R., Doherty, M. E. and Tweney, R. D. (1977). Confirmation bias in a simulated research environment: an experimental study of scientific inference.* Quarterly Journal of Experimental Psychology *29, 85-95.*

In the 1977 study, subjects saw computer generated displays on a screen (see Fig . 1) showing various shapes (circles, squares, triangles) of varying degrees of brightness (dim or bright). A "particle" could be fired across the screen (from a fixed position) in any direction, and it would be stopped when it approached some objects but not others. The subjects' overall task was to produce a hypothesis that would account for the behaviour of the particle. The correct answer was that the particle stopped on approaching dim shapes.

At first, subjects were allowed to formulate an initial hypothesis on the basis of the particle's behaviour with one particular configuration of objects (a configuration that favoured adoption of a wrong hypothesis in terms of object shape). They then chose between pairs of environments in one of which they could make observations which would probably confirm the typical wrong hypothesis and in the other of which they would test alternative hypotheses. Evidence for a confirmation bias, involving failure to choose environments allowing tests of alternative hypotheses, was found. However, if subjects did obtain explicit falsifying information, they generally used this information to reject incorrect hypotheses. Behaviour in this task was not affected by instructions stressing confirmation or disconfirmation.

In the 1978 study, subjects were allowed 10 hours to explore a very complex environment of 27 objects, varying in shape, size and brightness, in which particles were deflected on approaching objects. The angles of deflection were governed by a formula involving parameters whose values were determined by the shape, size and brightness of the objects. No one solved the problem and Mynatt *et al.* inferred a "confirmation bias" from the subjects' reaction to observations that falsified their hypotheses but the interpretation of these results (Table 5.4 below) is debatable.

Mynatt *et al.* had two groups of subjects. One group was instructed in Platt's "strong inference" approach to scientific methodology (this emphasizes developing and testing alternative hypotheses; especially with a view to falsification). A control group received no special instructions about scientific research strategy. No major differences emerged between the two groups' patterns of results, and so in Table 5.4 below I have merged the data from two groups.

Table 5.4. Summary of reactions to hypothesis disconfirmation. *(Reprinted by permission from Mynatt, C. R., Docherty, M. E. and Tweney, R. D. (1978). Consequences of confirmation and disconfirmation in a simulated research environment.* Quarterly Journal of Experimental Psychology *30, 395–406.)*

	Results of hypothesis tests	N cases	%
Responses following disconfirmation (N = 88)	Permanently abandoned hypothesis	26	(30)
	Temporarily abandoned hypothesis	11	(13)
	Revised hypothesis and retested	33	(37)
	Retested hypotheses without revision	18	(20)
		88	(100)

When falsifying data were obtained the subjects either abandoned or revised their hypotheses 67% of the time. On 33% of occasions the falsifying data do seem to have been discounted either immediately or after a delay during which forgetting could have intervened. So, if we allow hypothesis *revision* (as well as abandonment) to be a reasonable reaction to data that disconfirm a particular hypothesis, then subjects reacted in some appropriate way to 67% of falsifications. It seems unfair, on these data, to class the majority of subjects as showing "a strong tendency to discount or disregard falsification" (Mynatt *et al.*, 1978). However, it was clear from the subjects' thinking aloud records that deliberate attempts to falsify their own hypotheses almost never occurred. There was an overwhelming tendency to seek confirming data but the subjects in the 1978 study do seem to have reacted appropriately, on the whole, to the occurrence of disconfirming evidence. Perhaps because the environment was much more complex in the 1978 study there was less tendency to reject disconfirmed hypotheses totally and more of a tendency to modify than was evident in the 1977 results.

III. SUMMARY AND CONCLUDING COMMENTS

What conclusions, if any, can be drawn from the necessarily selective review of research on inductive reasoning presented above? A few themes seem to emerge consistently. These are, *(1)* a tendency to ignore potentially falsifying information, *(2)* a preference for "direct tests" of hypotheses using potentially confirming data but also, *(3)* a generally saving ability to take some appropriate action (abandonment or revision) when clear falsifying data are obtained. Let us now consider these points in more detail.

Available potentially falsifying information was generally not used in either the abstract version of Wason's four card task or in the more realistic settings of Mynatt *et al.*'s simulated research environments. Preference for direct tests of hypotheses emerged in Wason's (1960) reversed 20 questions task, the Mynatt *et al.*'s studies and in Bruner *et al.*'s studies of concept learning. Appropriate reactions to falsification were often (if not always) observed in both Bruner *et al.*'s and Mynatt *et al.*'s studies. The preference for direct tests of hypotheses is the best established of the three conclusions and a plausible explanation was suggested by Bruner *et al.* in terms of minimizing cognitive strain. The hypotheses being tested by the subjects in the relevant studies could be phrased as "equivalences" e.g. "if and only if the figure is red, is it a positive example of the rule" or "if and only if the series is arithmetic is it an instance of the experimenter's category" or "if and only if the particle approaches a triangle will it stop". The general form is "if and only if P then Q". To make a direct test one only has to seek or generate instances of P and check if they are also Qs. To make an indirect test on the other hand, one would have to decide which out of the possibly vast range of instances of not P to examine to check whether it was also not Q. Thus, it appears to be simpler to rely on direct tests. Such tests also have the benefit that they will usually succeed eventually and will only be seriously misleading if the hypothesis being directly tested is included completely in the correct hypothesis e.g. in concept learning, if the hypothesis "red" was tried when the correct answer was "red or square", or in the reversed 20 questions task if "arithmetic series" is tried when the correct answer is simply "increasing magnitude". Direct testing, which involves not deliberately seeking falsifying data, would thus usually be a reasonable cognitive strategy that would often succeed with low cognitive strain in real life. Ignoring available but potentially falsifying data may also arise from customary habits of hypothesis testing. In the case of the four card task, Wetherick (1970; 1971; *see also* Shapiro, 1971) has pointed out that it is "unrepresentative" of real life hypothesis testing. Wetherick argued that outside the thinking and problem solving laboratory a hypothesis of the "If p then q" variety would be formulated in order to facilitate *prediction* of "q" from "p" (e.g. predicting success at a particular job from test score). Thus, the normal procedure would be to seek "ps" and then check to see if they did *later* display "q" or not. The suggestion is that if subjects treat the four card task as representative of real life hypothesis testing they will tend to focus on the "p" card to see if "p" predicts "q" and will ignore the "q" and "q̄" cards as irrelevant to prediction.

It is interesting to note that studies of real life hypothesis testing in the sciences (Chalmers, 1978; Mitroff, 1974) suggest strongly that scientists are not overly disposed to seek falsifying data or to accept that favoured theories require revision or abandonment in the face of apparently falsifying results.

For example, Galileo ignored much data that was apparently inconsistent with Copernican theory and protagonists of Newton's theory did not abandon it in view of the "misbehaviour" of certain planets, such as Uranus. The typical reaction to observations inconsistent with a favoured theory is to seek an explanation that preserves the theory. In the case of Uranus's orbit a new undiscovered planet was postulated and in due course the theory received spectacular support from the discovery of Neptune in the predicted place. Other anomalies in Newtonian theory were never resolved, but the theory was not abandoned. In more recent times, Mitroff (1974) closely surveyed the attitudes and beliefs about scientific practice of a group of 43 geologists engaged in the study of lunar geology under the auspices of the Apollo space research programme. These well established scientists saw their aim as (mainly) confirming rather than falsifying hypotheses. The only hypotheses that they were interested in falsifying were the hypotheses of rival scientists! As Mitroff puts it, these scientists differed markedly from the "story book scientist" who is supposed to be completely disinterested and uncommitted to any particular hypothesis. The real scientists tended to be strongly committed to particular points of view and would only reluctantly abandon their views in the face of contrary evidence —rather than immediately, as a naive falsificationist position would suppose. Perhaps then, the laboratory subjects in Mynatt et al. are not untypical, in seeking confirmation rather than falsification. Indeed, the relatively high rate of appropriate reactions to falsifying data in Mynatt et al. (1977, 1978) may reflect the artificiality of the environment e.g. subjects could not doubt their "instruments" in the way that real scientists might. Mitroff's moon scientists pointed out that "commitment" was valuable from the point of view of motivating individual scientists. Also, since there would always be scientists with opposing commitments, the "scientific community" would not be biased as a whole and the rivalry of competing factions would ensure that opposing views would be thoroughly tested by the opposition. Even a few cases of extreme commitment or outright bias could be useful to have around, because those biased individuals would keep alive ideas that might prove useful again at a later date after having been abandoned by most researchers in a given area. These analyses of actual scientific practice suggest that the "simulated research environments" of Mynatt et al., have, so far, lacked the social psychological dimension that appears to be crucial in real life environments.

Although the inductive reasoning area, with the possible exception of concept learning (e.g. Williams, 1970; Hunt, Marin and Stone, 1966; Winston, 1975), does not seem to have been tackled by computer model makers, the general run of results and ideas outlined in our review are consistent with the usual information processing assumptions of small working memory, vast long-term memory and serial processing. Only in Evan's suggestion of *parallel* Type I ("irrational") and Type II ("rational") processes do we find a marked divergence from the usual assumptions. The original Wason and Evans (1975) statement of dual-process theory proposed alternating rather than parallel processes and that view would be more congenial to the standard information processing framework. The evidence for "parallelism" is rather indirect, in that it seems to depend on Evans's (1977) mathematical model. The committed "serialist" could point to the large number of parameters in Evans's model and conclude that this one piece of evidence is not firm enough to seriously shake the generally well established position that thinking at the level of problem-solving is serial. This issue will arise again in discussing creative processes (Chapter 7) and in our theoretical overview (Chapter 8). The topic of irrational (Type II) thinking will be taken up in the next Chapter on daydreaming. Finally, it may be noted here that Evans, in the course of developing his notions of Type I and II thinking, has criticized the use of subject reports as a source of evidence about information processing (since the reports may be misleading rationalizations, rather than accurate accounts). This point raises important questions concerning the meaning and utility of subjects' reports (whether "thinking aloud" or retrospectively justifying behaviour) and these matters will be discussed in the last Chapter, when we have a broader range of background information on which to draw.

IV. FURTHER READING

Mitroff, I. I. (1974). The subjective side of science. Elsevier, Amsterdam.
An intriguing empirical account of real life "inductive reasoning" among lunar research scientists.
Cohen, L. J. (1981). Can human irrationality be experimentally demonstrated? *Behavioral and Brain Sciences* 4, 317–331.
This paper, and the commentaries which follow it in the journal, debate the somewhat "bleak implications for human rationality" that have been drawn from studies of performance on Wason's four card task, syllogisms and other reasoning tasks.

6
Daydreaming

From early times a distinction has been made between two broad kinds of thinking. According to this distinction, on the one hand, we have thought directed toward some end or goal and on the other hand, undirected thought, such as occurs in daydreaming. The English philosopher Thomas Hobbes (1651/1919) expressed the difference over three centuries ago as follows.

> This train of thoughts, or mental discourse, is of two sorts. The first is *unguided, without design,* and inconstant . . . In which case the thoughts are said to wander, and seem impertinent [unrelated] one to another, as in a dream . . . And yet, in this wild ranging of the mind, a man may ofttimes perceive the way of it, and the dependence of one thought upon another . . . the second is more constant, as being regulated by some desire, and design.

Much later a related, influential distinction was made by Freud (1900) between primary and secondary process thinking. Primary process thinking is characterized as wish fulfilling, unfettered by logic or reality, and operating in accord with the pleasure principle of immediate gratification (though the gratification obtained may be in imagination only). This is the earliest form of thought in Freud's view. Secondary process thinking in contrast, is reality respecting, seeks real rather than imaginary satisfaction and is governed by logic. Secondary process thinking also ultimately serves the pleasure principle but does so with due respect to the reality principle of obtaining what is possible and safe, deferring gratification when necessary. In Freud's theory, night dreams are nearly pure representatives of primary process thinking and day dreams predominantly so, while real problem solving would predominantly involve secondary process thinking.

As one might expect, very similar distinctions have been made by many writers. A selection appears in Table 6.1.

Early in the development of psychology as an independent subject there was strong interest in the naturally occurring stream of consciousness, including its undirected flow (e.g. James, 1890). However, post Watson

Table 1. Classifying thought: a sample of distinctions.

Distinction	By whom proposed
Undirected v. directed	Many
Passive v. active reason	Aristotle
Unregulated v. regulated thought	Hobbes (1651)
Primary v. secondary process	Freud (1900)
Foreconscious v. conscious	Varendonck (1921)
Autistic v. reality	McKellar (1957)
Impulsive v. realistic	Hilgard (1962)
Autistic v. directed	Berlyne (1965)
Multiple v. sequential	Neisser (1963b)
Respondent v. operant	Klinger (1971)
Type I v. Type II	Evans (1980a)

experimental psychology, in so far as it dealt with thinking at all, focussed on directed thought as exemplified in studies of problem-solving and logical reasoning tasks. Perhaps this was because directed thinking seemed technically easier to investigate behaviourally or perhaps because directed thought was felt to be more educationally and socially useful than undirected day-dreaming, which might be judged time-wasting and foolish, if not actually pathological. Interest in daydreams and fantasy generally was kept alive in clinical rather than in experimental psychology until the early 1960's. At that point many psychologists felt ready, technically and theoretically, to try to make sense out of daydreaming, which, after all, is a very common and familiar mental activity. Much of the credit for the revival of scientific interest in this topic must go to Jerome Singer and his colleagues (*see* Singer, 1975a, b; 1978).

In the next sections of this Chapter the empirical work on daydreaming will be reviewed and then its theoretical significance will be considered.

I. PSYCHOMETRIC APPROACHES

A. Descriptive studies

The most basic questions concern the frequency and content of daydreams in the general population. Does everybody daydream? About how often? Are there differences in frequency or in content, depending on age, sex, cultural and personality factors? Some answers can be obtained by questionnaire methods (also called psychometric studies).

First, you may be relieved to learn that daydreaming is extremely widespread. An early survey by Singer and McCraven (1961) sampled 240 normal U.S. adults of whom 96% reported some form of daydream activity everyday. This investigation involved a General Daydream Questionnaire in which respondents indicate the frequency on a 6 point scale with which they have experienced each of a series of about 100 daydreams, e.g. "As a child, I imagined myself as a great detective"; "I suddenly find I can fly — to the amazement of passers by"; "I picture an atomic bombing of the town I live in". The results of this study indicated that daydreams took the form of fairly clear images, mainly of people, objects or events. Items dealing with *planning* for future actions, particularly interpersonal actions, were high in frequency. Daydreaming generally occurred, it was reported, when the person was alone and in a restful state. In addition to such environmental factors it may be noted that studies by Kripke and Sonnenschein (1978), in which subjects were asked to report their thoughts at intervals throughout the day, have suggested the existence of an intrinsic cycle, in which daydreaming peaks about every 90 minutes and is associated with heightened alpha waves in Electro-Encephalograph (EEG) and reduced eye movements. This cycle seems to hold both in laboratory studies and in real life settings.

Most people's high frequency daydreams involved practical, immediate concerns, with daydreams about sex and unusual good luck also common. Singer suggests that the range of items that have a high frequency do not exactly tally with the notion that daydreaming is purely unrealistic wish-fulfilling. Rather, daydreaming often reflects attempts at anticipating possible future events and it is oversimplifying to say that "daydreams are unrealistic". It seems that daydreams vary in reality orientation from the practical and plausible through to true fantasies.

More recently, Singer and Antrobus (1972), have developed a lengthy questionnaire known as the Imaginal Processes Inventory. This involves 400 items that are to be rated on 5 point scales. Example items are "The pictures in my mind are as clear as photographs"; "I often have the same daydream over and over"; "My daydreams have such an emotional effect that I often react with fear". The items fall into 29 groups or subscales dealing with different aspects, such as frequency of daydreaming, degree of acceptance of daydreaming, fear of failure, sex and hostile-aggressive content, guilty daydreams, visual imagery in daydreams and distractability associated with daydreams, among others.

Using large U.S. student samples, factor analysis of these scales produced 3 factors, suggesting 3 different styles of daydreaming. Factor 1 (guilty-dysphoric) high scorers are inclined to "tortured self examination", have strong achievement drives and negative fantasies. Subjects high on factor 2 (anxious-distractable) seem to be very anxious, self doubting, rather disorganized in thought and lack clear and elaborate daydreams. They are not oriented toward achievement and persistence. The high scorers on factor 3 have a positive attitude to daydreaming and fantasy and show a high level of "thoughtfulness". It appears that factor 1 and 2 scores decline with age but factor 3 scores remain steady. Future oriented and sexual daydreams seem to decline with age also.

Finally on the topic of descriptive psychometric studies, Singer found that different subcultural groups in U.S. seemed to differ in frequency of daydreaming. They were in order, from high to low frequency, Blacks, Italian, Irish and Anglo-German groups. (The subjects had been equated for class and education.) Singer suggests that such group differences in daydreaming may be associated with the degree to which the groups are accepted in the society as a whole. This hypothesis is open to test in other societies; however, as yet, the required studies do not appear to have been carried out in other countries.

B. Validity of daydreaming questionnaires

Daydreaming questionnaires, of the type discussed above, exhibit high degrees of test-retest *reliability*. The question of the extent to which they measure something outside of themselves, i.e. the question of their *validity* has also been investigated with promising results.

One way of validating daydream questionnaires is to see whether subjects whose questionnaire scores put them in high or low daydream frequency categories, differ from one other in various experimental tasks. For such research purposes, daydreaming has often been operationally defined as the report of "thoughts that involve a shift of attention away from an immediately demanding task" (Singer, 1975a). An example experiment is that by Antrobus, Cohen and Singer (1967) in which subjects who reported themselves to be high or low daydreamers were given a monotonous signal detection task. The high daydreamers indeed reported more thoughts unrelated to the task when "probed" at intervals throughout. Also, although high and low daydreamers did not differ in efficiency of initial performance, the high daydreamers missed more signals and reported more task-irrelevant thoughts as time went on. It is notable that even although this task involved monetary pay offs for correct detections, much of the time subjects daydreamed rather than attend to the external stimuli.

An interesting correlation that has turned up is that obese students have significantly lower scores than normal weight students on daydream vividness as measured by the Imaginal Processes Inventory. Singer (1975a) suggests that this result is consistent with the theory about obesity put forward by Schachter and Rodin (1974) which says that obese individuals are dominated by external stimulus cues and so, given any amount of food, will continue to eat as long as some food remains. If there is indeed a general tendency on the part of the obese to attend to external stimuli rather than to internal stimuli, then lower vividness ratings of daydreams would be expected from such subjects.

During daydreaming, a fixed leftward gaze is often adopted. This leftward orientation of the eyes indicates a predominance of activity in the right cortical hemisphere during daydreaming. Further evidence for the validity of the Imaginal Processes Inventory, then, comes from Meskin and Singer's (1974) observation that high scorers on the Inventory showed more leftward eye-shifts in response to imagery-evoking questions than did low scorers.

Overall, it appears that there is a reasonable amount of evidence for the validity of daydreaming questionnaires as indices of a style of thinking. Further supporting evidence also emerges in later sections of this Chapter.

II. EXPERIMENTAL APPROACHES TO DAYDREAMING

A. Task demands

As well as individual differences in frequency and style of daydreaming, situational factors also play a role. Roughly speaking, the more important it is to attend to the outer environment, the less likely one is to engage in daydreaming. A number of experimental studies support this generalization.

Singer and his colleagues have generally used signal detection tasks. These have the advantage that the task load can be easily varied in a number of ways. For example, rate of occurrence of signals (fast *v.* slow) and complexity of judgment (judge tone to be high or low *v.* judge tone to be same or different to preceding one) were varied in a study by Antrobus, Singer and Greenberg, 1966. As dependent measures, in addition to signal detection performance, they had subjects rate their frequency of task-irrelevant thoughts and obtained ratings of degree of verbal thinking, visual imagery and auditory imagery at intervals throughout the task. The major effects were as one might expect. Task-irrelevant thought declined with increase in speed of signals and with increase in complexity of judgment. Overall, the correct response rate was quite high (92.4%) and there was no particular correlation, in this experiment, between daydreaming frequency and signal detection performance. Subjects seemed to maintain a fairly stable rate of correct responses and varied daydreaming up or down depending on the amount of "spare mental capacity" left by the demands of the main task.

A second experiment in the same paper concerned the rate of daydreaming (i.e. task-irrelevant thought) depending on the rewards and costs of "hits" and "misses" in signal detection.

There were four groups of subjects and each group started off with 3 dollars but the groups differed in the penalties for errors, these being 0¢, 2¢, 4¢, or 8¢ respectively. After each block of 15 trials, the subjects had to make a simple yes/no report of whether they had had task-irrelevant thoughts or not. The probability of task-irrelevant thought being reported declined as the penalty for missing signals increased (*see* Fig. 6.1). So, it can be shown experimentally that the complexity and importance of a current task affects levels of daydreaming during performance.

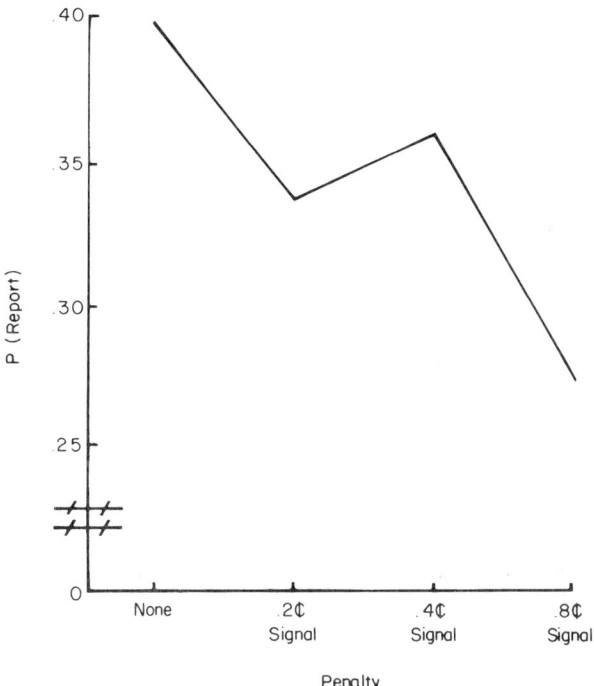

Fig. 6.1. Probability of reporting task-irrelevant thoughts during signal detection task as a function of penalty for missing signals. *(Reprinted with permission from Antrobus, J. S., Singer, J. L., and Greenberg S. (1966). Studies in the stream of consciousness: experimental enhancement and suppression of spontaneous cognitive processes.* Perceptual and Motor Skills *23, 399–417.)*

B. "Bad news"

It was mentioned earlier that, according to survey data, much daydreaming is concerned with anticipating or planning for future events. Antrobus, Singer and Greenberg (1966) explored this experimentally, by giving a group of subjects some information, which, if true, would have seriously affected their futures. This experimental group were then compared with controls in the amount of task-irrelevant thinking they reported during a signal detection task.

The "information" was given in the form of a special radio news bulletin that the experimental subjects overheard while in a waiting room before the

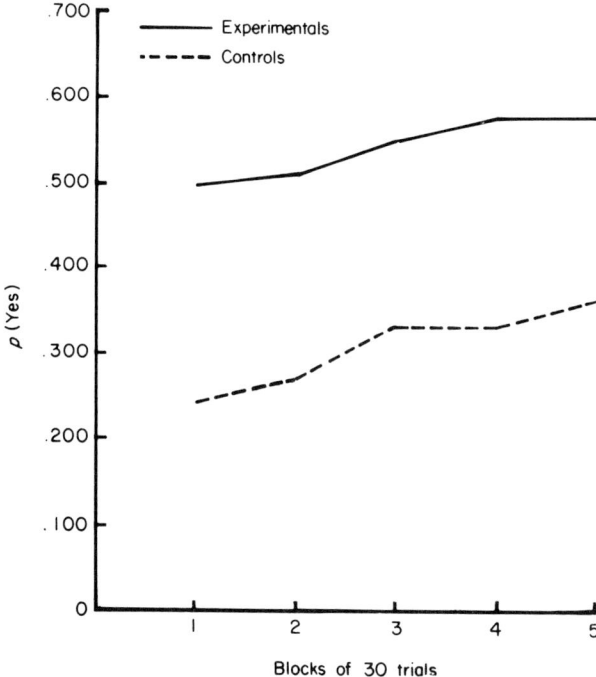

Fig. 6.2. Probability of reporting task-irrelevant thinking as a function of time within the detection session for experimental ("bad news") subjects and control subjects. *(Reprinted with permission from Antrobus, J. S., Singer, J. L. and Greenberg, S. (1966). Studies in the stream of consciousness: experimental enhancement and suppression of spontaneous cognitive processes.* Perceptual and Motor Skills *23, 399–417.)*

signal detection task got under way. Imagine you were an American male student in June 1965 and you heard the following.

> ... High military aides in Saigon have conceded that heavy damage has been inflicted upon our air base at Da Nang after the surprise massive air and ground attack earlier today. This action, in addition to last night's sinking of two Navy aircraft carriers by Chinese jets, has served to weaken seriously our offensive air postures in Southeast Asia . . . Meanwhile, the Associated Press reports that Defense Secretary McNamara has placed all active military units on emergency alert status . . . Allegedly, the communique also instructed the local (draft) boards to call in for physical examination as soon as possible, all unemployed youths over 18 and all eligible college graduates. (From Antrobus *et al.*, 1966).

As might be expected, the experimental group reported much higher levels of task-irrelevant thought throughout the 150 signal detection trials (*see* Fig. 6.2). Experimental subjects were also more likely to miss signals.

After the experiments the subjects wrote down examples of their task irrelevant thoughts. These generally concerned implications of the news for their future e.g. possibilities of themselves or their friends being drafted, possibilities of escaping to Canada etc. Another class of thoughts concerned images of the Vietnam war or war in general. Thus, by introducing a rather drastic change in subjects' expectancies about the future, the "stream of thought" was diverted toward making adjustments and anticipations in order to deal with the change. Of course, the subjects were "debriefed" after the experiment — no doubt to their relief!

C. Stress effects

Horowitz and colleagues have reported a number of experiments concerning the effects of stress on cognitive responses (as contrasted with physiological responses). The clinical literature suggested that after traumatic stress, "intrusive" thoughts that involve "stimulus repetition" are common reactions. These reactions are sometimes labelled "repetition compulsion" and involve repeated thoughts about the traumatic experience despite attempts to avoid such thoughts. Horowitz hypothesized that this "repetition compulsion" was an extreme version of a general tendency that occurs in normal populations even after relatively mild stresses.

In the study carried out by Becker, Horowitz and Campbell (1973) subjects did signal detection tasks after seeing a 6 minute stressful film and after a 6 minute neutral film. The signal detection tasks were split into 3 periods between which the subjects wrote down what they could recall of their mental contents during the preceding task period. It was expected that the stressful film would produce more signs of "repetition compulsion" than the neutral film. The stressful film was entitled "Subincision". It shows repeated scenes of circumcision rites among Australian bushmen and it features old men inflicting pain on young adolescents, nudity, injury, blood and anguished expressions. Prior studies have shown that this film is indeed stressful in terms of physiological measures. The neutral film was entitled "The Runner" and consists of a man running through the town he grew up in, having flashbacks along the way. It is said to be quietly interesting without being very exciting.

After the experiment, the subjects' mental reports were analysed by 3 independent judges for intrusions, film references and task irrelevant thoughts. Inter-judge reliability correlations were high ($r = .94$). An intrusive thought was defined as "any thought the subject experiences as *(a)* non-volitional; *(b)* hard to dispel; *(c)* something to be avoided, or *(d)* a repetition of the identical thought." (The other thought categories are self-evident.) The main results were that the stressful film significantly increased the number of intrusive thoughts and film references but did not significantly affect the total number of task-irrelevant thoughts compared to the neutral film. Both films increased number of irrelevant thoughts above a baseline level established before the films were shown.

It is interesting that in this experiment the stressful material did not have any direct implications for the subjects' futures, unlike Singer *et al.*'s (1966) "bad news" study, and yet similar effects were obtained. Perhaps because the "Subincision" film presented material very discrepant from the subjects' prior conceptions about human behaviour, cognitive work had to be done to adjust existing schemas to accommodate such events.

Whatever the explanation, it would seem that Singer and Horowitz and their colleagues, have produced experimental analogues of certain real life experiences viz., compulsive mulling over of "bad news" in the Singer *et al.* experiment and mental replaying of disturbing scenes from films or T.V. (even if they do not have any personal relevance) in the Horowitz *et al.* study.

D. Analysing daydream protocols

The daydreaming reports obtained in the earlier studies of daydreaming, discussed above, were typically retrospective and/or incomplete. Fuller report methods should produce finer grain information on the structure of daydreaming sequences. Eric Klinger (1971, 1978) at the University of Minnesota has experimented with a variety of thought sampling methods.

One of these methods, *"thinking out loud"* requires the subject to talk continuously for a period of 5 to 30 minutes. The subject is seated in a chair and simply asked to keep talking and talking aloud. The utterances are tape recorded for further analysis. An example 2 minute protocol is given below (from Klinger, 1971; reprinted by permission of author and publisher).

> Oh, I also think about how I wanted to die. I don't want to die you know, like ahm, by living in a hospital for six months, kept on by drugs. I don't want to die, um, on the golf course on the 9th hole, being struck by lightning or doing my daily jogging — Ahh, being hit by a car or something like that just being free . . . and be still young at heart. I don't know, I don't want to have to sit in a room like that, seeing my family watch me die, I don't know, that's, it's ridiculous. Isn't there some way we can say hell and let me die? How can people do that to other people? It's just like an old folks home. Can't stand to go there and watch. It scares me half to death seeing people like that. Usually . . . Almost like . . . T. and another couple, they're ahm just look at them and you could almost get hypnotized. I think one of the major things is . . . No, that's, where did I hear that? Oh. D. told me. Told him to quit smoking all you have to do is to go and get hypnotized for a cost of $50 or something but completely, completely quit smoking. No desire to smoke. All you do is get hypnotized. Hmm, my stomach's growling. Ha I think mmm . . . You know that one little dot right there seems so funny. Reminds me of a graba I saw in a, from a horror movie. Yeah, creepy films series again for this fall going to be. Consists of um, Frankenstein, King Kong, oh, all those really goodies, man.

Klinger has found that coders can reliably analyse such sequences into "main routines" or "themes" (e.g. "Dying" in above protocol), and further into "subroutines" or "subthemes" (e.g. "Dying on golf course" in above). Main routines define an area of concern, while subroutines either go to finer and finer levels, drift from one subtopic to another within a given level, return to the main theme or apparently stimulate new themes. Most routines are fragmented and are interrupted, before a natural conclusion is reached, by some new routine.

Klinger (1974) compared thinking aloud protocols from problem-solving sessions with thinking aloud protocols obtained under daydreaming instructions. In the problem-solving protocols there were many more utterances containing progress evaluations (e.g. "yep"; "Dammit"; "Now wait . . .") and attention directing statements (e.g. "Let's see"; "where was I"). At the least, these results indicate that the general method of obtaining and analysing thinking aloud records has some validity.

However, it must be acknowledged that the "thinking aloud" method has some possible drawbacks. The requirement to verbalize may slow down the apparent rate of the flow of thought and may make thinking seem more verbal than it is. A study discussed by Pope and Singer (1978) indicates that verbalization does affect the apparent nature of the stream of consciousness. Subjects were asked to report on shifts in thought by releasing a key each time a change in topic or direction of thinking occurred. These data suggested that thought shifts occurred every 5 or 6 seconds in average. In contrast, data from subjects who has been thinking aloud produced on average rate of one shift per 30 seconds. Thus, thinking aloud methods may produce a biased picture. In view of this point, *thought sampling* methods may be a useful option, in that they can yield fairly detailed data without affecting the flow as much as continuous verbalization. In thought sampling methods the subjects are cued at irregular intervals and describe their most recent thoughts, often by means of rating scales that can be completed quickly. This technique has been used to good effect in some recent studies by Klinger.

E. Thought sampling studies

1 Normal thought flow
Klinger (1978) reported a large scale, quantitative study of normal conscious thought that used thought sampling techniques both in and out of the laboratory. In both settings, subjects were periodically interrupted and asked to report their thoughts in terms of the fifteen scales that comprise the "Thought Sampling Questionnaire". The scales were as follows:
(1) estimated duration of the latest thought segment; *(2)* estimated duration of the previous segment; *(3)* vagueness *v.* specificity of the imagery; *(4)* amount of directed thought; *(5)* amount of undirected thought; *(6)* amount of detail in imagery; *(7)* number of things going on simultaneously; *(8)* visualness of imagery; *(9)* auditoriness of imagery; *(10)* attentiveness to external stimuli; *(11)* recall of recent stimuli; *(12)* degree to which imagery felt controllable; *(13)* degree of trust in accuracy of memory; *(14)* familiarity *v.* unfamiliarity or bizarreness of the latest experience; and *(15)* time of life associated with the experience. In the out-of-the-laboratory setting, scale 14 was divided into Usualness and Distortedness scales.

In the study conducted in the laboratory the subjects listened to dichotic tapes and were required to indicate by means of a toggle switch the channel that they were attending to. The tapes were interrupted at irregular intervals by a tone that signalled the subjects to report on their thoughts using the questionnaire. A total of 936 thought samples were obtained in the laboratory setting from a sample of 20 subjects.

Outside the laboratory, the subjects carried with them an alarm device (a "beeper") that emitted a soft tone at random intervals having a mean of

40 minutes. On hearing the tone, the subjects filled in a similar thought sampling questionnaire to that used in the laboratory studies. The beeper could be switched off, if the subject felt that its activation might prove embarrassing! This study yielded a total of 285 real life thought samples from 12 subjects.

Klinger proposed certain *a priori* dimensions in terms of which thoughts could be characterized and used these in interpreting his thought sampling data. The first dimension is the familiar one of "Directed *v.* undirected". The second is that of "Stimulus independent *v.* stimulus bound". As Klinger points out, these two dimensions are conceptually independent. A person may think in a very directed way about a problem which does not relate to his current stimulus field (e.g. a student trying to solve a maths problem in his head while riding in a bus). At the other extreme, a person might free associate to the stimuli in his immediate environment. Some of the earlier studies of daydreaming assumed that "stimulus independent" equalled "undirected" but this is not necessarily true. A further dimension is that of "Fanciful-realistic". Again, fanciful thinking about improbable events may or may not be directed. In some problem-solving techniques (e.g. brain storming, discussed in Chapter 7), the person deliberately tries to think of fanciful combinations and events. A fourth dimension is that of "integrated *v.* fused or degenerate". In normal waking thought, images and ideas remain intact, separate wholes, while in dream-like thought, images tend to flow together and merge. This latter sort of thinking can also occur in the waking state, especially under the influence of some drugs and during sleep deprivation. Nor are such thoughts at all uncommon, at least fleetingly, during normal waking states.

The main results from Klinger's thought sampling study may be summarized as follows:

(1) The median judged duration of thought segments was 5 seconds and the mean was around 10 seconds. These results agree quite well with those of other studies that have used toggle-switching to indicate change of thought topic.

(2) Thoughts rated as "Directed" were also rated as more specific, more related to external cues and more controllable than undirected thoughts. "Directedness" was not related to duration of the thought segment, amount of detail, presence of visual or auditory imagery, familiarity or time of life associated with the thoughts.

(3) Stimulus-bound thoughts tended to be "directed" but the connection was not a strong one. Degree of fancifulness of thought segments was not strongly related to their directedness (presumably because undirected thought can easily be either fanciful or realistic).

(4) There was a detectable baseline of "strange" or "degenerate"

thoughts, indeed 22 per cent of out-of-laboratory thoughts were so rated. "Strangeness" was negatively related to thought specificity, to relatedness to external cues and to controllability. "Strange" thoughts did occur during both directed and undirected segments.
(5) In general, compared with in-laboratory thoughts, out-of-laboratory thoughts were more specific, more directed, more related to external cues, more oriented to the present and led to better recall of external cues.
(6) Visual imagery was reported considerably more frequently than auditory imagery in both in- and out-of-laboratory settings.

These results, especially those obtained outside the laboratory give a broad picture of the normal thought stream and indicate that thought sampling is a useful technique.

2 The induction principle

It seems apparent from the above studies that the topic of thought changes quite rapidly in the normal course of events. What determines which topic will be taken up next?

Psychologists have generally assumed that moment-to-moment thoughts are determined by a combination of motivational factors and cues interacting with memory contents.

The motivational concept of a "current concern" has been found useful in considering the determinants of thought content. A "current concern" is defined as the state of an organism between the time it becomes committed to pursuing a goal and the time it either obtains the goal or abandons it. Another label for essentially the same concept as "current concern" is "unfinished business". Any individual is typically beset by many current concerns—most of which will not be in consciousness at a given time. However, it is proposed that the contents of consciousness at a particular time will tend to reflect one or other current concerns or pieces of unfinished business.

As well as current concerns, cues related to these concerns are also likely to play a role in steering thought. Klinger (1978) proposed an "induction principle" as follows:

> At any given moment, the next thematic content of thought is determined by the combination of a current concern and a cue related to that concern.

The cue may be of external origin or be a symbolic event in the individual's own stream of thought. Also it is surmised that people may be more perceptually sensitive to cues bearing on current concerns. Such "attentional tuning" would be of obvious utility.

Taking the induction principle as a starting point Klinger (1978) carried out the following experiment. First, the subjects were interviewed and from these interviews four current concerns were extracted for each subject. One or two days later the subjects were presented with dichotic tape messages. These consisted of literary extracts in which, at intervals, material relating to a current concern was introduced on one channel while material relating to a non-current concern was introduced into the other channel. The inserted passges lasted 25 seconds. Throughout the experiment, the subjects indicated by means of a switch the channel to which they were attending. Ten seconds after each inserted passage, a signal was given, whereupon the tape stopped and the subjects reported their latest thoughts in accordance with the Thought Sampling Questionnaire. They also reported their recollections of the most recent taped passages.

As would be predicted on the induction principle, the concern related passages received more attention than the non-concern passages. The subjects switched to them sooner and spent longer listening to them. Furthermore, the concern related passages had more effect on subsequent thought contents and were recalled better. It seems then, that people's current concerns dispose them to attend to and to retain and reflect in their thoughts, cues related to those concerns, as the induction principle predicts.

Some recent research (Hoelschler, Klinger and Barta, 1981) indicates that the induction principle even operates on thought content during sleep. Subjects were presented with concern and non-concern related words at low volumes during Rapid Eye Movement (REM) sleep. There was significantly more incorporation of concern stimuli than of non-concern stimuli in dream reports obtained shortly after stimulus presentation. Since people might be expected to dream more about concern than non-concern topics irrespective of any cues, the authors checked that the probability of a dream related to a particular concern was indeed higher immediately after the concern stimulus than after other stimuli. These results suggest that the induction principle is descriptive of a powerful tendency that affects cognitive processes both in waking and sleeping.

As it has been described so far, the induction principle is non committal with respect to the degree of influence that a person's various current concerns will have on thought flow. Most of the research has dealt with the role of cues and little with the effects of concern attributes. Klinger, Barta and Maxeiner (1980) have remedied this deficiency to some extent. Questionnaires were used to elicit topics thought about with varying degrees of frequency and the resulting topics were then rated by the subjects on a variety of scales (such as positive value of thing thought of; negative value; anticipated future effort; nearness in time and so on). Real life thought sampling (beeper studies) supported the validity of the questionnaires as measures of topic frequency in thought.

The main results may be summarized as follows. The frequency of thoughts about particular goals was predicted best by the person's self reported commitment to the goal, the value of the goal, the subjective probability of achieving the goal and the time left before action was required. Thoughts related to threatened personal relationships and unexpected difficulties were notably high in frequency. Although the particular thought contents reported in this study probably largely reflect the concerns of undergraduate students, the general findings should be widely applicable.

F. Functions of daydreaming

Given the frequency of daydreaming in everyday thought, an obvious question to ask is "what *functions* does this activity serve?"

As Singer (1975b, Chapter 5) points out, on Freud's psychoanalytic theory, daydreams are always connected, although sometimes indirectly, to drives considered to be basic (such as sex and aggression) and serve a temporary drive reducing function. The psychoanalytic theory proposes that daydreaming starts in infancy, when the hungry baby in the absence of immediate gratification, automatically engages in "primary process" thinking and hallucinates an image of breast or bottle. These images are presumed to have temporary drive-reducing effects.

A label used for such drive reduction brought about by imagery, fantasy or vicarious means is *catharsis*. Freud borrowed this term from Aristotle's theory of tragedy. Watching a play in which a character (Oedipus) discovers that he has murdered his father and married his mother is considered, on the psychoanalytic view, to help the audience to discharge repressed sexual and aggressive tendencies relating to their parents. On this approach then, daydreams act as safety valves, permitting the partial reduction of drives whose overt expression would be unacceptable. According to this catharsis view, the regular presentation of sex and violence in the mass media should be encouraged in order to help reduce the rates of actual rape and murder.

Alternatively, it can be argued that the witnessing of "pre-packaged fantasies" on T.V. or films has a stimulating effect on the relevant drives and that such stimulating effects might also hold for self-generated fantasies in daydreaming. Indeed, it seems from the general run of results from a number of studies by Berkowitz (1969) in which subjects were shown aggressive film scenes and then given opportunities to act aggressively, that those who witnessed the aggressive scenes showed an increase in aggressive activity, rather than the decrease that catharsis would suggest.

More directly related to daydreaming is a complex study by Paton, reported in Singer (1975b). A group of college student subjects took the Imaginal Processes Inventory and then later in the session were insulted while performing a task. Immediately after the insulting episode, one group were given pictures of aggressive material (such as battle scenes) to look at. A second group that had also been insulted were shown interesting non-violent pictures. Both groups then daydreamed and reported their thoughts. Next, they were given questionnaires which yielded measures of how angry and aggressive they felt about the person who had insulted them. There were also control groups. One control group had no opportunity for fantasy activity after being insulted, and the other control group was not insulted at all. These control groups made it possible to show that the insults really did anger the subjects. The insulted group without an opportunity to daydream showed a higher level of subsequent anger than did the group that had not been insulted.

The main question in this experiment was whether the opportunity to daydream after becoming angry would lead to a reduction in the amount of anger felt about the insulter. If there is an aggressive drive that is aroused and if daydreams related to the aggressive drive reduced that drive, then one would expect the greatest drop in aggression to occur if the subject has produced angry and hostile thoughts rather than non-violent thoughts. Alternatively, it might be that the effect of daydreaming after being insulted, would be mainly to divert the subject and produce an alternative mood that would reduce anger. In that case, one would expect that the subjects who produced non-violent daydreams would show a greater drop in subsequent aggressive tendencies toward the insulter than would those who produced aggressive fantasies. It would also be consistent with this view if both kinds of daydreams produced greater reductions in anger than did no opportunity for daydreaming.

The results supported the "diversion" hypothesis. Both groups who daydreamed showed less anger toward the insulter than the group who had no daydream opportunity. However there was a large difference in the effect between the conditions. Subjects who produced mainly neutral daydreams showed a greater drop in anger than those whose daydreams were aggressive. From this study it seems then, that the motivational effect of daydreaming is mainly one of diversion and mood shifting. The view that daydreaming brings about automatic reductions of the relevant drives was not supported.

If daydreams do not serve as simple drive reducing safety valves, what functions might they serve? On the basis of the existing literature, Singer

(1975b; 1978) suggests that daydreams may serve functions of *(1)* anticipation and planning, *(2)* reminding us of "unfinished business" which we may be trying to suppress, and *(3)* maintaining arousal in dull environments.

Whatever functions daydreams may serve, Singer suggests that their occurrence follows from widespread and continuous activity in the brain. His model is described in the following section.

III. A CONCEPTUAL MODEL OF DAYDREAMING

Singer (1975a; Pope and Singer, 1978) has proposed a simple model that can handle much of the data regarding daydreaming. This model claims that *(a)* there are two continuously available sources of stimulation, one internal and one external, and *(b)* that there is a limited capacity central processor that attends to only one of these sources at a time. The external source is the outside environment. The internal source that Singer proposes is a continuously active long-term memory in which information is not stored in some inert form but rather through continuous representational activity. Similar notions of an active long-term memory have also been put forward by other authors, e.g. Neisser (1963b) and Reitman (1965). Daydreaming, Singer suggests, involves attending to the normally unnoticed ("underground") flows of activity in long-term memory. Some support for the notion of continuous unconscious activity can be drawn from the occurrence of intrusive thoughts (as in Becker *et al.*, 1973) and from personal reports by scientists and artists of incubation and inspiration experiences (*see* Chapter 7). These phenomena suggest the existence of internal parallel processes that can occasionally "seize" attention. Of course the existence of such processes would be contrary to the serial activity assumption of the standard information processing approach to thinking.

Whatever the merits and problems of the "active long term memory" notion, there is much support for the view that daydreaming and external attending are incompatible and that a selection of one or the other form of activity has to be made on the basis of task demands. Daydreaming frequency drops as task complexity and the costs of errors go up (Antrobus *et al.*, 1966). On the other hand, if external inputs are severely restricted, as in sensory deprivation experiments, then daydreaming increases very markedly. Increased daydreaming could serve useful arousing functions in dull environments.

As a final point, this model suggests that individual differences in self reported daydreaming frequency, may be due either to differences in dominant attention strategies or to differences in amount of unconscious mental activity. Whether these two possibilities could be operationally separated is currently an open question.

IV. SUMMARY AND CONCLUDING COMMENTS

The material reviewed in this Chapter shows that undirected thinking can be successfully studied, although it has not yet been given the same degree of research attention as directed thought. The question of a definition of "daydreaming" was largely by-passed in the foregoing review and deserves some consideration at this point.

As Klinger (1978) has argued, thoughts may be independently, directed or not, realistic or not, related to current external stimuli or not and so on. Of these characteristics the major feature of daydreaming seems to be a lack of persistent direction. Daydreams are not necessarily unrealistic but tend to drift from one topic to another, whereas thinking in problem-solving is checked against feedback concerning progress toward the current goal and attention is "locked" on to the problem materials (Klinger, 1971). Daydreams are often concerned with anticipating future problems. So, for instance, in anticipating a dinner date with a girl, a boy may be seen as setting up an internal symbolic model representing the meeting, which he then runs in order to anticipate possible outcomes of going to alternative restaurants. To be classed as daydreaming, as against problem-solving, we would have to suppose a loose degree of control over the model running process—permitting departures from reality and switches to different, if associated, topics.

From the studies discussed above, daydreaming is a widespread and frequently occurring phenomenon, whose incidence varies with personal characteristics (e.g. social group membership; obesity) and with external demands (e.g. sitting in drab waiting room *v.* descending a sheer rock face). The moment-to-moment contents of daydreams seem to reflect both immediate and recent internal or external stimuli and the person's list of "current concerns". In terms of functions, daydreaming resists attempts to reduce it to a Freudian safety valve. Rather, it seems to serve functions of anticipating, reminding about outstanding concerns and maintaining arousal in uninteresting environments.

The model for daydreaming put forward by Singer (1975a; Pope and Singer, 1978) clashes with the "seriality" assumption intrinsic to the modal information processing approach to thought (e.g. Newell and Simon, 1972). Singer suggests that there is continuous activity within the long-term memory and that this activity is the source of daydreams. From the data discussed so far, the case for parallel processes in conjunction with the conscious mainstream of thought is perhaps most strongly supported by the occurrence of intrusive and unwelcome thoughts (Becker *et al.*, 1973).

A possible "serialist" argument would be that the mainstream of thought could be halted every so often and the list of current concerns scanned. This might lead to a switch in the thought stream in order to deal with one of those concerns (e.g. adjust concept of range of human behaviour to incorporate data from "Subincision" film in the case of Horowitz *et al.'s* subjects). The issue of serial *v.* parallel models for thinking will arise again in the next Chapter, which deals with creative processes, and it will also be discussed in the final Chapter in a broader context.

V. FURTHER READING

Singer, J. L. (1975). Daydreaming and fantasy. Allen and Unwin, London.
A very readable overview of much basic research in daydreaming in both normal and pathological cases. Developmental aspects are stressed, as are possible applications of daydreaming based techniques in education and therapy.
Singer, J. L. (1978). Studies of daydreaming. *In* "The stream of consciousness" (Eds K. S. Pope and J. L. Singer), pp. 187–223. John Wiley, New York.
A brief but comprehensive guide to recent research trends and results in the area of daydreaming.

7
Creative processes

Before discussing creative processes it is necessary to briefly consider what is meant by the term "creative" and its associate "creativity". It is perhaps easiest to start by defining creative products. Creative products, be they poems, scientific theories, paintings or technological advances, are both novel and acknowledged to be valuable or useful in some way. Whether a product is novel or not is relatively easy to determine, although an element of judgement does enter, in that some products are more obviously related to previous developments than others. Objective measurement of novelty is possible in laboratory settings, since the same task can be given to a large number of people (e.g. "think of ways of improving a doorknob"), and the degree of novelty of proposed solutions can be readily assessed by counting their frequencies of occurrence. In real life, however, only the "creator" may be working on a given self-set problem (e.g. an author seeking to represent the stream of consciousness of a Stone Age man, as in W. Golding's (1955) *The Inheritors*), and so frequency of production is not always available as a criterion. When we turn to the quality of a product, subjective judgment looms still larger than in the case of judging novelty. In science and technology the criteria for quality are clearer than in the arts. A new theory or gadget can be seen to "work" if it covers more phenomena with no more assumptions than its predecessors (e.g. Einstein's theory compared to Newton's) or meets the function for which it was devised (e.g. the first telephone). Notoriously, there is usually less agreement about the merits of artistic productions, both at the time of their emergence and over history. Initial reactions may well be negative to artistic products that either depart too far from established styles or, at the other extreme, are too conventional. Later generations are more likely to appreciate the boldness of developments that their ancestors decry as "insane", e.g. Surrealism, Cubism, Expressionism, etc.

It may also be suggested here, that judgments of "novelty" or "unusualness" will presumably relate to the degree to which the product can be fitted into an established style (in the arts) or "paradigm" (in the sciences). Highly creative products signal and exemplify a new style or approach.

Subsequent work within a given style or paradigm would generally be regarded as less creative than the initial style-defining work.

The above comments should serve to indicate what is meant here as a creative product. What of "creative processes" and persons blessed with "creativity"? Although it is a starting point, it is not very informative to say that creative processes are those processes that result in creative products. Later on I will be reviewing some attempts to be more detailed about such processes. At this stage though, it may be noted that psychologists hold to the belief that creative processes are composed of similar ingredients to those entering into less exalted forms of thinking. It is assumed that creative products result from multitudinous, small steps carried out by limited capacity cognitive systems that suffer from all the normal limitations of cramped working memory and imperfect retrieval from long-term memory. Indeed, most of the approaches to "small scale" problem solving (e.g. behaviourist, associationist and information processing) have something to say about creative thinking. It is an article of faith for theories of thinking that creative processes can be explained in terms of their basic processes (whatever the basic processes may be for any particular theory, e.g. associations or production rules) and that supernatural interventions in the form of "daemons" or "divine sparks" are ruled out. Turning now to "creativity", this is an attribute ascribed to those individuals who show a long-term tendency to generate novel products that are also influential (Albert, 1975). With a few extremely rare exceptions (such as Leonardo Da Vinci) most "creatives" display their valued characteristic within a particular speciality—but within that speciality they are marked for their combination of productivity (e.g. Picasso) and high quality of work (as indexed by its influence). Of course, in real life, for someone to be acknowledged as displaying "creativity" involves social processes, as well as purely within-individual cognitive processes. To become known, creative individuals must "promote" their products and convince enough others who control the communication media that these should be presented to a larger audience, (Stein, 1974). Given that wider presentation, further social processes leading to widespread acceptance and influence, or to apathy or rejection can begin.

In the rest of this Chapter, I will discuss some of the main approaches and topics that have arisen in the study of creative processes. First, there is the psychometric approach, which considers in what ways individuals acknowledged to be creative might differ in cognitive, personality or biographical characteristics from others. Second, there is the approach *via* personal accounts by artists and scientists of how the process seemed to them and this leads on to stage models for creative thinking based on personal accounts. Next, we turn to laboratory-based approaches that have examined ways of stimulating idea-production. Then, there will be a discussion of theoretical approaches and finally, a summing up.

I. STUDIES OF CREATIVE INDIVIDUALS

A. Psychometric studies

A number of studies have been made of people acknowledged to be creative, (e.g. Roe's (1952) study of scientists, MacKinnon (1962) on architects, and Barron (1955) on writers and artists). These studies were aimed at uncovering any common background or personality characteristics of these unusual groups of people.

In one of the earliest investigations of its kind, Ann Roe (1952) studied 64 American scientists who had been rated as eminent in their fields by expert panels. The 64 were roughly evenly split amongst physicists, biologists and social scientists. Each individual was subjected to long interviews, projective personality tests (Thematic Apperception Test (TAT) and Rorschach) and a conventional intelligence test. On the basis of this investigation Roe gave the following composite picture of the average eminent scientist.

The average eminent scientist was a first born son in a middle class Protestant family, with a professional man as a father. He was likely to have often been ill in childhood or to have lost a parent early. He had a very high Intelligence Quotient (IQ) and began reading avidly at an early age. He felt "lonely" and different from his school mates, did not have much interest in girls and married late, (27 years old on average). He usually decided on his career as a professional scientist as a result of a student project involving individual research. He worked hard and persistently, very often 7 days a week with few holidays.

This general picture seems to have held best for the physicists. The social scientists were on average somewhat more extroverted, and showed more concern for personal relationships. They displayed more aggression in the projective tests than members of the other scientific groups. A large proportion of social scientists came from homes with a dominant mother and they had a very high divorce rate (41%). Though different in these ways, they were also totally absorbed by their work and worked very long hours, as did the other groups of scientists.

Similar evidence on personality characteristics of creative people was gathered by Cattell and his colleagues. Before actually testing any "live" scientists Cattell (1959) scanned the biographies of many famous scientists and noted that the typical eminent scientists seemed to be introverted and stable. Although introverted, they were generally independent and self sufficient. They also tended to be solemn or restrained and rather dominant in personal relationships.

Cattell and Drevdahl (1955) selected groups of about 45 eminent researchers in physics, biology and psychology and had them complete the 16 Personality Factors (PF) test. Compared with the general population, the eminent researchers were more introverted, intelligent, dominant and inhibited; they were also more sensitive emotionally and more radical. These findings are in line with the suggestion of biographies and with the results of Roe's investigation.

A similar study of artists and writers (Drevdahl and Cattell, 1958) yielded a profile rather similar to that of the scientists. The artistic group were more emotionally sensitive than the scientists and exhibited more inner tension — but were otherwise similar.

Also relevant is Mitroff's (1974) study of scientists engaged in the analysis of lunar samples as part of the Apollo moon project. Mitroff noted a strong tendency toward a style of thinking often labelled "convergent" (Hudson, 1966). Any open ended question put to the scientists would be quickly transformed into a narrower, more tightly defined one. This tendency fits in with Hudson's finding that those boys who performed better on convergent (one answer) test questions than on divergent items (multiple possible answers) tended to specialize in science subjects. It was also noted that the lunar scientists strongly identified with the traditionally conceived "masculine" characteristics. They believed in hard work, dedication, striving, and did not disapprove of a touch of ruthlessness. Intriguingly, and contrary to earlier reports, Mitroff found evidence in his interviews of strongly aggressive tendencies. In discussing other scientists and rival groups, the desire to win glory at the expense of others and a fear of their rivals' over aggressive tactics (e.g. idea stealing) were evident. Aggressiveness was also clear in their attitude to promoting their own ideas. As one scientist remarked "if you want to get anybody to believe your hypothesis, you've got to beat them down with numbers: you've got to hit them again and again over the head with hard data until they're stupefied into believing it" (Mitroff, 1974).

Possibly, aggressiveness in scientists was not evident in previous studies that had relied on projective tests (e.g. TAT) because such tests are uncongenial to the scientists' preferred convergent style. McLelland (1962) noted the extreme dislike of scientists for the TAT and their tendency to analyse portions of the picture rather than empathizing with the characters and telling a story. In Mitroff's study, with material close to their hearts, few inhibitions were evident regarding aggression. Mitroff suggested that the scientists were somewhat one sided in emotional expression and he found that they were far less free in displaying soft emotions as against harsh or aggressive ones. The notion that science is an aggressive activity was also expressed in Freud's self description. He wrote ". . . I am not really a man of science, not an observer, not an experimenter, and not a thinker. I am nothing but by temperament a *conquistador*—an adventurer, . . . with the curiosity, the boldness, and the tenacity that belong to that type of being" (Jones, 1961).

Another interesting point emerges from a study of the *ages* at which creative accomplishments tend to occur. Data gathered by Lehman (1953) reveals that in many fields the most highly regarded contributions are produced between 30–40. The average age is younger in some subjects e.g. in chemistry it is at 25–30 and it is older in others such as psychology, philosophy, novel writing and architecture. Although these age trends were detectable it should be noted that good work was evident in all fields at a very wide range of ages. The 32-year old chemist is not necessarily "finished" as far as creative work is concerned.

B. Personal accounts of creative problem solving

Many scientists and artists have provided accounts of their experiences in solving complex problems (*see for example*, Ghiselin, 1952; Koestler, 1964, or Vernon, 1970). These personal accounts are of interest for evidence they may contain about features common to the creative process in a wide range of difficult tasks. Fairly consistent patterns do seem to emerge and these patterns have served as the bases for various analyses into stages of both creative thinking and more routine problem-solving.

It is worth noting that some well known thinkers have disclaimed any ability to tell us how they solved problems or thought creatively. For example, Bertrand Russell was once asked to contribute to a book on how to think clearly. He replied that he could not help because, for him, thinking was instinctive, like digestion. He said that he simply filled up with relevant information, went about his business, doing other things and later, with time and good luck, he found that the work had been done. Perhaps Russell was too modest on this occasion. His brief account broadly matches those of others who have tried to be more detailed. It is only possible to consider a small number of these more detailed reports here and I have selected accounts by Poincaré, Helmholtz and Tchaikovsky.

1 Poincaré's account
Henri Poincaré was a prominent French mathematician of the nineteenth

century. He reported (1908) once struggling for a long time to prove a certain theorem without getting any results. One evening he drank black coffee before going to bed and it seemed to him that ideas of possible ways of solving the problem combined and recombined in one way after another before he finally got to sleep. In the morning, he clearly saw how the problem was to be solved, and after two hours had completed the detailed proof. The solution to the initial problem raised further problems and Poincaré noted that these problems were solved as a result of ideas that occurred while he was not actively engaged on them, e.g. while riding in a bus, walking along a street or beach.

2 *Helmholtz's account*
The nineteenth century scientist Herman Helmholtz who contributed to physics, neurology and psychology, volunteered the following report of his problem-solving experience in a speech made at a dinner in honour of his seventieth birthday in 1896 (Woodworth and Schlosberg, 1954).

> So far as my experience goes, 'happy thoughts' never came to a fatigued brain and never at the writing desk. It was always necessary, first of all, that I should have turned my problem over on all sides to such an extent that I had all its angles and complexities 'in my head' and could run through them freely without writing. To bring the matter to that point is usually impossible without long preliminary labour. Then, after the fatigue resulting from this labour had passed away, there must come an hour of complete physical freshness and quiet well being, before the good ideas arrived. Often they were there in the morning when I awoke, just according to Goethe's oft cited verses, and as Gauss also once noted. But they especially liked to make their appearance while I was taking an easy walk over wooded hills in sunny weather.

3 *Tchaikovsky's account*
Peter Ilich Tchaikovsky attempted to describe his experience of composing in a series of letters (extracts of which are reprinted in Vernon (1970). Here are three examples;

> Do not believe those who try to persuade you that composition is only a cold exercise of the intellect. The only music capable of moving and touching us is that which flows from the depths of a composer's soul when he is stirred by inspiration. There is no doubt that even the greatest musical geniuses have sometimes worked without inspiration. This guest does not always respond to the first invitation. We must *always* work, and a self respecting artist must not fold his hands on the pretext that he is not in the mood. If we wait for the mood without endeavouring to meet it half way, we easily become indolent and apathetic. We must be patient, and believe that inspiration will come to those who can master their disclination.

Generally speaking, the germ of a future composition comes suddenly and unexpectedly. If the soil is ready—that is to say, if the disposition for work is there—it takes root with extraordinary force and rapidity, shoots up through the earth, puts forth branches, leaves and, finally blossoms. I cannot define the creative process in any other way than by this simile. The great difficulty is that the germ must appear at a favourable moment, the rest goes of itself. It would be vain to try to put into words that immeasurable sense of bliss which comes over me directly a new idea awakens in me and begins to assume a definite form. I forget everything and behave like a madman. Everything within me starts pulsing and quivering; hardly have I begun the sketch ere one thought follows another.

Yesterday, when I wrote to you about methods of composing, I did not sufficiently enter into that phase of work which relates to the working out of the sketch. This phase is of primary importance. What has been set down in a moment of ardour must now be critically examined, improved, extended, or condensed, as the form requires. Sometimes one must do oneself violence, must sternly and pitilessly take part against oneself, before one can mercilessly erase things thought out with love and enthusiasm.

II. STAGE ANALYSES

A. Wallas's stage analysis

On the basis of reports such as those of Poincaré, Helmholtz and others, and on the basis of his own experiences as a university teacher, administrator and writer, Graham Wallas (1926) proposed a 4 stage analysis of creative problem-solving in a book entitled *The Art of Thought*. In this book Wallas was concerned with the natural course of thought and with how thinking might be made more effective. So, in addition to proposing certain typical stages he also offered advice on how these stages could be made more fruitful. The stages extracted by Wallas were as follows.

1 Preparation
In this stage the problem-solver familiarizes himself with his problem and engages in conscious, effortful, systematic and usually fruitless work on the problem. Although this stage may well not lead to solution in itself, it is widely believed to be very important in influencing the likelihood that the next stage will result in a useful idea. Much personal testimony indicates that inspiration will not be forthcoming without this preliminary labour; or as Edison, the prolific inventor, is reported to have said, "No inspiration without perspiration".

2 Incubation

This is a period during which the task is set aside. No conscious work is done on the problem during this stage. Poincaré and others have hypothesized that unconscious work is carried out during this phase. On the other hand, it may be that this is simply a necessary rest period which enables a later period of conscious work to proceed more effectively than it would have without the break. Wallas suggested that this phase could be made more or less effective, depending on the intervening activity. Light work on minor problems or duties could be beneficial. Better still, he thought was complete mental rest, coupled with mild exercise. He felt that the habit of filling every spare minute with reading was especially detrimental.

3 Illumination or inspiration

This is the point when a fruitful idea, or "happy thought" in Helmholtz's phrase, occurs to us. The inspiration is not usually a complete solution to the problem but points in the direction in which the complete solution may be found.

This phase may be preceded by a vague feeling of "intimation", a feeling that the solution is nigh. Wallas suggests that if thinkers can recognize this feeling, then they should relax, cut out possible distractions and let the inspiration come. If the intimation feeling is not recognized then the possible inspiration may be lost on account of distracting stimuli.

4 Verification

This stage is much like preparation, in that conscious work must be done in order to develop and test the inspiration.

These 4 stages are visible in the personal reports of Helmholtz, Poincaré and Tchaikovsky. Their reports, however, do not stress "intimation" and rather suggest that inspiration comes very suddenly and without warning. Wallas suggests that the "intimation" experience is easily forgotten in the excitement of inspiration. It may also be noted that Poincaré proposed a 4 stage view like Wallas's but with the omission of "intimation".

Wallas's stage analysis could be interpreted as proposing a strict 1, 2, 3, 4 order that is gone through once and once only in solving a problem. Such a formulation is open to the criticism of being overly rigid. However, Wallas (1926) did not intend such a rigid interpretation. He wrote "In the daily stream of thought these 4 different stages constantly overlap each other as we explore different problems. An economist reading a Blue Book, a physiologist watching an experiment, or a businessman going through his morning's letters, may at the same time be 'incubating' on a problem which he proposed to himself a few days ago, be accumulating knowledge in 'preparation' for a second problem, and be 'verifying' his conclusions to a third problem. Even in exploring the *same* problem, the mind may be unconsciously incubating on one aspect of it, while it is consciously employed in preparing for or verifying another aspect".

Some attempts have been made to bring Wallas's stages into the laboratory, notably by Patrick (1935, 1937) whose work is reviewed in the next section. The incubation stage has been singled out as the specific focus of some laboratory studies that will be discussed in a later section.

B. Patrick's laboratory studies of stages

In the 1930's Catherine Patrick attempted to gather more systematic data on the stages of creative problem-solving than were available in retrospective reports. Her method involved having subjects produce poems in response to a painting (1935) and sketches in response to a poem (1937). In each case, Patrick recorded all that the subject said and did between presentation and completion of the task. I will discuss here the 1937 study of the sketching task. The 1935 study of poetic composition was similar in method and in results.

Two groups of subjects were tested. One group consisted of 50 experienced painters, all of whom had exhibited their paintings publicly. A comparison or control group consisted of 50 non-artist subjects who had no or only very slight experience of art work. The two groups were similar in ages, sex distribution and intelligence test scores.

The subjects were tested in their own homes. After a brief conversation period to put subjects at their ease and to accustom them to having their words noted down, they were presented with an extract from Milton's poem "L'Allegro" and asked to draw a sketch about the poem or anything it suggested to them. There was no time limit and subjects were encouraged to "think aloud" throughout. When the sketch was finished the artist subjects were questioned about their normal working methods.

To get objective evidence on stages of thinking, Patrick divided each thinking aloud record (protocol) into 4 equal time quarters. The protocol quarters were then analysed for *(a)* the number of *thought changes*, *(b)* the number of *general shapes drawn for the first time* and *(c)* the number of instances of *revision* in each quarter.

Thought changes were taken to indicate *Preparation* stage thinking and 75% of thought changes occurred in the first quarter. *Illumination* was taken to be indexed by drawing a general shape for the first time and 66% of such events occurred in the 2nd and 3rd quarters. Revisions were taken to indicate a *Verification* stage and 75% of revisions occurred in the 3rd and

and 4th time quarters. The incidences of these types of events, then, were in accord with Wallas's stage analysis.

Incubation was taken to be indicated if an idea occurred early in the protocol, recurred one or more times, while the subject spoke of other things and finally appeared as the chief topic of the picture. Approximately 85% of the protocols showed such evidence of incubation.

According to the questionnaire given to the artists after the experiment, about 94% reported using incubation at least some of the time in their *normal* work (76% usually, 18% some times). The reported time periods of real life incubation ranged from days to years.

In the experimental data, there were no differences between the artist and the control subjects in amount of incubation. In fact, there were no differences between artist and non-artist groups in any of the performance measures, except in the rated quality of the sketches. The artist's sketches were rated far higher than those of the control subjects, as one would hope.

Patrick's data are in accord with Wallas's 4 stage analysis. However, any incubation that occurred in this study was very brief compared to the retrospective reports by noted thinkers. Furthermore, the main problem was never wholly put aside, but rather, was worked on continuously for an average of 18 minutes. In typical reports by artists and scientists of incubation phenomena, the problem is often set aside for lengthy periods. The one example of incubation that Patrick gives in detail (1937), might be explained by the problem-solving strategy of scanning a number of possibilities first, before returning to the most promising one to develop it further. That sort of strategy emerged in other protocol studies of problem-solving, e.g. Duncker (1945) and De Groot (1965). This "progressive deepening" (*see* Chapter 2) strategy could account for the effects that Patrick attributed to incubation. The difficulty here seems to be that the criterion used by Patrick for incubation effects was too weak.

To sum up, Patrick's data are certainly of interest and support the broad stages of Preparation (in which possible directions are surveyed), Illumination (in which one possibility is decided on) and Verification (in which revisions occur). The protocol data are less convincing on Incubation effects since at no time was the main task set aside during the average 18 minutes spent on it. However, the artists' questionnaire reports *did* support incubation as a real life phenomenon, despite the difficult of trapping it in the confines of the sketching task. Finally, Patrick notes, as did Wallas, that the stages appear to overlap and recur.

C. Laboratory studies of incubation

As we have seen, the notion of incubation plays a prominent role in the recollections of artists and scientists. Despite its importance in personal accounts of creative thinking, incubation has not, as yet, attracted much experimental study. However, some data are available and will now be discussed.

Murray and Denny (1969) investigated the effects of incubation-opportunity on subjects of high and low problem-solving ability. Subjects were divided into high and low ability on the basis of the Gestalt Transformation Test. This test requires the selection of objects for unusual uses — e.g. "From which object could you make a hose: a tree, cigarette, shirt, bicycle, eye glasses?"

Subjects were also divided into control and experimental groups. Both were given a rather complicated problem, devised by Saugstad, in which the subject is given a nail, pliers, a length of string, a pulley, some elastic bands and several newspapers.

Eight feet from the subject was a glass containing metal balls and standing on a movable frame. Next to the glass was a steel cylinder. The subject had to find a way of transferring the steel balls from the glass to the cylinder without going nearer than 8 feet to the glass or the cylinder.

The solution involves 2 stages. First, bend the nail into a hook, attach the hook to the string and throw it into the frame. The frame can then be dragged back to the line and the balls removed. The second stage is to construct a long hollow tube by rolling up the newspapers and connecting them telescope fashion by elastic bands, and then roll the balls down the tube to the steel cylinder.

Control subjects were given 20 minutes continuously to solve the problem. While the experimental subjects worked 5 minutes on the task, then had 5 minutes on an unrelated pencil and paper task. They were then given a further 15 minutes on the main task.

Neither incubation nor ability level significantly affected the frequency of solutions — but there was a significant interaction in that high ability solvers were *hindered* by incubation-opportunity while low ability solvers were aided by an incubation-opportunity. Murray and Denny interpreted these results by suggesting that low ability subjects quickly became fixated, and incubation allowed their inappropriate sets to die out, while the high ability subjects may have been working more systematically through various possibilities, without fixation, but this orderly process was disrupted by an incubation opportunity.

Murray and Denny suggest, then, that incubation will be most effective when the problem is very difficult for the solver — as for their low ability subjects tackling the tube and balls problem and presumably, for famous scientists and artists tackling major problems and projects.

Incubation effects appear to be difficult to obtain in the laboratory. Dominowski and Jenrick (1972) carried out a follow up of Murray and Denny using a different problem involving manipulation of objects but found no significant effect of incubation. However on a divergent task, Fulgosi and Guildford (1968) found significant effects of 20 minutes incubation on the quantity of solutions provided, but no effect on the quality of solutions. Clearly, research remains to be done, by for example, varying problem types, preparation time and length of incubation period. If incubation opportunities are sometimes useful, how might the benefit be brought about?

The two main ideas that have been put forward, are those of *(a)* unconscious work and *(b)* the decay of inappropriate sets during incubation.

Poincaré (1908) provided a graphic attempt at describing possible unconscious work during incubation periods. He proposed that the course of unconscious activity would be influenced by prior preparation or conscious work. Imagine ideas to be like hooked atoms, then Poincaré says, conscious work selects certain atoms/ideas as relevant to the problem and tries to organize them to reach solution. When the problem is put aside, the atoms continue to move about hooking up with each other and with other atoms not activated during conscious work. Eventually, a solution combination may be reached — but it will generally involve at least one of the atoms/ideas which were selected during conscious work.

In contrast, Woodworth and Schlosberg (1954) suggested that incubation simply involves a decay in misleading tendencies that interfere with problem solution. At present, both the "decay" and the "unconscious work" hypotheses remain open.

III. INCREASING IDEA-PRODUCTION

Are there any ways of increasing the production of novel ideas? Numerous proposals have been put forward (*see* Stein, 1974, 1975) for stimulating the idea production stage of creative thinking. Probably the most famous, and certainly the most researched, method is that known as "brainstorming".

A. Brainstorming

1 Basic results
In the 1940's and 1950's a practical businessman, Alex Osborn, developed a package of recommendations known as the brainstorming method. This

was intended mainly for use in group problem-solving and as a means of increasing idea production. The method can be adapted for individual use and is described in Osborn's (1953) book *Applied Imagination*. Brainstorming has been taken up quite widely in a variety of organizations and has also been extensively investigated in laboratory settings.

Osborn adopts the standard view that problem-solving and creative thinking involve *(1)* problem formulation, *(2)* idea-finding and *(3)* evaluation of ideas to find a likely solution. Brainstorming aims at facilitating the middle, idea-finding, stage and it can be summarized as involving 2 main principles and 4 rules.

Principles
1. Deferment of judgment.
2. Quantity breeds quality.

Rules
1. Criticism is ruled out.
2. Free wheeling is welcomed.
3. Quantity wanted.
4. Combination and improvement sought.

The "Deferment of judgment" principle meant that evaluation of ideas was to be postponed until a set period of idea production had elapsed. The untutored thinker will tend to evaluate each idea as it is produced. Osborn suggests that this can be inhibiting and may lead to premature abandonment of ideas that, although not useful in themselves, may lead on to possible solutions. The "Quantity breeds quality" principle states that the more ideas produced the larger the absolute number of useful ones there are likely to be, even if the proportion is very low. The rules listed above remind "brainstormers" not to criticize their own ideas or those of others, to free associate to ideas already produced, to aim for quantity and to combine and improve already generated suggestions.

The method was originally devised for group use but can be adapted for individual applications. A number of questions arise, e.g. Does the method lead to better productivity *(a)* for groups and *(b)* for individuals? Does group brainstorming lead to better results than would be obtained by pooling the ideas produced by the appropriate number of individual brainstormers?

Numerous studies support the hypothesis that groups using brainstorming produce more ideas than similar groups that work along conventional lines. Brainstorming instructions strongly affect the quantity of ideas produced and although effects on *average* quality are not so evident, reports of more high quality ideas have been obtained (as would be expected by virtue of the "quantity effect"). An example study is the following by Meadow, Parnes and Reese (1959). They compared the effects of brainstorming instructions with the effects of instructions that stressed the quality of ideas produced. The tasks set the subjects were to think of as many uses as they could for *(1)* a broom and *(2)* a coathanger. Ideas were rated independently for *uniqueness* (the degree to which the suggested use differed from normal use) and for *value* (social, economic or aesthetic) "Good" ideas were defined as those rated highly on both uniqueness and value. The results indicated that significantly more good ideas were produced with the brainstorming instructions than with the non-brainstorming instructions.

Favourable results on individual brainstorming have also been reported by Parnes and Meadow (1963). In one study, subjects were individually required to think up possible solutions to problems for 5 minutes. On one problem they operated conventionally, evaluating ideas as they thought of them, on the other problem, they used deferred judgement. The first method produced an average of 2.5 "good" ideas, while the second produced an average of 4.3 "good" ideas. Parnes estimated that in this case about 72% better productivity resulted from deliberate deferment of judgment during idea production.

2 Brainstorming: real v. nominal groups
Given that both individual and group brainstorming seem to be effective, the question arises of whether brainstorming in a group produces better results than would be obtained by pooling results from individual brainstormers? It could be argued either that the group procedure would lead to beneficial mutual stimulation or alternatively, that participants would be inhibited by fear of implicit criticism even although overt criticism is not permitted.

Taylor, Berry and Block (1958) tackled this question with an experiment in which 12 groups of 4 men and 48 individuals followed the basic rules of brainstorming while working on the same 3 problems. The problems were *(a)* "think of as many ways as possible of encouraging European tourists to visit the U.S.; *(b)* "what would be the consequences if all future children were born with an extra thumb on each hand?", (a diagram of the new hand structure was provided); *(c)* "how could the education system cope with the effects of a 'bulge' in the school age population?" (as was being experienced at the time of the study).

After the idea production stage, the 48 individual subjects' data were assigned to 12 *nominal* groups of size 4. The performance of each such nominal group was then scored as though the members had in fact worked together. The achievement of such nominal groups provided a base-line level of performance which would be achieved if group work were neither facilitating nor inhibiting. As can be seen from Fig. 7.1, the nominal groups produced more unique ideas than the real groups. More distinct "good" ideas were also produced by the nominal groups—largely by virtue of the quantity effect.

It was concluded from these data that group participation in brainstorming inhibited creative thinking relative to individual brainstorming.

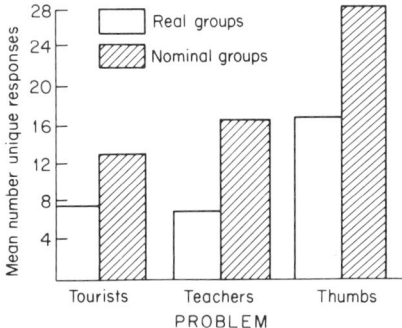

Fig. 7.1. Results from Taylor, Berry and Block's (1958) study of real versus nominal groups using brainstorming on three problems.

Perhaps, then, individuals feared implicit criticism even when open criticism was not permitted. Also, individuals working in a real group are more likely to develop the same set or direction in their thinking than the same number of individuals working alone. Individuals working alone will probably develop "sets" but these sets are likely to differ from person to person.

The "nominal group superiority effect" first revealed in Taylor *et al.*'s experiment, has held up over a number of procedural variations. For example, Dunette, Campbell and Jaastad (1963) used a similar design to Taylor *et al.*, but their subjects were research scientists and advertising people who had extensive prior experience of working with each other. Thus the groups were more like real groups in a working environment than were Taylor *et al.*'s student groups. The same three problems as those in the Taylor *et al.* study were used, plus the so-called "People" problem (i.e. "what adjustments and consequences would follow if people's average height increased to 80 inches and their average weight doubled?"). The performance of real brainstorming groups of size 4 was compared with that of nominal brainstorming groups of 4. Again, the nominal groups produced more ideas and more good ideas than the real group. This led Dunnette *et al.* to conclude that brainstorming is most effective when undertaken by individuals working *alone* in an atmosphere free from the apparently inhibiting influence of group interaction.

Four-person groups, as in the above two studies, are at the low end of group size. Perhaps larger groups would show an advantage over nominal groups? Bouchard and Hare (1970) addressed this possibility in a study in which 84 male students individually brainstormed the "thumbs" problem while a further 84 were assigned to groups of 5, 7 or 9 persons. The results indicated that as group size increased, the advantage of the nominal groups also increased, both in terms of quantity and quality.

The problems used in the foregoing studies were rather artificial, or unreal, and possibly not very involving for the subjects. Dillon, Graham and Aidells (1972) used a topic that was both real life and "hot" at the time. This was "how might people influence U.S. foreign policy as a result of the U.S. invasion of Cambodia in 1970?" Once more, nominal groups out-scored real groups on quantity of ideas for dealing with this question.

The nominal group superiority effect seems to be very robust and, in addition to the manipulations already described, it has withstood variations in sex of experimenter, presence of experimenter, and written v. tape-recorded responses (*see* Stein, 1975, for further details).

3 Deferment v. separation of judgement
Whether undertaken by individuals or groups, deferment of judgment is a key tenet of Osborn's description of brainstorming. Some research has considered whether it is really the deferment of judgment or simply the *separation* of judgment from production that is the effective feature. Brilhart and Jochem (1964) compared three different patterns of stages in problem-solving. Pattern A was labelled "ideas-criteria" and conformed to the normal brainstorming sequence of events i.e. *(1)* analysis of problem, *(2)* brainstorming production of ideas, *(3)* consideration of criteria, *(4)* evaluation and *(5)* report of best idea. Pattern B ("Criteria-ideas") reversed the order of steps 3 (criteria consideration) and 2 (idea production) but was otherwise the same as Pattern A. In Pattern C ("problem-solution") the following three steps were followed, *(1)* analysis, *(2)* simultaneous generation and evaluation of ideas, *(3)* selection of best solution.

Five-man groups worked on three problems using three different patterns of steps and all group results were scored for quantity and quality of ideas produced. Patterns A and B resulted in many more ideas than Pattern C and Pattern A was best in terms of numbers of good ideas. So, it seems that separation of idea producing and criteria-considering is useful in terms of quantity irrespective of the order of these two steps. However, the standard order used in brainstorming (i.e. "ideas-criteria"), seems most effective in terms of quality of ideas, as compared to the other two patterns.

B. Checklists and morphological synthesis

The brainstorming technique was not very expicit on *how* to generate ideas, apart from urging free association. Warren and Davis (1969) compared three more specific methods that are suitable for individual use. Subjects were set the task of thinking of ideas for changing or improving a particular object, viz. a doorknob. One group of subjects was given a short checklist of general "idea-spurring" suggestions (e.g. Add something; subtract something; change colour; change materials . . .). A second group was given a long checklist of 73 idea spurring questions organized into 9 categories (e.g. *Magnify?* (add what?, time, frequency, strength . . . .) *Modify?* (meaning, colour, motion . . . .)). The third group were instructed in a technique known as *Morphological Synthesis* (Zwicky, 1969). This technique requires the problem-solver to list ideas for one aspect of the object in question along one axis and ideas for another aspect of the problem along a second axis. Novel ideas would then be found in the matrix formed by combining the two axes. For example, if the problem was to invent a new type of vehicle, this could be tackled by creating a matrix with ideas for power sources along one dimension (axis) and ideas for the medium of transport along the other dimension. See Fig. 7.2 for a possible morphological synthesis of the "new vehicle" problem.

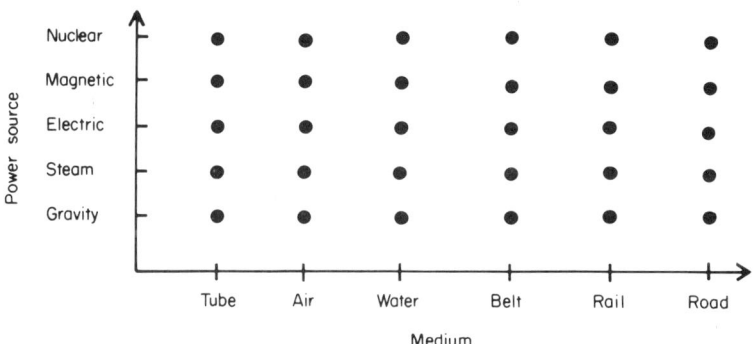

Fig. 7.2. Morphological synthesis applied to the "new vehicles" problem.

Each point in the matrix (Fig. 7.2) represents some combination of power source and medium. Some are familiar, and some impossible; but others may be new and useful. Evidently the number of combinations increases rapidly with the number of ideas per dimension. More than two dimensions may be used, leading to further increases in the number of combinations.

A fourth, control group were given no particular instructions in problem-solving methods. Of the 4 groups, the short checklist and morphological synthesis groups produced the highest number of ideas and the greatest number of high quality ideas. Surprisingly, perhaps, the long checklist produced no improvement over the control conditions. The morphological synthesis instructions produced the greatest number of ideas and had the highest rate of production; and so, when time is taken into account this method appeared to be the most effective of those studied.

C. Synectics

A method which has been extensively taken up, especially in the U.S., by industrial and other organizations that have practical and pressing needs for innovative ideas is known as synectics (Gordon, 1961). Despite its wide use in practice, it does not seem to have attracted much laboratory investigation. Thus data on its utility are largely in the form of anecdotes. However, it is an interesting and plausible technique and seems worth describing here, albeit briefly.

Synectics involves the joining together of different and apparently irrelevant elements by the use of metaphors and analogies. An unfamiliar problem may be better understood when it can be represented by an analogy with something familiar (i.e. "making the strange familiar"). Conversely, a problem that is overfamiliar, and about which we have difficulty generating fresh ideas, can often be usefully handled by means of an unusual metaphor ("making the familiar strange"). These two uses of metaphor are helpful in developing formulations of problems. Four types of analogy are proposed for use in generating further ideas toward solutions; these are, *(1)* personal analogy, *(2)* direct analogy, *(3)* symbolic analogy, and *(4)* fantasy analogy. The personal analogy requires that the problem-solver identify him or herself with part or all of the problem and its solution (e.g. imagine how it would feel to be a zip fastener, if the problem was to improve on such a device). Direct analogy attempts to find parallel facts in other fields (e.g. considering biological examples of apertures that close up tightly in the zip fastener problem). The symbolic analogy involves a compressed description of the problem or of a possible solution, and may be verbal, or in the form of an image. For example, according to Stein (1974) one group used the Indian rope trick as a symbolic analogy in developing a new jacking mechanism. Fantasy analogy allows purely wish-fulfilling and unrealistic proposals to be put forward. For example, on the problem of making a vapour-proof closure for space suits, (earlier referred to as the zip fastener problem), one participant expressed a fantasy analogy as follows, ". . . wish fulfillment. Childhood dream . . . you wish it closed, and invisible microbes, working for you, cross hands across the opening and *pull* it tight".

Little work appears to have been published evaluating synectics, apart from anecdotal accounts of successes. However, Bouchard (1972) did find that use of the personal analogy technique led to improved performance in brainstorming as compared to a brainstorming without use of personal analogy. This result then, lends some laboratory support to the use of synectics.

IV. THEORETICAL APPROACHES

So far our discussion of research on creative processes has been somewhat atheoretical. In this section I will consider some attempts to explain creative processes within the frameworks of theoretical approaches established in other areas. The approaches dealt with here are those of associative, Piagetian and information processing theory.

A. Associative theories

1 Mednick

Mednick (1962) defines the creative thinking process as the "forming of associative elements into new combinations which either meet specified requirements or are in some way useful". On this view then, the creative thinker comes up with useful combinations of ideas that are already in the thinker's repertoire but which have not been previously brought together (e.g. Salvador Dali combining the idea of a "watch" with that of "softness", producing the novel combination "a soft watch"). In accord with the standard associative approach, ideas are assumed to be linked to each other, more or less directly and with varying degrees of strength, in a vast associative network. Thus "watch" and "clock" would tend to be strongly associated, while "watch" and "soft" would not be. Mednick suggests that the more weakly or indirectly connected two combined ideas are, the more original is their combination. As he puts it, "The more mutually remote the elements of the new combination, the more creative the process of solution" (1962). Three ways are suggested in which "mutually remote" ideas could be brought together.

(a) Serendipity. This is the accidental occurrence of environmental stimuli that evoke the requisite ideas in close proximity. Accidental events do seem to have played a role in a number of scientific discoveries and inventions,

e.g. discovering the vulcanization of rubber, X-rays and penicillin.

Deliberate use of serendipity is not unknown in the arts and sciences. Mednick cites a physicist who keeps in a fishbowl large numbers of slips of paper each having some physical fact written on it. Every so often, he randomly draws pairs of facts from the bowl in the hope of finding new and useful combinations. The avant-garde author William Burroughs made good use of his "cut up" method, which involved snipping portions from newspapers and randomly arranging and rearranging them until a suitable effect was obtained. Similarly, painting, collages and *objets trouvés* can also deliberately involve chance elements.

(b) Similarity. The required elements may be evoked close together by similarity on some dimension. Examples would include rhymes, alliterations and homonyms.

(c) Mediation. The required ideas may be evoked through the mediation of associates that they have in common. For example, the idea of using a vacuum cleaner to remove a cloud of small flies that has settled on the ceiling may come about through an associative sequence such as "ceiling-floor-vacuum cleaner" where the "ceiling-vacuum cleaner" connection is mediated by their common associate "floor".

Given this view, Mednick proposes explanations of individual differences in creativity principally in terms of differences in associative organization. In particular, it is suggested that individuals may be characterized by the "steepness" of their "associative hierarchies". Take the word "table". Two individuals may have the same set of associates to table, ordered in the same way, but one may have a steep hierarchy in which the most associated word ("chair") is much more strongly associated with "table" than is the second associate ("cloth"). The other person may have a much flatter hierarchy in which the differences in strength between successive associates to "table" are much less. Fig. 7.3 represents two such hierarchies.

Mednick suggests that creative individuals may be characterized by relatively flat associative hierarchies which enable them to connect together remote ideas more readily than people with steep hierarchies. On the basis of this theory, Mednick devised the Remote Associates Test (RAT). In this test each of the 30 items consists of 3 words, known to be mutually remote. The subject's task is to produce a fourth word which is a common associate of all 3 remote words. An example item is "surprise, line, birthday", and the answer is "party". People with "flat" hierarchies should find this test easier than those with "steep" hierarchies. The test displays satisfactory levels of reliability (around 0.91) and validation studies have been quite encouraging. Mednick reported a correlation of 0.7 between RAT score and rated creativity of design students. Other, weaker, but statistically significant connections were reported between RAT scores and creativity ratings of psychology graduate students, originality assessments of eminent architects and "non conformist" tendencies among students. Furthermore,

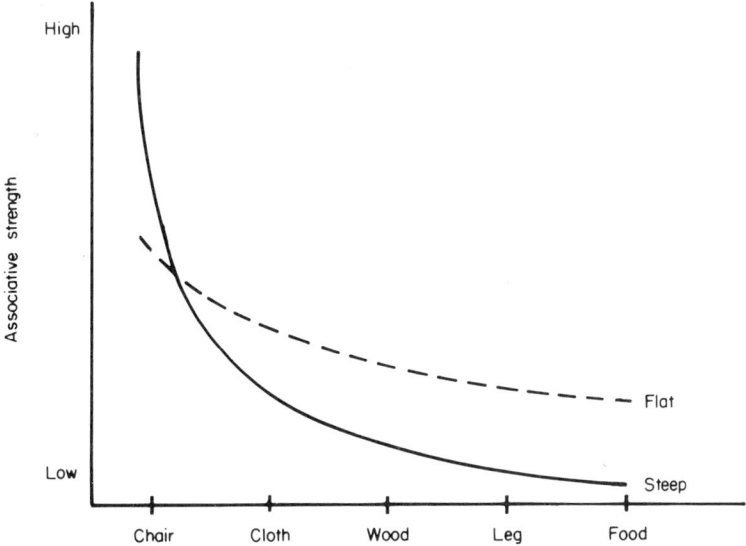

Fig. 7.3. Steep and flat associative hierarchies to the word "table". *(After Mednick, 1962.)*

high scorers on the RAT have been found to detect and use incidentally presented information to a greater degree than low RAT scorers (Mendelsohn and Griswold, 1964; Laughlin, Docherty and Dunn, 1968). This suggests that a broad, less focussed attentional style may underlie the development of the presumed flatter hierarchies of high RAT scorers.

Despite the plausibility of Mednick's theory and the early promise of the RAT, little further development seems to have occurred in this approach since the late 1960's. This may reflect a general disenchantment with simple associative theories of memory and thought. Before moving on to consider some approaches that allow more to mental organization than purely associative links a quite influential associative theory due to Koestler (1964) will be briefly discussed.

2 Koestler

Arthur Koestler (1964) has put forward a somewhat more sophisticated associative theory than Mednick's. However, perhaps because it derives very largely from case studies of numerous "acts of creation" and has not led to laboratory tests, this theory has had little impact on psychology, although it has been well received by the lay public. Koestler's *bisociative* theory claims that a creative act involves linking together two previously unconnected "frames of reference" (also known as "associative contexts", "universes of discourse" or "matrices"). Koestler proposes that, in given associative contexts, ideas are connected by fixed rules, and that normal problem-solving involves working with the established rules within one context (e.g. applying rules of chess, exploring permissible moves in an 8-puzzle problem, etc.). The (possibly apocryphal) case of Archimedes solving the problem of measuring the volume of an irregular object (a crown) serves to illustrate the bisociation of different associative contexts. None of the rules in Archimedes' habitual "frame of reference" for measuring volume would yield the volume of a valuable crown without damaging it (e.g. by melting it down or by hammering it into a regular shape). Presumably, all the time, Archimedes also had rules relating to the "bathing" context. One of the bathing rules would be that if one got into a full bath, the water would spill out. The volume-measuring "frame of reference" and the bathing "frame of reference" were suddenly linked when Archimedes noticed the water level rise as he stepped into a bath after thinking about the volume problem for a considerable time. It became clear that immersion of a body in a full container (as in bathing) would displace liquid whose volume could then be measured by the rules already well established in the volume-measuring "frame of reference".

Koestler interpreted as cases of bisociation numerous other examples of scientific creativity (e.g. the discovery or invention of vaccination, printing, the notions of elliptical planetary orbits and evolution by natural selection). However, no predictions that could be tested in laboratory settings, or possible measures of individual differences that might be relevant to predicting creativity, have arisen from this theory. (An interesting creative task would be to think up possible tests of the bisociation theory!)

B. Gruber's Piagetian approach

Gruber (1980) has painstakingly analysed the case of Charles Darwin's development of evolutionary theory from a Piagetian point of view. Piagetian theory is, of course, mainly concerned with the development of concepts (e.g. that of the conservation of mass) in children, but Gruber shows that the approach can be usefully applied to conceptual growth in adults. Gruber points to the long time periods involved in developing significant new ideas. The emphasis on "acts of creation" and "moments of insight" has, perhaps, been misleading and diverted attention from the long-term growth-like processes in which the "moments of insight" are embedded. Analysis of Darwin's notebooks indicates a series of changes in his "system of ideas" concerning the relationship of biological and geological phenomena. Initially, the dominant conceptual scheme was that the physical world and the species inhabiting it were fixed at creation. However, evidence from geology more and more indicated a changing physical world. This led to a conceptual conflict. How could species fixed at creation remain adapted to changing environments? Darwin's first theory—the monad theory—suggested that simple living forms (monads) appeared through spontaneous generation from inanimate matter and then evolved to match the environment. This was fairly quickly abandoned and Darwin then sought other ways in which species could change. Hybridization seemed possible and led Darwin to a study of plant and animal breeding which increased his knowledge of artificial selection. The transmission of acquired characteristics was another possible solution and led Darwin into a study of mental processes and behaviour in animals and humans. Although this approach did not produce the desired answer to the question of heritable variation it produced much evidence that later on would be related to the completed theory. Studying the evolution of mental processes also raised forcibly the issue of materialism. This was a somewhat suspect and dangerous idea at the time and Darwin expressed fear of persecution on account of his materialist notions. After many years of prior study and experience, Darwin read Malthus's *Essay on Population* on September 28, 1838, and this seems to have led him to realize that natural selection could work in favour of variants that were better suited to their environments than their ancestors had been. The idea of natural selection as a "conservative" force, weeding out weak or maladapted variants was well known but the positive aspects of natural selection, favouring the best adapted variants, had not been emphasized before Darwin's insight.

Darwin was not quite satisfied with the theory because it did not explain variation but rather took variation and heredity as unexplained assumptions. A further 20 years work and the stimulus of Wallace's independent conception of "evolution by natural selection" were required before Darwin finally published his evolutionary theory.

Gruber emphasizes the slowness of the changes in Darwin's system of ideas and he interprets the process of change in terms of Piaget's notions of "assimilation" and "accommodation". "Assimilation" involves the incorporation of new information into existing conceptual structures, while "accommodation" involves changes in conceptual structure brought about by new information. Gruber argues that what appear to be dramatic breaks with the past, can also be seen as the culmination of numerous small changes. This approach then, places "moments of insight" within their long-term context and would suggest that little understanding of high order creativity will result from laboratory studies of small-scale problem-solving.

C. Simon's information processing approach

Simon (1966) has indicated how the information processing approach might tackle the topic of creativity in science. He points out that high level creativity in science is a very rare event and that scientific discovery is a very slow process (as Gruber has also argued). A theory of scientific creativity therefore should account not only for the occurrence of major conceptual advances but also for their rarity of occurrence. Simon proposes that the information processing theory of small-scale problem-solving can also be applied to highly creative scientific thinking. The information processing theory of problem-solving is basically that outlined in Chapters 2 and 3 of this book. Thinking is seen as a hierarchical organization of elementary processes carried out one at a time. Considerable search is postulated, limited by selective heuristics, such as means-end analysis. Only a very limited working memory capacity is assumed, backed up by a vast long-term memory.

Scientific biographies generally reveal considerable trial and error search through a vast space of alternative hypotheses before the breakthrough occurs. Persistence and strong motivation are marked characteristics of successful scientists. Some apparently have better heuristics than others and can reach solutions more rapidly on that account. A prime source of heuristics are good representational or observational methods. For instance, many advances followed the inventions of telescopes and microscopes. These devices presumably helped in formulating the nature of the relevant problems more clearly and in ruling out possible alternative hypotheses more decisively than had been possible previously.

What of incubation and possible unconscious processes in discovery and invention? Simon argues that incubation and inspiration phenomena may be explained in terms of two mechanisms he labels *familiarization* and *selective forgetting*. Familiarization is a slow process of building up a representation of the problem and relevant data in long-term memory. It is assumed that, in seeking information, the person is guided by a goal tree that is stored and developed in working memory. In the course of pursuing goals, information is obtained and added to the long term memory. This information in turn is used in constructing new goals and subgoals. Thus there is a continuous interaction between goal information in working memory and problem information in the long-term memory. When the problem is set aside the goal information is lost and has to be reconstructed again. However, when the problem is taken up again, there is more information about the task in the long-term memory than there was before, so a different set of goals and subgoals will likely be erected and these may lead to a quick solution where the previous goals did not.

There is no need for parallel processing in this theory. Inspiration would be explained by a switch of attention to the problem, followed by rapid solution. Attention-switching could be accomplished by a time sharing scheme that checked on outstanding goals or tasks at regular intervals and decided whether the current task should continue to occupy attention or whether to switch for a while to a different task. Such systems are common in computer installations and ensure that all outstanding claims on processing time get a fair share of attention. Further discussion of this topic will be found in the next Chapter, where the issue of parallel *v.* serial thought processes is considered in the general context of research on thinking.

To sum up, Simon's analysis is plausible and although far from a detailed simulation, it does indicate in broad terms how the information processing approach would set about tackling creative processes.

V. SUMMARY AND CONCLUDING COMMENTS

This Chapter has concerned the kinds of thinking involved in generating creative products, where a creative product was defined as being both novel and valuable, in some way. Studies of individuals acknowledged to be creative, (i.e. to have a tendency to make creative products) noted tendencies toward dominance, radicalism and high intelligence as conventionally measured (Cattell and Drevdahl, 1955). In the sciences, creative individuals tended to be first born or only sons (Roe, 1952). Aggression was not far below the surface, especially in connection with rival scientists. However, aggressive tendencies usually did not show up in projective test responses, probably because such tests were not congenial to the scientists' preferred "convergent" style of thinking (Mitroff, 1974; Hudson, 1966).

Personal accounts by scientists and artists suggested four broad phases in creative work that Wallas (1926) labelled "Preparation", "Incubation", "Illumination" and "Verification". Patrick's (1935, 1937) laboratory studies indicated some support, at least for the conscious phases or stages of preparation, illumination and verification. Her results on incubation were less clear, perhaps because the problems were too small scale in terms of the time involved. Incubation has largely resisted capture in the laboratory, although Murray and Denny (1969) and Fulgosi and Guilford (1968) did find some beneficial effects of incubation opportunities. Even if incubation opportunities do facilitate later solution, the mechanisms involved are not clear. Both unconscious work and selective forgetting are viable explanatory candidates and will remain so until the appropriate experiments have been devised.

Various schemes for increasing idea production have been promoted. Many studies have focussed on Osborn's brainstorming method, which involves deferment of idea evaluation until after a period of free-wheeling idea production. Brainstorming seems to be beneficial on many problems and appears to work both for groups and for individuals. However, from many experiments it seems that the group version of the method is inhibiting compared to individual brainstorming (Stein, 1975). Other individual-oriented techniques, such as, short idea-spurring checklists and Zwicky's (1969) morphological synthesis, appear to be useful (Warren and Davis, 1969). Although they have been widely adopted in practice, there has been little experimental evaluation of Gordon's (1961) synectics techniques, which are based on using various forms of analogy (personal, direct, symbolic and fantasy). Bouchard (1972) did find results in favour of using the personal analogies technique in brainstorming sessions.

A number of theoretical approaches were considered. Associative theory, as developed by Mednick (1962) gained some empirical support from the apparent validity of the Remote Associates Test, which was constructed on the basis of the theory. However, perhaps because of a general disenchantment with associative theories of thinking, this approach has not been further developed. Koestler's (1964) bisociative theory allows more complexity to mental organization than Mednick's associative theory and postulates "associative contexts" or "frames of reference". He proposes that normal, noncreative, thought procedes *within* particular contexts or frames and that the creative act involves linking together previously unconnected frames. Although Koestler's ideas are attractive they remain unexplored in the laboratory or by computer modelling. Like Koestler, Gruber (1980) has based his analysis on case studies. He has focussed especially on Darwin's development of the Theory of Evolution. Using Piagetian notions, such as assimilation and accommodation, Gruber shows how Darwin's system of ideas changed very slowly over a period of many years. "Moments of insight", in Gruber's analysis, were the culminations of slow long-term processes. If this approach is accepted, laboratory analysis of high level creativity would seem to be ruled out in favour of meticulous case studies. Finally, the information processing approach, as represented by Simon (1966), was considered. Simon indicates how the apparent phenomena of incubation and inspiration could be explained in information processing terms by using the notions of "familiarization" and "selective forgetting". No parallel processing is required by Simon's scheme. He points out the importance of good problem representations — both to ensure search is in an appropriate problem space and to aid in developing heuristic evaluations of possible research directions. As Simon notes, many advances in science have followed improved representational technology (e.g. microscopes and telescopes). Also, he reminds us that the rate of progress in science is generally slow and this fact fits well with the information processing notion of the thinker as a limited capacity, serial system slowly searching for solutions in a vast space of possibilities.

VI. FURTHER READING

Barron, F. and Harrington, D. M. (1981). Creativity, intelligence and personality. *Annual Review of Psychology* **32**, 439–476.
A thorough review of developments in the psychometric approach to creativity.
Koestler, A. (1964). The act of creation. Hutchinson, London. (A paperback edition has been published by Picador (Pan Books) London, 1975.)
This work is a highly readable presentation of Koestler's bisociative theory of creativity, applied to numerous examples of scientific and artistic innovation.
Gruber, H. E. (1980). Darwin on Man: a psychological study of scientific creativity. 2nd edition. University of Chicago Press.
Gruber details a very promising Piagetian approach to creative processes in science and provides a thorough case-study of the development of Darwin's thinking on evolution.

8
Thinking: theoretical overview, progress and prospects

In this book thinking has been taken to be a form of information processing, and on this view, models of thinking should fit in with more general frameworks for understanding human information processing. A number of broad frameworks (e.g. Bower, 1975; Hunt, 1971, 1973; Atkinson and Shiffrin, 1968) have been proposed, but the differences between such schemes are generally matters of detail only, and certain assumptions have been widely accepted by different theorists (at least until recently). These common assumptions form important parts of what I have referred to as the "modal model" for thinking. According to the modal model, individuals have a vast long-term memory and a small capacity working memory. These two memories are supplemented in the overall system by high capacity but short-lived sensory memories (e.g. Sperling, 1960) which are not usually regarded as very important for thinking and may be ignored for our present purposes. Thinking is seen as the manipulation of symbols both within working memory and between long-term and working memory. The manipulations are assumed to be in accord with rules stored in long-term memory. At a given time, the rule selected from long-term memory will depend on which goals are current and on the contents of working memory. It is assumed that only one thinking step occurs at a time (the *seriality* assumption). This modal model of thinking, just outlined, is consistent with many broader frameworks for the whole human information processing system. However, here the important questions are:
  (1) "How well does the modal model of thinking stand up in view of the experimental data?"
  (2) "Do developments in our general understanding of human information processing have implications for the modal model of thinking?"
In addition to these questions, this Chapter will also discuss theoretical progress and likely research trends in the thinking area.

I. MODAL MODEL ASSUMPTIONS

A. Memory and symbol manipulation

First, the memory assumptions of the modal model do not appear to be challenged. Quite sharp limits on mental search were indicated by the data from both adversary and nonadversary problems. Thus, working memory can only sustain a limited size of symbol structure representing sequences of possibilities. These working memory limitations quite likely underlie the preference for depth-first searches, in which memory load grows slowly, compared to breadth first searches. The "progressive deepening" strategy observed in chess play (De Groot, 1965) may reflect a familiarization process that builds up a structure in long-term memory to represent explored paths (Simon, 1966). Through a process of "chunking", ultimately quite long paths can be represented by single symbols in working memory. Differences in long-term memory contents between individuals are important in explaining skill differences in many areas of problem-solving. For example, the data from studies of memory for game-positions indicate that game playing expertise resides in vast collections of familiar patterns in long-term memory rather than in any quantitative superiority in working memory capacity beyond average levels. It was very notable that De Groot's (1965) chess masters searched to about the same depth as did less skilled players and this result suggests essentially equal working memory capacities in both groups. The greater effectiveness of the master players' mental explorations reflected the superior structuring they imposed on the initial problem configuration, compared to that of the good, but amateur, players.

The view of thinking as symbol manipulation is fundamental to the information processing approach and is not challenged by the research results that have been reviewed here. The further specification that manipulations are either within working memory (e.g. rearranging letters in a short anagram) or between working memory and long-term memory (e.g. in mental arithmetic, retrieving an intermediate sum from long-term memory and placing it in working memory) discounts manipulations occurring purely within long-term memory. On this point, the modal model clashes with notions of spontaneous activity within long-term memory as proposed by Freud (1900), Neisser (1963b), Singer (1975a) and Gestalt memory theorists (*see* Baddeley, 1976, Chapter 4) among others. Theorists who have postulated activity within long-term memory have usually also considered that this activity could occur in parallel with the main stream of conscious thinking. Since the notion of within long-term memory activity thus also clashes (potentially at least) with the seriality assumption, this matter will be discussed more fully in a later section on the issue of parallelism.

The notion that thinking is goal directed is non-controversial, at least in the case of problem-solving. However, difficulties for the model do arise in connection with goal scheduling and with urgent interruptions to single-minded goal seeking, that demand attention in real time (Neisser, 1963b; Simon, 1967). Again, these questions relate to the serial v. parallel thinking issue and will be discussed shortly. Even the apparently undirected thoughts involved in daydreaming are in fact often related to goals (or "current concerns") although the thought sequence is not constrained by higher level goals of "keeping to the topic" or "sticking to practical possibilities". However, the occurrence of "intrusive thoughts", reported in the daydreaming literature, is a possible problem for the modal serial model, in that such thoughts suggest parallel processes "breaking through" into consciousness. From this brief survey, then, the assumption of serial processing emerges as a very problematic aspect of the modal model. Hence, the seriality issue will now be considered in more detail.

B. Serial or parallel thought processes?

This question is very important for modelling thought in that the answer chosen influences the model maker's treatment of many other topics e.g. interpretation of "incubation" data, daydreaming (especially intrusive thoughts), goal scheduling and goal interruptions. This issue also impinges on the utility of verbal reports. If all thinking is serial, then verbal reports could give a good view of, at least, that large portion of thought which is in a verbal code or readily translatable into verbal terms (Ericsson and Simon, 1980). However, if parallel streams of thought exist and people can only report on that stream going through working memory, then much thought could not be reported and less direct methods would be needed to tap the "underground" thought streams. Of course, the seriality assumption is simpler, more parsimonious and more testable than the alternative and has the advantage of leading to models for particular tasks that can be readily explored on existing available computer systems which are completely serial devices. So, there is much to be said for adopting the seriality assumption as an initial hypothesis. Also, as Newell has argued (1962), an awkward possibility arises when parallel activities are permitted, in that information processing may become like an "Alice in Wonderland croquet game, with porcupine balls unrolling themselves and wandering off, and flamingo mallets asking questions at inopportune times". Newell is here pointing to the chaotic possibilities of parallel systems; however, other theorists have not been so deterred, and although some have willingly embraced chaos (e.g. as a potential source of novel ideas), yet others have striven to show how order and parallel activity can co-exist within a single system. Consideration of some of these proposals and the "serialist" treatment of the relevant data is now in order.

1 Neisser and Simon on the "multiplicity" of thought

In a paper entitled "The imitation of man by machine", Neisser (1963a) argued that thought is intimately linked with emotions and usually serves more than one goal at a time. He charged that information processing models cast in the form of computer programs lack any representation of emotion and are overly single minded in seeking relentlessly for a single top level goal. Simon (1967) replied with suggestions for incorporating some emotional phenomena and for dealing with multiple goals. In the case of emotion, Simon proposed that emotion is associated with interruption of the current activity sequence by an urgent stimulus demanding real-time attention (e.g. shouts of "Fire" while working on an algebra problem). However, to handle "interruptions" Simon did allow that a low level monitoring process may take place along with the main stream of thought. In his own words, "A certain amount of processing must go on continuously or almost continuously, to enable the system to *notice* when conditions have arisen that require ongoing programs to be interrupted. The noticing processes will be substantially in parallel with the ongoing goal attaining program of the total system, although this parallelism may be realized in fact, by the high frequency time sharing of a single serial processor" (Simon's italics).

Thus, Simon raised the possibility of parallel "noticing" processes that scan for "danger" signals, but he kept open the serialist option of "time sharing". The notion of "time sharing" is simply that the system rapidly switches from one program to another and so gives the appearance of doing two things at once without true simultaneity. Time sharing requires a higher level program to determine which lower level program should take over next and for how long. Time sharing is one way in which real computer systems allocate processing to the various jobs that come in and queue for attention. So, it is a method of known utility for serial systems.

Neisser's point about humans having multiple goals and being other than single minded is more easily tackled without parallelism. Simon showed that multiple goals can be readily generated in computer game playing, for instance, and that current goals can be set aside for other goals on the basis of time- and effort- limits put on the search for goal states.

Thus, Neisser's anti-serialist points in the 1963a paper were acknowledged and largely "defused" by Simon, but in a second paper in the same year, Neisser (1963b) espoused the radical notion of multiple simultaneous thought processes and this concept cannot be accommodated within a serial framework.

Neisser proposed that a number of more or less independent trains of thought co-occur but that there is a "main sequence" corresponding to the ordinary flow of consciousness. The main sequence, except perhaps in pathological cases, has control of motor activity. It was suggested that the unconscious trains of thought might generally follow the rules of Freud's primary process thinking and interact together in a chaotic way. However, when the main sequence is not too demanding the unconscious sequences may attain high degrees of complexity and do useful unconscious work — the results of which can later be made available to consciousness. Accounts of incubation and inspiration in creative thinking were taken by Neisser as supporting these ideas. Serialist rejoinders (Simon, 1966; Ericsson and Simon, 1980) have tended to *(a)* play down the solidity of reports of incubation, and *(b)* to propose alternative explanations for any apparently well-founded claims of incubation phenomena. So, for instance, Ericsson and Simon pointed out that reports of incubation have frequently been given many years after the supposed events occurred. It could be that the scientists, inventors or artists concerned did start to consciously muse on their problems but on the critical occasion of "inspiration" rapidly solved, forgot the details of their own thought processes and then reported the event as one of sudden insight occurring without warning (Woodworth and Schosberg, 1954). The occurrence of a rapid solution on trial $n + 1$ after n failures may be attributed (Simon, 1966) to beneficial forgetting of misleading sub-goals in the rest period between trial n and $n + 1$. The topic of "incubation" is clearly very important for theories of thinking but unfortunately the supposed phenomenon has proven difficult to capture in the laboratory. Apart from a very few published experimental studies (e.g. Patrick, 1937; Murray and Denny, 1969; Fulgosi and Guilford, 1968; Dominowski and Jenrick, 1972) there are only anecdotal data on which to rely. Of course, if incubation is a real phenomenon but is only associated with high-level creativity, psychologists are unlikely to be able to observe it with the usual laboratory tools of small-scale, often artificial, puzzles presented to normal subjects for short periods. Intuitively, incubation does seem to play a role in less exalted, more everyday forms of problem solving, and it may yet be possible to get leads on this elusive process, either in laboratory settings or perhaps through naturalistic "diary" studies using more ordinary people than those whose recollections fill the anthologies on creative thinking experiences (e.g. Ghiselin, 1952). However, at present, the

very existence of the phenomenon, let alone its explanation, is uncertain.
 The question of "intrusive" thoughts also arises in connection with the "parallelism" issue. Becker *et al.* (1973) and Antrobus *et al.* (1966) found that unwelcome thoughts appear to intrude onto consciousness following exposure to disturbing information. This phenomenon is certainly consistent with Neisser's multiple thinking scheme. The rival serial position could propose, along with Simon's (1967) reply to Neisser (1963a), that goals of "assimilating the disturbing information" are set up and given high priority. Thus, a time sharing system could switch from external task goals to the "intrusive" goals quite frequently. It is conceivable that a long standing high-level goal is to process disturbing information even if it is painful, and that this goal is not easily ignored.

2 Dissociations between verbal reports and behaviour?
If the important thought processes involved in problem-solving are serial then it is reasonable to hope that verbal reports could be informative about the course of those processes. On the other hand, if parallel thought streams are importantly involved, the best verbal reports can only be very incomplete, being restricted to the main conscious stream. Thus, the status of verbal reports on mental processes is relevant to the serial *v.* parallel issue.
 The question of the accuracy of verbal reports of mental activity has generated considerable controversy, since the era of the Introspectionists until the present time. A major critique of verbal reports as a source of information on cognitive processes was presented by Nisbett and Wilson (1977) and this article stimulated a reply from Ericsson and Simon (1980) who attempted to detail the circumstances under which the "modal model" of thinking would expect verbal reports to be valid.
 Nisbett and Wilson reviewed a dauntingly large collection of studies, mainly from the social psychological literature. The experiments reviewed by Nisbett and Wilson involved such varied topics as subjects changing their opinions (Goethals and Reckmann, 1973), coming to eat grasshoppers (Zimbardo, Weisenberg, Firestone and Levy, 1969), taking electric shocks (Zimbardo, Cohen, Weisenberg, Dworkin and Firestone, 1969) and selecting which of 4 pairs of stockings they preferred. When subjects in these various studies were asked about the cognitive processes that had led them to make their responses, their verbal reports did not refer to the stimuli that the experimenters could demonstrate to be influencing their behaviour. In view of the very low accuracy of the verbal reports in these studies, Nisbett and Wilson concluded that reports on cognitive processes are not based on genuine "privileged" information of a type only available to introspection, but rather, are based on implicit and widely held causal

theories of which stimuli could cause given responses. This latter point draws its support from studies in which control subjects are asked to say which factors they think will be effective in particular experiments. Control groups' predictive judgments of the effectiveness of experimental variables were highly correlated with experimental subjects' judgements — but both sets of judgments were equally inaccurate. Nisbett and Wilson qualify their condemnation of verbal reports and allow that such reports may be accurate if confined to mental *contents* (e.g. contents of focal attention, current sensations, plans, etc.) but they maintain that verbal reports will be woefully inaccurate regarding mental *processes*. Thus, they are claiming that the most important processes underlying behaviour in a variety of tasks are unavailable to consciousness and that the conscious thought stream is largely epiphenomenal.

Even if Nisbett and Wilson's conclusions are accepted, a serial model could still be tenable, if the unreportable processes could be seen as not using working memory but as being run off in a "ballistic" or "compiled" mode, such as has been postulated for highly practised actions. However, this explanatory escape-route seems implausible, in view of the unfamiliar nature of many of the tasks in which inaccurate verbal reporting has been claimed. Ericsson and Simon (1980) take a difficult tack and on the basis of the modal, serial model, they propose conditions under which accurate verbal reports should and should not occur. In particular they suggest that verbalization can only be expected to be accurate to the degree that the report is made *concurrently* with the task-related cognitive activity. Furthermore, for maximum validity the report should be made in a free manner i.e. in the subject's own words, not confined to some experimenter-set categories which may not match the subject's own representational schemes. The basic notion put forward by Ericsson and Simon is that only information in focal attention can be verbalized. This principle limits "verbalizable" information to that in working memory and further it predicts that information about the inputs and outputs of current processes will receive priority in free concurrent verbal reports. Ericsson and Simon point out that almost all the studies discussed by Nisbett and Wilson involved retrospective reports, often some considerable time after the behaviour concerned had occurred. The serial modal model would not predict accurate reports in such circumstances since the contents of working memory during processing are very transitory and so, subjects asked to give retrospective reports have to fall back on inferences based on their implicit causal theories of behaviour. Under more favourable conditions, such as in Newell and Simon's (1972) study of cryptarithmetic problem-solving, Ericsson's (1975) own studies of 8-puzzle performance, and De Groot's (1965) studies of chess play, concurrent verbal reports appear quite consistent with behaviour and lead to coherent models of underlying processes.

From Ericsson and Simon's analysis, it follows that processes not using working memory will not be reportable. This would be true for highly practised sequences of operations. Beginners at writing say, would perhaps be able to report how they wrote a "t", at least to the level of "draw vertical" then "put cross bar through vertical", whereas skilled writers would probably not be able to say with confidence which operation had been carried out first. Highly practised motor sequences become "automatic" and seem to run off as wholes without reference to working memory. Of course, this is a generally useful development, though it can contribute to accidents since intermediate steps are not monitored and may be based on assumptions that no longer hold (*see* for instance, Reason, 1979; and Norman, 1981a, on behavioural slips and accidents). On this view, the depth of detail with which processes can be verbally reported will depend on their degree of automaticity. Where subprocesses have not been "compiled" or automatized into larger wholes, extensive detail would be expected. A further point of contention lies in Nisbett and Wilson's claim that although mental *processes* can never be reported, mental *contents* can sometimes be reported. This may be disputed. For example, if we set people the task of multiplying 11 × 15 while thinking aloud, the labels of various processes are likely to be mentioned, e.g. "*multiply* 5 × 11" or "*add* 15 to 150". Reports will tend to mention inputs, outputs *and* process labels. Admittedly, if we ask "how did you multiply 5 by 11" the answer will likely be "I don't know how—I just know it's 55". The relevant "look up" or retrieval process from long-term memory is automatized in the practised numerate person. It seems that processes *can* be reported, down to the level of those component subprocesses that have been automatized.

Overall then, it seems that much information on mental contents and processes can be accurately reported, in the proper conditions, up to the point at which automatized subprocesses come into play. The proper conditions include both the conditions of the main task and of the verbalization task. For accurate reports the task must not be too highly practised and free concurrent verbalization should be used since this will be much more likely to yield valid introspective reports than delayed retrospections to vague or inappropriate probes.

Thus, on the issue of serial *v.* parallel processing, it appears that the data from studies of subjective report validity are not absolutely decisive. In certain circumstances, detailed by Ericsson and Simon, and summarized above, valid reports of working memory contents, including process labels, can be given, in accord with the serialist position. A parallel model would interpret cases of valid verbal reporting to mean that, in the appropriate circumstances, behaviour is controlled by the introspectible main sequence. What of inaccurate verbal reports? The serialist position could account for many of these cases in terms of delays in reporting short lived working memory contents, leading to retrospective rationalizations rather than to valid introspections, since the relevant information may have been lost before the query was made. Also, failures to report accurately may be due to the relevant processes being automatized and so not using working memory. The parallel alternative would propose that the effective processes were unconscious in the cases of inaccurate verbal reports and so were never available even for concurrent reports. In the face of the controversy over verbal report accuracy, it may be noted that an obvious research possibility is to carry out the relevant experiments reported by Nisbett and Wilson, but to obtain verbal reports in accord with the conditions that Ericsson and Simon deem ideal for valid introspective reports. If the results remained as before (i.e. inaccurate reports) then the view that important thought processes can be unconscious and parallel to the conscious stream would be upheld. In the absence of such experiments, perhaps a resolution of the serial v. parallel issue might be obtained by looking at the broad context of human information processing? Within this wider area (including sensory-motor skills, for instance) a number of theorists have proposed schemes that incorporate parallel processes, yet still possess a degree of orderliness. The serialist position in thinking has generally derided the parallel alternative, as being a recipe for chaos, while the opposite insult is that the serial model is mechanistically single-minded. In conflicts like this, compromise positions are worth exploring and I will briefly consider some possible mergers of parallel and serial views.

3 Orderly parallelism?
The favourite analogy for an orderly parallel system is probably that of the bureaucracy. In bureaucratic systems, upper levels decide on broad forms of action while lower levels attend to the details. The various levels inter-communicate information and instructions. Most interestingly, the subsystems at each level can work simultaneously and largely independently of each other.

So, while the chief executive of a large company is pondering the next five-year plan, numerous shop floor workers, clerks and intermediate level managers pursue their own functions. The levels must interact, of course, to avoid chaos developing. Thus, the upper levels have to monitor lower level performance, send instructions down the line and receive information from below. Instructions from above are only as detailed as need be since they can be unpacked by lower level specialists. So if the top level decrees, "increase production of Brand Y and phase out Brand X", lower level specialists will attend to the details of say, increasing orders of some raw materials and reducing others, shifting workers and changing equipment, etc.

Indeed the upper levels do not need to know how the lower levels actually execute their orders ("principle of executive ignorance", Becker, 1975). Similarly, on this type of model, within an individual person an upper level process may initiate an action sequence (e.g. picking up a cup), but no information about the lower-level, detailed sensory-motor processes that execute the sequence is available to the upper levels.

The motivation for multilevel parallel models of human information processing becomes more apparent if one steps back from the "thinking" domain and looks more broadly at human behaviour. The "thinker", after all, may be driving a car, walking, or carrying out any other routine activity at the same time as mentally exploring a chess problem. These abilities to carry out two or more tasks simultaneously can be readily explained in terms of different levels and types of processing which can procede simultaneously as long as they do not require the same input and output channels. The multi-level approach explains why some task combinations are easier than others (i.e. those not requiring the same input and output channels) and also helps explain why drugs and stress may have unexpected effects, e.g. depressants, such as alcohol, may knock out an upper level and lead to increased activity by lower level processes normally controlled by the upper (*see* Broadbent, 1977, for very relevant general discussion), producing the apparent paradox of a depressant drug increasing overt activity rather than decreasing it. These points about task compatibility and differential (and unexpected) effects of drugs, stress, fatigue, brain damage and so on, do not seem to be so readily met by the thorough going serialist proposal that *all* appearances of parallel activity are due to the "time sharing" of a single central processor.

Approaching the question from the neuropsychological angle, a number of theorists have put forward possible schemes of parallel neural activity (e.g. Arbib, 1972, and Shallice, 1972; 1978). The brain, of which thought is a product, appears to be highly parallel in its operations and Allport (1980a) has recently argued strongly in favour of the view that processing is distributed throughout the brain. On the bases of neurological data, of experiments on divided attention (e.g. Spelke, Hirst and Neisser, 1976), and of production systems notions in AI, Allport proposes that the human information processing system can best be represented by a highly parallel model in which productions can "fire" independently and simultaneously. On this scheme no central processor is required. A "withering away" of the executive is attractive in view of the unfortunate homuncular properties of the "central processor/executive" in most prior models. Conflicts between productions calling for the same output systems could be handled by means of other productions which are triggered by conflict states and which specialize in resolving conflicts. Thus a special executive or decision maker does not need to be postulated since the decision making functions can be taken over by production rules identical in form to all the other production rules stored in long-term memory.

Given this approach, what limits might there be on parallel mental activity? Allport (1980b) suggests that various forms of inter-process interference impose limitations. Physically incompatible actions cannot occur simultaneously and so must be "queued" or alternated. Slightly more subtly, on the production system approach, if two activities have similar conditions, there is a grave risk of "cross talk" such that the stimuli meant to be dealt with by activity 1 actually elicit activity 2 and vice versa. Such "data-specific" limitations would clearly restrict the degree to which the activities concerned could be carried out effectively in parallel with each other.

How might these limitations affect thinking? In the case of problem solving, it may well be that data-specific limitations would restrict parallel, mental exploration of alternative courses of action within a single problem. If parallel exploration was attempted then the productions involved in generating and assessing the different alternatives would be in danger of calling on similar data (i.e. the task definitions) and so interfere with one other. So simultaneous exploration of different lines of attack on the same problem seems unlikely. However, when a problem has been thoroughly familiarized and can be explored mentally without references to outside sensory channels or to external memories *and* the main stream of thought is concerned with some other goal, it is possible that some work could take place on the familiarized problem in parallel with the main stream. These conditions for successful parallel streams of thought are essentially those reported for successful incubation. So, although this particular parallel processing approach does not predict simultaneous thought streams on the same problem, it would be compatible with some parallel thinking on different problems. In conclusion it seems that a broad range of data favours a parallel or distributed processing approach to human information handling but there are severe limits on the degree of parallelism in thinking. Thus, in many cases, especially of directed thinking, a serial model will be consistent with the data.

II. THEORETICAL PROGRESS?

Has the information processing approach to thinking led to genuine progress in our understanding of thought? Certainly, within the framework of the modal model, H. A. Simon and his colleagues at Carnegie-Mellon University have succeeded in interpreting an ever widening range of thinking tasks over the last 25 years or so. Their task analyses have ranged from symbolic logic (Newell, Shaw and Simon, 1958), cryptarithmetic, chess (Newell and Simon, 1972), and understanding task instructions (Simon and Hayes, 1976) to the accuracy of introspective data (Ericsson and Simon, 1980). So, it would seem that steady progress has been demonstrated by this research team. However, as discussed in the previous sections, there is some dissatisfaction with the limited, rather one-dimensional, perspective of the modal model. It seems that richer models are under development and that the serial model will be encompassed as a special case within a broader, distributed processing scheme. However, even should such a theoretical development occur, the work of the Carnegie-Mellon group will still have been very useful and their model will survive as a special case.

Despite the good example of the Carnegie-Mellon group, it must be admitted that the thinking field of research could be accused, with some justice, of being excessively "phenomenon-driven" and not sufficiently concerned with general theory (as Newell, 1973, charged of cognitive psychology in general). It is quite easy to list a string of phenomena that have attracted research e.g. "state-action problems"; "memory for game positions"; "atmosphere effect"; "matching bias"; "verification set"; "intrusive thoughts"; "incubation"; "brain storming" and "introspective accuracy" among others. Unfortunately, a truly general theory that would tie these topics together convincingly is lacking. Although some theoretical progress has been made, particularly by the Carnegie-Mellon group, and distributed processing notions look promising, the overall problem of accounting for thought in all its manifestations still stands as a challenge to future researchers and theorists.

III. RESEARCH TRENDS?

Will future research be essentially "more of the same"? Recent concerns about the state of the field suggest that a change in emphasis away from laboratory settings is likely.

It is notable that many of the studies reviewed in earlier chapters used very artificial tasks (e.g. missionaries-and-cannibals; Wason's 4 card task). Arguments for using simple, artificial materials are generally in terms of equating subjects' prior task experience and helping to ensure uniform interpretations of task materials. Of course, experimenters hope that the artificial tasks do reflect aspects of real life problem-solving such as, "looking ahead" or "testing hypotheses". In Neisser's (1976) terminology, "ecological validity" is hoped for—but it is rarely demonstrated. To complement laboratory studies, it could be very worthwhile to examine more cases of real life problem-solving. For instance, Mitroff's (1974) study of moon scientists indicated that "verification" tendencies were by no means limited to artificial laboratory conditions. This study also helped explain why verification tendencies arise in view of the positive, motivating functions of a personal commitment to a hypothesis. Furthermore, Mitroff highlighted the long-term and social dimensions of much real life problem-solving—factors which have generally been ignored in laboratory investigations. So, it would seem desirable for more effort to go into studies of real life problem-solving and thinking.

Signs of increasing efforts to tap real life thinking may be found in Klinger's (1978) work, using thought sampling methods, on thinking in natural settings, including basketball play (Klinger, Barta and Glas, 1981), in Reitman's studies of computer programming skill (McKeither, Reitman, Reuter and Hirtle, 1981), and in Csikszentmihalyi's (1975) research on the experience of self-motivated problem-solving. Csikszentmihalyi found that people reported very enjoyable "flow" experiences when totally absorbed in self-set problems that matched their skill levels. So, the mountaineer, the chess player and the surgeon for instance, find enormous satisfaction when they are working on problems just within their skill limits. If the problems are too easy, boredom results and if they are too difficult, anxiety is produced. A better understanding of motivation for problem-solving may come from such out-of-the-laboratory studies. In the laboratory, the motivation is supplied by an outside agent, the experimenter. It may be that the levels of performance obtained (e.g. depth of look-ahead) would be much greater with self-motivation and when the problem is enjoyed for its own sake. That problem-solving is often enjoyable is evident from the reports cited by Csikszentmihalyi and also from the high circulation figures of puzzle magazines, the enduring popularity of crossword puzzles and the recent success of the Rubik cube and derivatives thereof.

As a part of the increasing concern with real life thinking there may well be more emphasis on applied research aimed at training problem tackling skills. Of course, a certain amount of research of this type has been carried out, especially into idea-production techniques, such as brainstorming and synectics. There have also been courses at some North American universities in more "directed" forms of techniques (e.g. use of search trees, problem reduction, means-end analysis, etc.). Although promising, these latter courses have not been subject to much evaluation and there is considerable debate (Tuma and Reif, 1980) about the relative utility of teaching general problem-solving methods (which are usually "weak" in practice) as against area-specific knowledge (which may be very limited in application). At any event, the area of teaching problem-solving skills seems likely to be a major target of future research on thinking.

Finally, as Simon has recently pointed out (1981) the search for *the* way in which people tackle particular problems is likely to broaden into research concerned with the *variety* of strategies employed by different individuals and by the same individual at different times. Signs of such developments may be found in Charness's studies in chess (1981a, b, c) and in Anzai and Simon's work on the Tower of Hanoi task (1980).

IV. CONCLUDING COMMENTS

I will finish by summarizing very briefly my conclusions about the recent past and the possible future of studies of thinking. Although the serial model of human thinking has coped with a wide range of data, there are anomalies (e.g. incubation; intrusive thoughts), that tax the serial scheme. These, together with difficulties for the general serialist framework (e.g. Allport, 1980a, b) suggest that there will be an increasing trend toward explicitly parallel or distributed processing models. In terms of research techniques, more out-of-laboratory studies seem likely and would be very useful complements to laboratory methods. Finally, it is expected that the future will see both an increased emphasis on individual differences and the growth of an applied psychology of thinking which could lead to soundly based methods of training in problem solving skills.

V. FURTHER READING

Miller, G. A. (1981). Trends and debates in cognitive psychology. *Cognition* **10**, 215–225.

One of the pioneers in the field reviews the progress of the information processing approach. Miller includes a discussion of the validity of verbal reports that may be found to be a useful adjunct to the treatment of this issue in this text.

Norman, D. A. (1981b). Twelve issues for cognitive science. *In* "Perspectives on cognitive science" (*Ed.* D. A. Norman), pp. 265–296. Ablex Publishing Corporation, New Jersey.

A leading figure in the field outlines his view of promising lines of development in cognitive research, including thinking.

References

(Nos. in square brackets give the page numbers where the references are mentioned in this text.)

Adamson, R. E. and Taylor, D. W. (1954). Functional fixedness as related to elapsed time and set. *Journal of Experimental Psychology* **147**, 122-126. [9]

Albert, R. S. (1975). Toward a behavioral definition of genius. *American Psychologist* **30**, 140-151. [124]

Allport, D. A. (1980a). Patterns and actions: Cognitive mechanisms are content-specific. *In* "Cognitive Psychology" (*Ed.* G. Claxton), pp 26-64. Routledge and Kegan Paul, London. [159, 163]

Allport, D. A. (1980b). Attention and performance. *In* "Cognitive Psychology" (*Ed.* G. Claxton), pp 112-153. Routledge and Kegan Paul, London. [160, 163]

Anderson, J. R. (1978). Arguments concerning representations for mental imagery. *Psychological Review* **85**, 249-277. [3]

Antrobus, J. S., Singer, J. L. and Greenberg, S. (1966). Studies in the stream of consciousness: Experimental enhancement and suppression of spontaneous cognitive process. *Perceptual and Motor Skills* **23**, 399-417. [108, 110, 120]

Antrobus, J. S., Coleman, R. and Singer, J. L. (1967). Signal detection performance by subjects differing in predisposition to daydreaming. *Journal of Consulting Psychology* **31**, 487-491. [107]

Anzai, Y. and Simon, H. A. (1979). The theory of learning by doing. *Psychological Review* **86**, 124-140. [39, 46, 163]

Arbib, M. (1972). The metaphorical brain. John Wiley and Sons, New York. [159]

Atkinson, R. C. and Shiffrin, R. M. (1968). Human memory: A proposed system and its control process. *In* "The Psychology of Learning and Motivation" (*Eds* K. W. Spence and J. T. Spence), Vol. 2, pp 90-195. Academic Press, London and New York. [150]

Atwood, M. E. and Polson, P. G. (1976). A process model for water jug problems. *Cognitive Psychology* **8**, 191-216. [31]

Atwood, M. E., Masson, M. E. J. and Polson, P. G. (1980). Further exploration with a process model for water jug problems. *Memory and Cognition* **8**, 182-192. [35]

Baddeley, A. D. (1976). *The Psychology of Memory*. Basic Books, New York. [151]

Barron, F. (1955). The disposition toward originality. *Journal of Abnormal and Social Psychology* **51**, 478-485. [125]

Barron, F. and Harrington, D. M. (1981). Creativity, intelligence and personality. *Annual Review of Psychology* **32**, 439-476. [149]

Baylor, G. W. and Gascon, J. (1974). An information processing theory of aspects of the development of weight seriation in children. *Cognitive Psychology* **6**, 1-40. [43]

Becker, J. D. (1975). The formal representation of behaviour. In "Representation and Understanding" (*Eds* D. G. Bobrow and A. Collins). Academic Press, London and New York. [159]

Becker, S., Horowitz, M. and Campbell, L. (1973). Cognitive responses to stress: Effects of changes in demand and sex. *Journal of Abnormal Psychology* **82**, 519-522. [111, 120, 121, 154]

Begg, I. and Denny, J. P. (1969). Empirical reconciliation of atmosphere and conversation interpretations of syllogistic reasoning errors. *Journal of Experimental Psychology* **81**, 351-354. [71, 83]

Bell, A. G. (1978). The machine plays chess? Pergamon Press, Oxford. [50]

Berkowitz, J. (1969). The roots of aggression. Lieber-Atherton, New York. [118]

Berlyne, D. E. (1965). Structure and direction in thinking. John Wiley, New York. [9, 10, 105]

Bhaskhar, R. and Simon, H. A. (1977). Problem solving in semantically rich domains: An example from engineering thermodynamics. *Cognitive Science* **1**, 193-215. [42]

Birch, H. G. (1945). The relation of previous experience to insightful problem solving. *Journal of Comparative Psychology* **38**, 367-383. [7]

Birch, H. G. and Rabinowitz, H. S. (1951). The negative effect of previous experience on productive thinking. *Journal of Experimental Psychology* **41**, 122-126. [9]

Boden, M. A. (1977). Artificial intelligence and natural man. The Harvester Press, Hassocks. [47]

Bouchard, T. J., Jr. (1972). A comparison of two group brainstorming procedures. *Journal of Applied Psychology* **56**, 418-421. [141, 148]

Bouchard, T. J., Jr. and Hare, M. (1970). Size, performance, and potential in brainstorming groups. *Journal of Applied Psychology* **54**, 51-55. [138]

Bower, G. H. (1975). Cognitive psychology: An introduction. In "Handbook of Learning and Cognitive Processes" (Ed. W. K. Estes), Vol. 1. [150]

Bracewell, R. J. (1974). Interpretation factors in the four card selection task. Paper presented at the Selection Task Conference, Trento, Italy, April 17-19. [93]

Bracewell, R. J. and Hidi, S. E. (1974). The solution of an inferential problem as a function of stimulus materials. *Quarterly Journal of Experimental Psychology* **26**, 480-488. [90]

Brilhart, J. K. and Jochem, E. M. (1964). Effects of different patterns on outcomes of problem solving discussions. *Journal of Applied Psychology* **48**, 175-179. [138]

Brown, J. (1958). Some tests of the decay theory of immediate memory. *Quarterly Journal of Experimental Psychology* **10**, 12-21. [57]

Broadbent, D. E. (1977). Levels, hierarchies, and the locus of control. *Quarterly Journal of Experimental Psychology* **29**, 181-201. [159]

Bruner, J. S. (1957). On going beyond the information given. In "Contemporary Approaches to Cognition", pp 41-69. Harvard University Press, Cambridge, Massachusetts. [1]

Bruner, J. S., Goodnow, J. J. and Austin, G. A. (1956). A study of thinking, Wiley, New York. [96]

Cattell, R. B. (1959). The personality and motivation of the researcher from measurements of contemporaries and from biography. *In* "The 1959 University of Utah Research Conference on the Identification of Creative Scientific Talent" (*Ed.* C. W. Taylor) University of Utah Press. [125]

Cattell, R. B. and Drevdahl, J. E. (1955). A comparison of the personality profile (16PF) of eminent researchers with that of eminent teachers and administrators, and of the general population. *British Journal of Psychology* **46**, 248-261. [126, 127]

Ceraso, J. and Provitera, A. (1971). Sources of error in syllogistic reasoning. *Cognitive Psychology* **2**, 400-410. [74, 77, 84]

Chalmers, A. F. (1978). What is this thing called science? The Open University Press, Milton Keynes. [101]

Chapman, J. L. and Chapman, J. P. (1959). Atmosphere effect re-examined. *Journal of Experimental Psychology* **58**, 220-226. [70, 83]

Charness, N. (1976). Memory for chess positions: Resistance to interference. *Journal of Experimental Psychology: Human Learning and Memory* **2**, 641-653. [56, 57, 65]

Charness, N. (1979). Components of skills in bridge. *Canadian Journal of Psychology* **33**, 1-16. [61, 62, 65]

Charness, N. (1981a). Aging and skilled problem solving. *Journal of Experimental Psychology: General* **110**, 21-38. [57, 58, 65, 66, 163]

Charness, N. (1981b). Search in chess: Age and skill differences. *Journal of Experimental Psychology: Human Perception and Performance* **7**, 467-476. [21, 51, 57, 58, 64, 65, 66, 163]

Charness, N. (1981c). Visual short term memory and aging in chess players. *Journal of Gerontology* **36**, 615-619 [58, 65, 163]

Chase, W. G. and Simon, H. A. (1973a). Perception in chess. *Cognitive Psychology* **4**, 55-81 [54, 56, 58]

Chase, W. G. and Simon, H. A. (1973b). The mind's eye in chess. *In* "Visual information processing" (*Ed.* W. G. Chase), pp 215-282. Academic Press, London and New York. [54, 58, 65]

Cohen, L. J. (1981). Can human irrationality be experimentally demonstrated? *Behavioral and Brain Sciences* **4**, 317-331. [103]

Collins, A. M. and Loftus, E. F. (1975). A spreading activation theory of semantic processing. *Psychological Review* **82**, 407-428. [14]

Collins, A. M. and Quillian, M. K. (1969). Retrieval time from semantic memory. *Journal of Verbal Learning and Verbal Behavior* **8**, 240-247. [14]

Craik, K. J. W. (1943). The nature of explanation. Cambridge University Press, Cambridge. [2]

Csikszentmihalyi, M. (1975). Beyond boredom and anxiety. Jossey-Bass, San Francisco. [162]

De Groot, A. D. (1965). Thought and choice in chess. Mouton, The Hague. [10, 21, 51, 53, 58, 64, 132, 151, 156]

Dillon, P. C., Graham, W. K. and Aidells, A. L. (1972). Brainstorming on a "hot" problem: Effects of training and practice on individual and group performance. *Journal of Applied Psychology* **56**, 487-490. [138]

Dominowski, R. L. and Jenrick, R. (1972). Effects of hints and interpolated activity on solution of an insight problem. *Psychonomic Science* **26**, 335-338. [134, 154]

Doran, J. W. and Michie, D. (1965). Experiments with the graph traverser program. *Proceedings of the Royal Society (A)* **294**, 235-259 [22]

Drevdahl, J. E. and Cattell, R. B. (1958). Personality and creativity in artists and writers. *Journal of Clinical Psychology* **14**, 107-111. [126]

Duncker, K. (1945). On problem solving. *Psychological Monographs* **58**, whole No. 270, 1-113. [3, 7, 8, 24, 132]

Dunnette, M. D., Campbell, J. and Jaastad, K. (1963). The effects of group participation on brainstorming effectiveness for two industrial samples. *Journal of Applied Psychology* **47**, 10-37. [137]

Egan, D. W. and Greeno, J. G. (1974). Theories of rule induction: Knowledge acquired in concept learning, serial pattern learning, and problem solving. *In* "Knowledge and Cognition" (*Ed.* L. W. Gregg), pp 43-104. New York. [14, 36]

Eisenstadt, M. and Kareev, Y. (1977). Perception in game playing. *In* "Thinking" (*Eds* P. N. Johnson-Laird and P. C. Wason), pp 548-564. Cambridge University Press, Cambridge. [59]

Engle, R. W. and Bukstel, L. (1978). Memory processes among bridge players of differing expertise. *American Journal of Psychology* **91**, 673-689. [61, 62, 65]

Erickson, J. R. (1974). A set analysis theory of behavior in formal syllogistic reasoning tasks. *In* "Theories of Cognitive Psychology: The Loyola Symposium" (*Ed.* R. Solso). Lawrence Erlbaum Associates, New Jersey. [75, 84, 85]

Erickson, J. R. (1978). Research in syllogistic reasoning. *In* "Human Reasoning" (*Eds* R. Revlin and R. E. Meyer), pp 39-50. John Wiley, New York. [75, 76, 80, 83, 84]

Ericsson, K. A. (1975). Instruction to verbalize as a means to study problem solving processes with the 8-puzzle: A preliminary study. Reports from the Department of Psychology, No. 458, The University of Stockholm, Sweden. [156]

Ericsson, K. A. and Simon, H. A. (1980). Verbal reports as data. *Psychological Review* **87**, 215-251. [152, 154, 155, 156]

Ernst, G. W. and Newell, A. (1969). GPS: A case study in generality and problem solving. Academic Press, New York. [24]

Evans, J. St. B. T. (1972). Interpretation and matching bias in a reasoning task. *Quarterly Journal of Experimental Psychology* **24**, 193-199. [94]

Evans, J. St. B. T. (1977). Towards a statistical theory of reasoning. *Quarterly Journal of Experimental Psychology* **29**, 621-635. [94, 102]

Evans, J. St. B. T. (1980a). Current issues in the psychology of reasoning. *British Journal of Psychology* **71**, 227-239. [94, 105]

Evans, J. St. B. T. (1980b). Thinking: Experimental and information processing approaches. *In* "Cognitive Psychology: New Directions" (*Ed.* G. Claxton), pp 275-299. Routledge and Kegan Paul, London. [95]

Evans, J. St. B. T. and Lynch, J. S. (1973). Matching bias in the selection task. *British Journal of Psychology* **64**, 391-397. [93]

Evans, J. St. B. T. and Wason, P. C. (1976). Rationalization in a reasoning task. *British Journal of Psychology* **67**, 479-486. [94]

Findler, N. (1978). Computer poker. *Scientific American* **239**, 112-119. [63, 65]

Frey, P. W. and Adesman, P. (1976). Recall memory for visually presented chess positions. *Memory and Cognition* **4**, 541-547. [56, 65]

Freud, S. (1900). The interpretation of dreams. *In* "Standard Edition", Vols. IV and V. Hogarth Press, London 1953. (First German edition, 1900). [104, 105, 151]

Frijda, N. H. and De Groot, A. D. (1981). Otto Selz: His contribution to psychology. Mouton Publishers, The Hague. [10]

Fulgosi, A. and Guilford J. P. (1968). Short term incubation in divergent production. *American Journal of Psychology* **81**, 241-246. [134, 148, 154]

Gilhooly, K. J. and Falconer, W. (1974). Concrete and abstract terms and relations in testing a rule. *Quarterly Journal of Experimental Psychology* **26**, 355-359. [90]

Ghiselin, B. (1952). The creative process. University of California Press. [127, 154]

Glucksberg, S. and Danks, J. H. (1968). Effects of discriminative labels. *Journal of Verbal Learning and Verbal Behavior* **7**, 72-76. [9]

Glucksberg, S. and Weisberg, R. W. (1968). Verbal behavior and problem solving. *Journal of Experimental Psychology* **71**, 659-664. [9]

Goethals, G. R. and Reckman, R. F. (1973). The perception of consistency in attitudes. *Journal of Experimental Psychology* **9**, 491-501. [155]

Golding, E. (1980). Non-dominant hemisphere ECT and reasoning. Paper presented at The British Psychological Society annual conference, Aberdeen, Scotland, 27-31 March, 1980. [95]

Golding, E. (1981). The effect of unilateral brain lesion on reasoning. *Cortex* **17**, 31-40. [95]

Golding, W. (1955). The Inheritors. Faber and Faber, London. [123]

Goodwin, R. Q. and Wason, P. C. (1972). Degrees of insight. *British Journal of Psychology* **63**, 205-212. [89, 94]

Gordon, W. J. J. (1961). *Synectics*. Harper, New York. [140, 148]

Gruber, H. E. (1980). Darwin on man: A psychological study of scientific creativity, 2nd edition. University of Chicago Press. [144, 148, 149]

Hayes, J. R. and Simon, H. A. (1974). Understanding written problem instructions. *In* "Knowledge and Cognition" (*Ed.* L. W. Gregg), pp 167-200. Lawrence Erlbaum Associates, Potomac, Md. [44]

Hayes, J. R. and Simon, H. A. (1977). Psychological differences among problem isomorphs. *In* "Cognitive Theory" (*Eds* N. J. Castellan Jr., D. B. Pisoni and D. M. Potts), pp 21-42. Erlbaum, Hillsdale, New Jersey. [45]

Hearst, E. (1977). Man and machine: Chess achievements and chess thinking. *In* "Chess Skill in Man and Machine" (*Ed.* P. W. Frey), pp 167-200. Springer-Verlag, New York. [52]

Henle, M. (1962). On the relation between logic and thinking. *Psychological Review* **69**, 366-378. [72, 73, 84, 85]

Henle, M. (1978). Foreword. *In* "Human Reasoning" (*Eds* R. Revlin and Mayer), pp xiii-xviii. John Wiley, New York. [84]

Hilgard, E. R. (1962). Impulsive versus realistic thinking: An examination of the distinction between primary and secondary processes in thought. *Psychological Bulletin* **59**, 477-489. [105]

Hobbes, T. (1951). *Leviathan*. 1919 edition. p. 9. J. M. Dent and Sons, London. [104, 105]

Hoelscher, T. J., Klinger, E. and Barta, S. G. (1981). Incorporation of concern and nonconcern related verbal stimuli into dream content. *Journal of Abnormal Psychology* **90**, 88-91. [117]

Hudson, L. (1966). Contrary Imaginations. Methuen, London. [126, 147]

Hull, C. L. (1934). The concept of the habit-family hierarchy and maze-learning. *Psychological Review* **41**, 33-52, 134-152. [9]

Hunt, E. (1971). What kind of computer is man? *Cognitive Psychology* **2**, 57-98. [150]

Hunt, E. B. (1973). The memory we must have. *In* "Computer Models of Thought and Language" (*Eds* R. C. Shank and K. M. Colby), pp 343-371. Freeman, San Francisco. [150]

Hunt, E. B., Marin, J. and Stone, P. J. (1966). *Experiments in induction*. Academic Press, London and New York. [102]

James, W. (1980). The principles of psychology. Henry Holt, New York. [104]
Jeffries, R., Polson, P. G., Razran, L. and Atwood, M. E. (1977). A process model for missionaries-cannibals and other river crossing problems. *Cognitive Psychology* 9, 412-420. [33, 46]
Johnson-Laird, P. N. (1975). Models of deduction. *In* "Reasoning: Representation and process" (*Ed.* R. C. Falmagne), pp 7-54. Lawrence Erlbaum Associates, Hillsdale, New Jersey. [77, 80, 84]
Johnson-Laird, P. N. (1981). Mental models in cognitive science. *In* "Perspectives on cognitive science" (*Ed.* D. A. Norman), pp 147-192. Ablex Publishing Corp., New Jersey. [85]
Johnson-Laird, P. N., Legrenzi, P. and Legrenzi, M. S. (1972). Reasoning and a sense of reality. *British Journal of Psychology* 63, 395-400. [91]
Johnson-Laird, P. N. and Steedman, M. (1978). The psychology of syllogisms. *Cognitive Psychology* 10, 64-99. [77, 80, 83, 84]
Johnson-Laird, P. N. and Wason, P. C. (1970). A theoretical analysis of insight into a reasoning task. *Cognitive Psychology* 1, 134-148. [89, 92]
Jones, E. (1961). The life and work of Sigmund Freud (*Eds* L. Trilling and S. Marcus), p. 227. Hogarth, London. [127]
Klinger, E. (1971). Structure and function of fantasy. p. 97. Wiley, New York. [105, 112, 121]
Klinger, E. (1974). Utterances to evaluate steps and control attention distinguish operant from respondent thought while thinking out loud. *Bulletin of the Psychonomic Society* 4, 44-45. [112]
Klinger, E. (1978). Modes of normal conscious flow. *In* "The Stream of Consciousness" (*Eds* K. S. Pope and J. L. Singer), pp 225-258. John Wiley, New York. [112, 114, 116, 117, 121, 162]
Klinger, E. Barta, S. G. and Maxeimer, M. E. (1980). Motivational correlates of thought content frequency and commitment. *Journal of Personality and Social Psychology* 39, 1222-1237. [117]
Klinger, E., Barta, S. G. and Glas, R. (1981). Thought content and gap time in basketball. *Cognitive Therapy and Research* 5, 109-114. [162]
Kochen, M. and Badre, A. N. (1974). Questions and shifts of representation in problem solving. *American Journal of Psychology* 87, 369-383. [4]
Koestler, A. (1964). The act of creation. Hutchinson, London. [127, 143, 148, 149]
Kohler, W. (1925). *The mentality of apes*. Harcourt Brace, New York. [7]
Kosslyn, S. M. (1981). The medium and the message in mental imagery: A theory. *Psychological Review* 88, 46-66. [3, 15]
Kosslyn, S. M. and Pomerantz, J. R. (1977). Imagery, propositions, and the form of internal representations. *Cognitive Psychology* 9, 52-76. [3]
Krechesky, I. (1935). Brain mechanisms and "hypotheses". *Journal of Comparative Psychology* 19, 425-462. [7]
Kripke, D. F. and Sonnenschein, D. (1978). A biologic rhythm in waking fantasy. *In* "The Stream of Consciousness" (*Eds* K. S. Pope and J. L. Singer), pp 321-332. John Wiley, New York. [106]
Laughlin, P. R., Doherty, M. A. and Dunn, R. F. (1968). Intentional and incidental concept formation as a function of motivation, creativity, intelligence and sex. *Journal of Personality and Social Psychology* 8, 401-409. [143]
Legrenzi, P. (1971). Discovery as a means to understanding. *Quarterly Journal of Experimental Psychology* 23, 417-422. [90]
Lehman, H. C. (1953). Age and achievement. Princeton University Press, Princeton, New Jersey. [127]

Levy, D. (1978). Computers are now chess masters. *New Scientist* 27th July, 256–258. [51, 52]

Lopes, L. (1976). Model based decision and inference in stud poker. *Journal of Experimental Psychology: General* **105**, 217–239. [62, 65]

Luchins, A. W. (1942). Mechanization in problem solving: The effect of Einstellung. *Psychological Monographs* **54**, Whole No. 248. [8]

Luger, G. F. (1976). The use of the state-space to record the behavioural effects of subproblems and symmetries on the Tower of Hanoi problem. *International Journal of Man-Machine Studies* **8**, 411–421. [36, 37, 46]

McKellar, P. (1957). Imagination and thinking. Basic Books, New York. [105]

McKeithen, K. B., Reitman, J. S., Rueter, H. H. and Hirtle, S. C. (1981). Knowledge organization and skill differences in computer programmers. *Cognitive Psychology* **13**, 307–325. [162]

MacKinnon, D. W. (1962). The personality correlates of creativity: A study of American architects. *In* "Proceedings of the 14th Congress of Applied Psychology", Vol. 2, pp 11–39. Munksgaard. Excerpts reprinted (1970) *In* "Creativity" (*Ed.* P. E. Vernon). Penguin Books, London. [125]

McLelland, D. C. (1962). On the dynamics of creative physical scientists. *In* "Contemporary Approaches to Creative Thinking" (*Eds* H. E. Gruber, G. Terrell and M. Wertheimer), pp 141–174. Atherton, New York. [126]

Maltzman, I. (1955). Thinking: From a behavioristic point of view. *Psychological Review* **62**, 275–286. [9]

Manktelow, K. I. and Evans, J. St. B. T. (1979). Facilitation of reasoning by realism: Effect or non-effect? *British Journal of Psychology* **70**, 477–488. [91]

Meadow, A., Parnes, S. J. and Reese, H. (1959). Influence of brainstorming instruction and problem sequence on a creative problem solving test. *Journal of Applied Psychology* **43**, 413–416. [135]

Mednick, S. A. (1962). The associative basis of the creative process. *Psychological Review* **69**, 220–232. [141, 148]

Mendelsohn, G. A. and Griswold, B. B. (1964). Differential use of incidental stimuli in problem solving as a function of creativity. *Journal of Abnormal and Social Psychology* **68**, 431–436. [143]

Meskin, B. B. and Singer, J. L. (1974). Daydreaming, reflective thought and laterality of eye movements. *Journal of Personality and Social Psychology* **30**, 64–71. [108]

Miller, G. A. (1956). The magical number seven, plus or minus two: Some limits on our capacity for processing information. *Psychological Review* **63**, 81–87. [12, 54, 65]

Miller, G. A. (1960). Psychology: The science of mental life. Penguin Books, London. [5]

Miller, G. A. (1981). Trends and debates in cognitive psychology. *Cognition* **10**, 215–225. [163]

Miller, G. A., Galanter, E. H. and Pribram, H. H. (1960). *Plans and the structure of behavior*. Holt, New York. [10]

Mitroff, I. I. (1974). The subjective side of science. p. 144. Elsevier, Amsterdam. [101, 103, 126, 147, 162]

Murdock, B. B., Jr. (1971). Short term memory. *In* "The Psychology of Learning and Motivation" (*Ed.* G. Bower), pp 67–127. Academic Press, London and New York. [13]

Murray, H. G. and Denny, J. P. (1969). Interaction of ability level and interpolated activity in human problem solving. *Psychological Reports* **24**, 271–276. [133, 147, 154]

Mynatt, Cr. R., Doherty, M. E. and Tweney, R. D. (1977). Confirmation bias in a simulated research environment: An experimental study of scientific inference. *Quarterly Journal of Experimental Psychology* **29**, 85-95. [98, 102]

Mynatt, C. R., Doherty, M. E. and Tweney, R. D. (1978). Consequences of confirmation and disconfirmation in a simulated research environment. *Quarterly Journal of Experimental Psychology* **30**, 395-406. [98, 100, 102]

Neisser, U. (1963a). The imitation of man by machine. *Science* **139**, 193-197. [153, 154, 155]

Neisser, U. (1963b). The multiplicity of thought. *British Journal of Psychology* **54**, 1-14. [13, 94, 105, 120, 151, 152, 154]

Neisser, U. (1976). Cognition and reality. Freeman, San Francisco. [162]

Newborn, M. M. (1979). Recent progress in computer chess. In "Advances in computers" (*Ed.* M. C. Yovits), **18**, 59-118. Academic Press, London and New York. [66]

Newell, A. (1962). Some problems of basic organization in problem solving programs. In "Self Organizing Systems" (*Eds* M. C. Yovits, G. T. Jacobi and G. D. Goldstein). p. 398. Spartan Books, Washington. [152]

Newell, A. (1973). You can't play 20 questions with nature and win. In "Visual Information Processing" (*Ed.* W. G. Chase), pp 283-302. Academic Press, London and New York. [161]

Newell, A. (1981). Physical symbol systems. In "Perspectives on Cognitive Science" (*Ed.* D. A. Norman), pp 37-86. Ablex Publishing Corp., New Jersey. [15]

Newell, A. and Simon H. A. (1972). Human Problem Solving. Prentice-Hall, Inc., Englewood Cliffs, New Jersey. [14, 21, 40, 46, 48, 50, 51, 121, 156, 161]

Newell, A., Shaw, J. C. and Simon, H. A. (1958). Elements of a theory of human problem solving. *Psychological Review* **65**, 151-166. [161]

Newell, A., Shaw, J. C. and Simon, H. A. (1962). The processes of creative thinking. In "Contemporary Approaches to Creative Thinking" (*Eds* H. E. Gruber, G. Terrell and M. Wertheimer), pp 63-119. Atherton, New York. [23]

Nilsson, N. J. (1971). Problem solving methods in artificial intelligence. McGraw-Hill, New York. [18]

Nisbett, R. E. and Wilson, T. D. (1977). Telling more than we can know: verbal reports on mental processes. *Psychological Review* **84**, 231-259. [155]

Norman, D. A. (1981a). Categorization of action slips. *Psychological Review* **88**, 1-15. [157]

Norman, D. A. (1981b). Twelve issues for cognitive science. In "Perspectives on cognitive science" (*Ed.* D. A. Norman), pp 265-275. Ablex Publishing Corp., New Jersey. [163]

Oldfield, R. C. (1966). Things, words and the brain. *Quarterly Journal of Experimental Psychology* **18**, 340-353. [56]

Osborn, A. F. (1953). Applied Imagination. Scribners, New York. [135]

Parnes, S. J. and Meadow, A. (1963). Development of individual creative talent. In "Scientific creativity: Its recognition and development" (*Eds* C. W. Taylor and F. Barron). Wiley, New York. [136]

Patrick, C. (1935). Creative thought in poets. *Archives of Psychology* **26**, 73. [131, 147]

Patrick, C. (1937). Creative thought in artists. *Journal of Psychology* **4**, 35-73. [131, 132, 147, 154]

Peterson, C. R. and Peterson, M. J. (1959). Short-term retention of individual verbal items. *Journal of Experimental Psychology* **58**, 193-198. [57]

Platt, J. R. (1964). Strong inference. *Science* **146**, 347-353. [98]

Poincare, H. (1908). Science et Methode. Flammarion, Paris. [128, 134]
Pollard, P. and Evans, J. St. B. T. (1981). The effect of prior beliefs in reasoning: An associational interpretation. *British Journal of Psychology* **72**, 73-82. [91]
Pope, K. S. and Singer, J. L. (1978). Regulation of the stream of consciousness: Toward a theory of ongoing thought. *In* "Consciousness and Self-regulation" (*Eds* G. E. Schwartz and D. Shapiro), Vol. 2, pp 101-138. John Wiley, New York. [114, 120, 121]
Popper, K. R. (1959). The logic of scientific discovery. Hutchinson, London. [97]
Pylyshyn, Z. W. (1973). What the mind's eye tells the mind's brain: a critique of mental imagery. *Psychological Bulletin* **80**, 1-24. [2]
Pylyshyn, Z. W. (1981). The imagery debate: analogue media versus tacit knowledge. *Psychological Review* **88**, 16-45. [3, 15]
Quillian, M. R. (1968). Semantic memory. *In* "Semantic Information Processing" (*Ed*. M. Minsky). MIT Press, Cambridge, Massachusetts. [13]
Raphael, B. (1976). The thinking computer. W. H. Freeman, San Francisco. [36]
Reason, J. (1979). Actions not as planned: the price of automatization. *In* "Aspects of Consciousness" (*Eds* G. Underwood and K. Stevens), pp 67-90. Academic Press, London and New York. [157]
Reitman, W. R. (1965). Cognition and Thought. Wiley, New York. [3, 4, 120]
Reitman, J. (1976). Skilled perception in Go: deducing memory structures from inter-response times. *Cognitive Psychology* **8**, 336-356. [59, 65]
Restle, F. and Davis, J. H. (1962). Success and speed of problem solving by individuals and groups. *Psychological Review* **69**, 520-536. [29]
Roe, A. (1952). A psychologist examines sixty-four eminent scientists. *Scientific American* **187**, 21-25. [125, 147]
Ruger, H. (1910). The psychology of efficiency. *Archives of Psychology (New York)* **15**, [6]
Sells, S. B. (1936). The atmosphere effect: An experimental study of reasoning. *Archives of Psychology* **200**, 1-72. [70]
Sells, S. B. and Koob, H. F. (1937). A classroom demonstration of "atmosphere effect" in reasoning. *Journal of Educational Psychology* **72**, 197-200. [70]
Shallice, T. (1972). Dual functions of consciousness. *Psychological Review* **79**, 383-393. [159]
Shallice, T. (1978). The dominant action system: an information-processing approach to consciousness. *In* "The stream of consciousness" (*Eds* K. S. Pope and J. L. Singer) pp 117-158. John Wiley, New York. [159]
Shannon, C. (1950). Programming a computer to play chess. *Philosophy Magazine* **41**, 256-275. [51]
Shapiro, D. (1971). "Representativeness", structure and content in a reasoning problem. *Bulletin of the British Psychological Society* **24**, 43-44. [101]
Shepard, R. N. and Metzler, J. (1971). Mental rotation of three-dimensional objects. *Science* **171**, 701-703. [2]
Simon, H. A. (1966). Scientific discovery and the psychology of problem solving. *In* "Mind and Cosmos: Essays in Contemporary Science and Philosophy" (*Ed*. R. G. Colodny). University of Pittsburgh Press, Pittsburgh. [146, 148, 151, 154]
Simon, H. A. (1967). Motivational and emotional controls of cognition. *Psychological Review* **74**, 29-39. [152, 153, 155]
Simon, H. A. (1975). The functional equivalence of problem solving skills. *Cognitive Psychology* **7**, 268-288. [37, 40]
Simon, H. A. (1979). Information processing models of cognition. *Annual Review of Psychology* **30**, 363-396. [47]

Simon, H. A. (1981). Cognitive science: the newest science of the artificial. *In* "Perspectives on cognitive science (*Ed*. D. A. Norman), pp 13-26. Ablex Publishing Corp., New Jersey. [15, 163]

Simon, H. and Barenfeld, M. (1969). Information-processing analysis of perceptual processes in problem solving. *Psychological Review* **76**, 473-483. [55]

Simon, H. and Gilmartin, K. (1973). A simulation of memory for chess positions. *Cognitive Psychology* **8**, 165-190. [55, 65]

Simon, H. A. and Hayes, J. R. (1976). The understanding process: problem isomorphs. *Cognitive Psychology* **8**, 165-190. [4, 45, 46, 81, 83, 84, 161]

Simon, H. A. and Reed, S. K. (1976). Modelling strategy shifts on a problem solving task. *Cognitive Psychology* **8**, 86-97. [29]

Singer, J. L. (1975a). Navigating the stream of consciousness: Research in daydreaming and related inner experience. *American Psychologist* **30**, 727-738. [105, 107, 120, 121, 151]

Singer, J. L. (1975b). Daydreaming and fantasy. pp 113-114. Allen and Unwin, London. [105, 118, 119, 120, 122]

Singer, J. L. (1978). Studies of daydreaming. *In* "The Stream of Consciousness" (*Eds* K. S. Pope and J. L. Singer), pp 187-223. John Wiley, New York. [105, 120, 122]

Singer, J. L. and Antrobus, J. S. (1972). Daydreaming, imaginal processes, and personality: A normative study. *In* "The function and nature of imagery" (*Ed*. P. Sheeham). Academic Press, London and New York. [106]

Singer, J. L. and McCraven, V. (1961). Some characteristics of adult daydreaming. *Journal of Psychology* **51**, 151-164. [106]

Smalley, N. S. (1974). Evaluating a rule against possible instances. *British Journal of Psychology* **65**, 293-304. [92]

Spelke, E., Hirst, W. and Neisser, U. (1976). Skills of divided attention. *Cognition* **4**, 215-230. [159]

Spence, K. W. (1936). The nature of discrimination learning in animals. *Psychological Review* **43**, 427-449. [7]

Sperling, G. A. (1960). The information available in brief visual presentation. *Psychological Monographs* **74**, Whole No. 498 [150]

Stein, M. (1974). Stimulating Creativity. Vol. 1, p. 189. Academic Press, London and New York. [124, 134, 140]

Stein, M. (1975). Stimulating Creativity. Vol. 2. Academic Press, London and New York. [134, 138, 148]

Taylor, D. W., Berry, P. C. and Block, C. H. (1958). Does group participation when using brainstorming facilitate or inhibit creative thinking? *Administrative Science Quarterly* **3**, 23-47. [136]

Thomas, J. C. Jnr. (1974). An analysis of behavior in the hobbits-orcs problem. *Cognitive Psychology* **6**, 257-269. [25, 34]

Thorndike, E. L. (1898). Animal Intelligence. Macmillan, New York. [6]

Thouless, R. H. (1953). Straight and Crooked Thinking. pp 24. Pan Books, London. [73]

Tolkien, J. R. R. (1966). The Hobbit. 3rd edition. Allen and Unwin, London. [25]

Tuma, D. T. and Reif, R. (Eds) (1980). Problem solving and education: issues in teaching and research. Lawrence Erlbaum Associates, Hillsdale, New Jersey. [162]

Van Duyne, P. C. (1974). Realism and linguistic complexity in reasoning. *British Journal of Psychology* **65**, 59-67. [91]

Van Duyne, P. C. (1976). Necessity and contingency in reasoning. *Acta Psychologica* **40**, 85-101. [91]

Varendonck, J. (1921). The Psychology of Daydreams. Macmillan, New York. [105]

Vernon, P. E. (1970). Creativity. pp 57-60. Penguin Books, London. [127, 128]

Von Neumann, T. and Morgenstern, O. (1944). Theory of games and economic behavior. Princeton University Press, Princeton. [48]

Wagner, D. A. and Scurrah, M. J. (1971). Some characteristics of human problem solving in chess. *Cognitive Psychology* **2**, 451-478. [21, 51]

Wallas, G. (1926). The Art of Thought. p. 81. Jonathan Cape, London. [129, 130, 147]

Warren, T. F. and Davis, G. A. (1969). Techniques for creative thinking: an empirical comparison of three methods. *Psychological Reports* **25**, 207-214. [139, 148]

Wason, P. C. (1960). On the failure to eliminate hypotheses in a conceptual task. *The Quarterly Journal of Experimental Psychology* **12**, 129-140. [97, 100]

Wason, P. C. (1966). Reasoning. *In* "New Horizons in Psychology" (*Ed.* B. M. Foss). Penguin, London. [86]

Wason, P. C. (1968). Reasoning about a rule. *Quarterly Journal of Experimental Psychology* **20**, 273-281. [86, 90]

Wason, P. C. (1969). Regression in reasoning? *British Journal of Psychology* **60**, 471-480. [89]

Wason, P. C. and Evans, J. St. B. T. (1975). Dual processes in reasoning? *Cognition* **3**, 141-154. [93, 102]

Wason, P. C. and Johnson-Laird, P. N. (1970). A conflict between selecting and evaluating information in an inferential task. *British Journal of Psychology* **61**, 509-515. [89]

Wason, P. C. and Johnson-Laird, P. N. (1972). Psychology of Reasoning: Structure and Content. pp 139. Batsford, London. [72, 75]

Wason, P. C. and Shapiro, D. (1971). Natural and contrived experience in a reasoning problem. *Quarterly Journal of Experimental Psychology* **23**, 63-71. [90]

Watson, J. B. (1913). Psychology as the behaviorist views it. *Psychological Review* **20**, 158-177. [5]

Wertheimer, M. (1945). Productive Thinking. Harper and Row, New York. [6]

Wetherick, N. E. (1970). On the representativeness of some experiments in cognition. *Bulletin of the British Psychological Society* **23**, 213-214. [101]

Wetherick, N. E. (1971). "Representatives" in a reasoning problem: a reply to Shapiro. *Bulletin of the British Psychological Society* **24**, 213-214. [101]

Wetherick, N. E. (1979). The foundations of psychology. *In* "Philosophical Problems in Psychology" (*Ed.* N. Bolton), pp 89-110. Methuen, London. [2]

Wickelgren, W. (1974). How to solve problems. pp 85-88. W. H. Freeman, San Francisco. [18, 47]

Wilkins, M. (1928). The effect of changed material on ability to do formal syllogistic reasoning. *Archives of Psychology* **16**, 83. [68, 72]

Williams, G. F. (1971). A model of memory in concept learning. *Cognitive Psychology* **2**, 158-184. [102]

Winograd, T. (1972). Understanding natural language. *Cognitive Psychology* **3**, 1-191. [14]

Winston, P. H. (1975). Learning structural descriptions from examples. *In The Psychology of Computer Vision* (*Ed.* P. H. Winston). McGraw-Hill, New York. [102]

Winston, P. H. (1977). Artificial Intelligence. Addison-Wesley, New York. [22]

Woodworth, R. S. and Sells, S. B. (1935). An atmosphere effect in formal syllogistic reasoning. *Journal of Experimental Psychology* **18**, 451–460. [69]

Woodworth, R. S. and Schlosberg, H. (1954). *Experimental Psychology*, 3rd Edition, p. 838. Methuen, London. [128, 134, 154]

Young, R. (1974). Production systems as models of cognitive development. *Bionics Research Reports* **No. 22**. Bionics Research Laboratory, School of Artificial Intelligence, University of Edinburgh. [43]

Zangwill, O. L. (1980). Kenneth Craik: the man and his work. *British Journal of Psychology* **71**, 1–16. [2]

Zimbardo, P. G., Cohen, A., Weisenberg, M., Dworkin, L. and Firestone, I. (1969). The control of experimental pain. *In* "The Cognitive Control of Motivation" (*Ed*. P. G. Zimbardo). Scott, Foresman: Glenview, Illinois. [155]

Zimbardo, P. G., Weisenberg, M., Firestone, I. and Levy, B. (1969). Changing appetites for eating fried grasshoppers with cognitive dissonance. *In* P. G. Zimbardo (Ed.), "The Cognitive Control of Motivation" (*Ed*. P. G. Zimbardo). Scott, Foresman: Glenview, Illinois. [155]

Zwicky, F. (1969). Discovery, invention, research. Macmillan, New York. [139, 148]

Index

A

Age
  chess ability and, 57–58
  creativity and, 127
Aggressiveness, 126–127, 147
Algorithms, 21
Analogy, in creative thinking, 140–141, 148
Approaches to thinking, 4–14
  behaviourism, 5–6
  Gestalt, 6–9
  information processing, 10–14
  introspectionism, 5
  neo-behaviourism, 9–10
Arithmetic series task, 6
Automatized processes, 157–158

B

Best first search, 22
Breadth first search, 20–21, 151
Bridge memory tasks, 61–62

C

Candle problem, 8
Catharsis, 118–120
Chess
  age and skill in, 57–58
  artificial intelligence approaches to, 49–51
  Bernstein chess program, 50
  chess 4–6 program, 50–51
  chunk sizes in, 54–55
  depth of processing in, 57
  expertise, nature of, 51–55, 57–58, 151
  human play of, 51–59
  maniac chess program, 49
  memory and perception in, 53–57, 64–65
  memory aided pattern-perceiver model, 55–57
  perceiver program, 55
  search in, 51–53, 58, 64
Chunking, 54, 151
Concept learning, 95–97, 100
Conditional rules, *see* Four card selection problem
Confirmation bias, *see* Verification bias
Convergent thinking, 126, 147
Creative processes, 123–149
  brainstorming, 134–138, 148
  checklists, 139–140, 148
  Gruber's Piagetian approach, 144–146, 148
  incubation experiments, 133–134, 147–148
  Koestler's bisociative theory, 143–144, 148
  Mednick's associative theory, 141–143, 148
  morphological synthesis, 139–140, 148
  personal accounts, 127–129, 147
  psychometric studies, 125–127, 147
  Simon's information processing approach, 146–147, 148–149
  synectics, 140–141, 148
  Wallas's stage analysis, 129–131, 131–132, 147
Cryptarithmetic tasks, 40–43

D

Darwin, development of his ideas, 144–145, 148
Daydreaming, 104–122, 152
  "bad news", effects on, 110–111
  conceptual model of, 120
  experimental approaches, 108–120

frequency of, 105-106
functions of, 118-119
induction principle, 116-118
normal thought flow, 114-116
protocol analysis, 112-114
psychometric approaches to, 105-107
stress effects, 111-112
styles of, 106-107
task demands, 108-109
thought sampling studies, 114-118
validity of questionnaires, 107-108
Depth first search, 19-20, 151
Divergent thinking, 126, 134

E

Ecological validity, 162
Eight-puzzle task, 18-19, 20-21, 22
Evaluation functions, 22, 33, 34, 35, 50, 58
"Executive ignorance" principle, 159

F

Familiarization, 146, 149, 151
Falsification, 87, 100-102
"Flow" experiences, 162
Four card selection problem, 86-95, 100-101
  basic results, 88-89
  explanation of task, 86-88
  insight model, 91-92
  interpretation factors, 92-93
  matching bias in, 93-95
  procedural variations, 89-91
  thematic effect in, 90-91
Functional fixity, 8

G

Game trees, 48-49
General Problem Solver program, 24
Go and Go-moku, 59-61

H

Habit family hierarchies, 9-10
Helmholtz, H., on creativity, 128
Hemispheres, cortical, 95, 108
Heuristics, 18, 80, 146
Hobbits-orcs problem, 25-29
Hypothesis generation, 86, 95-100
Hypothesis testing, 86, 95-100, 101-102
Hypothetico-deductive method, 86

I

Illumination or inspiration stage, 130, 131, 147
Implication rules, *see* Four card selection problem
Incubation stage, 130, 132, 133-134, 147, 148, 154-155
Information processing approach, 10-14
  artificial intelligence, 13-14
  basic notions, 10-11
  capacity limitations, 12-13
  simulation, 11
Insight, 6-8, 91-92
Intrusive thoughts, 111

L

List structures, 45, 81, 83
Long-term memory, 12, 55, 56, 65, 66, 85, 120, 121, 150, 151-152

M

Means-end analysis, 23-24
Mediation, in creative thinking, 142-143, 148
Minimax principle, 48-49
Missionaries-and-cannibals tasks, 25-31, 33-35
  see also Hobbits-orcs problem
Move problems, 25-40

N

New vehicle problem, 139
"Nominal group" effect, 136-138
Noticing processes, 152

P

Poincaré, H., on creativity, 127-128, 134
Poker play, 62-64
  draw poker, 63-64
  stud poker, 62-63
Preparation stage, 129, 131, 147
Problem Behaviour Graphs (PBGs), 41-43
Problem reduction
  problem reduction approach, 22-24
  Tower of Hanoi, 35-39
Problems
  adversary problems, 48-66
  adversary *v.* non-adversary, 4

definitions, 3-4
non-adversary problems, 16-47
problem space, 40-41, 43
state-action representations, 17-22
well v. ill defined, 3
Production systems, 43, 53, 65, 159-160
Progressive deepening, 21, 52, 132, 151
Puzzle box task, 6

Q
"Quantity effects", 135, 137

R
Rationalizations, 94, 103
Reasoning
 deductive, 67-85
 inductive, 86-103
Repetition compulsion, 111-112
Reversed 20 questions task, 97, 100-101

S
Saugstad's ball task, 133
Selective forgetting, 146, 148, 149
Serendipity, 141-142
Serial v. parallel processing, 13, 85, 102, 120, 121-122, 147, 152-155, 155-158, 158-160
Set effects, 8, 89, 90, 133-134
Short term memory, 54, 55, 56-57, 65
 see also Working memory
Simulated research environments, 97-100, 102
State-action representation, 17-22
 basic search methods, 19-22
 graphs and trees, 17-19
Syllogisms
 ambiguity of premises in, 74, 75, 85
 figures of, 76-77
 moods of, 79
 validity of, 67-68
Syllogistic reasoning, 67-85
 analogical model, 77-83, 84
 "atmosphere" effects, 69-70, 71-72
 concreteness effects in, 68-69
 conversion errors in, 70-71, 83
 Erickson's set-theoretic model, 75-77
 figural bias effect in, 77, 79
 Henle's defense of "rationality" in, 73-74, 84
 premise misinterpretation, 74-75, 84
 probabilistic inference in, 70-71, 83

T
Tchaikovsky, P.I., on creativity, 128-129
Teachers problem, 136-137
Thinking
 definition, 1-3
 directedness in, 104-105, 113, 115, 121
 internal symbolic models, 1-2, 63, 64, 65
 modalities, 2-3
 modal model, 13, 150-160
 primary and secondary process, 104
 research trends, 161-163
 theoretical progress, 160-161
 type I and II processes, 94-95, 102-103, 105
Thumbs problem, 136-137
Time sharing, 153
Tourists problem, 136-137
Tower of Hanoi problem, 35-40
Travelling salesman task, 18
Trial-and-error, 6

U
Unconscious work, 134, 148, 154
Understand program, 43-45

V
Verbal reports, validity of, 155-158
Verification bias, 89, 90, 92, 93, 96, 97, 99, 162
Verification stage, 130-131, 147

W
Waterjug tasks, 8, 31-35
Working memory, 12, 65, 151

X
X-ray task, 7-8